N. Bhaskara Rao is a pioneer of social research in India. He is Founder-Chairman of the Centre for Media Studies (CMS) and of Marketing and Development Research Associates (MDRA). Earlier, he built up the equally prestigious Operations Research Group (ORG) as its CEO. He was a member, with Dr M. S. Swaminathan, of the high-level government committee that drafted the National Population Policy, and an expert-member of the committee that reorganized the media units of the Information and Broadcasting Ministry.

His published books include *Controlled Mass Communication in Interstate Conflicts* (1970), *India 2021* (1985), *Social Impact of Mass Media* (1996), *A Handbook of Poll Surveys in Media: An Indian Perspective* (2009), *Sustainable Good Governance, Development and Democracy* (2018), *Citizen Activism in India* (2018) and *The TRP Trick: How Television in India was Hijacked* (2019).

THE THIRD EYE OF GOVERNANCE

RISE OF POPULISM, DECLINE IN SOCIAL RESEARCH

DR N. BHASKARA RAO

SPEAKING TIGER BOOKS LLP
4381/4, Ansari Road, Daryaganj
New Delhi-110002

First published in hardback by Speaking Tiger 2021

Copyright © Dr N. Bhaskara Rao 2021

ISBN: 978-93-89958-83-6
eISBN: 978-93-89958-82-9

10 9 8 7 6 5 4 3 2 1

The views and opinions expressed in this work are the author's own and the facts are as reported by him, and the publisher is in no way liable for the same.

All rights reserved.

No part of this publication may be reproduced, transmitted, or stored in a retrieval system, in any form or by any means, electronic, mechanical, photocopying, recording or otherwise, without the prior permission of the publisher.

This book is sold subject to the condition that it shall not, by way of trade or otherwise, be lent, resold, hired out, or otherwise circulated, without the publisher's prior consent, in any form of binding or cover other than that in which it is published.

This book is dedicated to:

Dr P.N. Vasanti, in appreciation of her commitment to unbiased and meticulous research and her deep sense of social responsibility;

and

The Economic & Political Weekly (EPW), a truly unique institution, for consistently publishing original research-based analyses of public policies for decades.

FOREWORD

Dr Bhaskara Rao has been India's preeminent public opinion analyst, applied social researcher, and a pioneer in social audit and countrywide surveys. He has played a crucial leadership role in premier research organisations such as ORG and CMS, as well as in ministries of the Government of India. This book captures his incredible insights and his invaluable wisdom concerning our present day challenges in public policy making and execution, remarkably articulated in the title of his book itself, *The Third Eye of Governance: Rise of Populism, Decline in Social Research*.

Dr Rao begins by reflecting on how India pursued planned development and shows how, in the early years, India had understood the relevance of public policy based on research and evidence which are essential elements for socio-economic transformation.

Dr Rao traces the origins and scope of public policy research through his own incisive lens. He powerfully articulates the relevance and role of research in formulating policies, designing programmes, optimising schemes and their utilisation, and ascertaining their impact. Not only that, he also lays out a roadmap to revive the social sciences as per the trajectory of governance, development, and democracy.

The significance of enlightened political leadership cannot be denied. In that context, he provides a nuanced discussion of the sensitivity towards research demonstrated by the Prime Ministers of India over five decades of Indian history.

Dr Rao emphasises that political parties cannot be the final arbitrators of policies and priorities, overriding citizens, communities, and civil society and that public opinion and consensus building play critical roles. The idea of field surveys, feedback, data, and analysis as a form of an interlocutor is as important as scientists, technocrats, and economists operating with complete freedom of thought. Strong institutions for research, data, and statistics with autonomy and independence are critical for economic and social development, which includes citizen participation and empowerment.

Dr Rao laments that 'evaluative' research (not just 'supportive' research) is critical but there has been a decline in robust data-based analysis and independent research. He observes that key reasons for this decline include politicisation of governance; tendency towards populism by prioritizing image building; short-sighted decisions, quest for control, command, and centralisation; shift in the balance of power; and a decline in the representative character of parties. He also analyses the role of the influx of foreign consultants with vested interests.

Dr Rao's personal analysis of what he terms as 'data crisis or crisis of data in 2018–19' offers many lessons for the future. In recent times, he points out, there has indeed been a cry for 'credible data' and 'impartial study of data'. World renowned policymakers such as Dr Vijay Kelkar have even suggested that the National Statistical Commission (NSC) should be given an autonomous constitutional status on the lines of the Election Commission of India.

Having summarised the essence of Prof. Rao's book, allow me to take the liberty of making three personal statements.

First, some views on policy making in a broader context. These have been elaborated in our recent book (co-authored with Ravi Pandit) published earlier this year, titled *Leap frogging to pole vaulting: Creating the magic of radical yet sustainable transformation*. We have shown that executable or actionable ideas require the support of four levers, public policy being just one of these. The four levers are technology, policy, social engagement, and economic model.

Technology, because we are unlikely to see successful

solutions for any of our big problems without technological interventions. Policy, because a bold, consistent, and enabling regulatory environment with adequate government support is a critical imperative for driving positive change. Social engagement, because the people at large have to accept policy intervention, be a part of the change, and be its stakeholders to finally accept and affect change. And finally, economic model is important because only a solution that makes economic sense to all the stakeholders involved will survive. We call this a STEP model. We have illustrated in the book the interactive and strong coupling of these four levers, along with demonstrating how even one level of the STEP missing can lead to failure. I do believe this view and analysis is complimentary to Dr Rao's comprehensive articulation on policy making and execution in the present book.

Second, I myself have learnt some lessons during my involvement in policy making in my own areas of expertise, namely science, technology, and innovation. I have participated in this as a member of the Science Advisory Council to the Prime Minister of India for over three decades since the mid-80s. I have also chaired 14 so-called Mashelkar Committees, many of them involved policy making in diverse fields, from environment to education to agriculture to health to intellectual property rights. Take, for instance, the National Auto Fuel Policy Committee of the Government of India that I chaired in 2003 where, among other things, a road map for new and tighter emission norms for India was laid down.

There was a strong perception at the time that the improvement in air quality in Delhi was solely due to the introduction of CNG in buses. We established a group of leading national research laboratories who invested about 10,000 man hours on data collection and research. It was concluded that CNG had just contributed to slightly over 10% improvement, while the rest had resulted from new engine technologies, better fuel, etc. So evidence based analysis is critical, as Dr Rao emphasizes in this book.

Third, our experience at Pune International Centre (PIC).

This is a think tank that is currently led by me and Dr Vijay Kelkar who himself provides a visionary personal leadership to PIC's policy research unit. Since its formation in 2011, PIC has introduced approximately 25 PIC policy papers addressing issues ranging from better corporate governance to containing black money to FDI 2.0 to reforming the GST to accelerating agriculture growth.

PIC's strategy is to deliberate, engage, and influence. Although it is early days, we have seen some encouraging success with PIC policy papers influencing national and state level policies in some respects. The role for many such truly 'independent' think tanks in policy making, as Dr Rao has championed in the book, cannot be overemphasised.

Let me finally turn to some valid questions that Dr Rao has raised. How do we create a citizen-centric, society-sensitive future instead of a market- and consumer-oriented one? How do we make research a reliable tool for pro-active initiatives, enhancing the chances of government policies becoming inclusive and participative, rather than giving space to manipulate initiatives and promoting centralisation?

Dr Rao has made a valiant effort in his book to respond to these thought-provoking questions, and I am sure this will be a 'work in progress' as our nation advances.

I am convinced that this book will also make a difference, just as Dr Rao has made a difference in the past. To cite just one example, despite various studies examining the delivery of basic public services, no study has focused on the challenge of the country's below-poverty-line population not being able to avail basic public services because of corruption. The subject was broached for the first time by Dr Rao when he led '*CMS India Corruption Survey*' that was conducted state-wise, first in 2005 and then in 2007. These new data analyses and research then led to public policies gaining new relevance and weightage.

In a similar vein, we hope that his deep analysis and concerns reflected in the book will lead to extensive introspection, debate, and new solutions that can improve the extent and quality of research at all stages including creation, strategy evolution, and execution. This will lead to the much-needed creation of a robust public policy research eco system while reinventing and reimaging the strong role of public policy research institutes, thereby benefiting the Indian society.

The nation owes its gratitude to Dr Rao for his valiant efforts towards rejuvenating the policy research culture and environment. Indeed, as he aptly puts it, we must succeed in this so that public policy research can assume its rightful and powerful role as the third eye of governance.

R.A. MASHELKAR*

---

*Honoured with the Padma Vibhushan, Mashelkar is one of India's most prominent scientists. He has been Director-General of the Council of Scientific and Industrial Research, President of the Indian National Science Academy and the Global Research Alliance, and Chairperson of the Academy of Scientific and Innovative Research.

PREFACE

RESEARCH FOR WHOM, WITH WHAT PURPOSE?

Abraham Lincoln, the 16th President of the U.S. was a tall man—a full six feet and four inches. Add a stovepipe hat, and he towered as a seven-footer. Struck by Lincoln's height, a soldier of the Union Army once remarked: 'Mr. President, you are tall! How tall are you?' Lincoln's response went something like: 'Son, like you, tall enough that my feet reach the ground.'

As a social researcher, and one who is deeply honoured to pen the Foreword to this volume, I find Lincoln's uncharacteristic response to be profoundly instructive. With his tallness being self-evident, Lincoln chose to emphasize the 'common ground' on which he stood with the soldier(s). He purposely suspended the titular trappings of being the President, Commander-in-Chief, or a Tallness Expert to favour a familial tone ('Son, like you')—accompanied by humanity and humility ('tall enough'). Philosophically-speaking, Lincoln privileges the voice and wisdom that is rooted in the common ground—a system of governance far removed from the lures of a monarchy, aristocracy, or autocracy, and instead one that subscribes to democratic ideals—'of the people, by the people, and for the people.' Methodologically speaking, Lincoln favours a richer, deeper, and more nuanced reading of measurement and data (beyond the precision of 6'4'), valuing and espousing alternative perspectives, viewpoints, and approaches. Policy and praxis-wise, Lincoln's perspective is steeped in humanity—a call to purposely bring forth the 'better angels of our nature', an enduring belief in the value of 'ballots' over 'bullets', a privileging of civil discourse over populist demagoguery.

Some 55 years after Lincoln's passing, when alighting at Motihari railway station in District Champaran in India, Mahatma Gandhi was asked by a reporter: 'Mr Gandhi, why do you travel third class?' Gandhi replied, 'I travel third class because, as you know, there is no fourth class.' I narrate Gandhi's story here to make the point that Lincolnian 'common ground' democratic ideals were integral to Mahatma Gandhi's philosophy, methodology, and praxis in India. Gandhi was one with the common man—the *daridranarayan*, spinning the *charkha*, traveling by third class, producing and wearing *khadi*, and taking on the British government to repeal the salt tax, which mostly hurt the common man who toiled in the field.

While both Lincoln and Gandhi are long gone, the ideals they espoused of democratic governance, humanistic policy-making, and civic participation find utterance in this rich and comprehensive analysis undertaken by Dr Bhaskara Rao of the Indian case in this book, *The Third Eye of Governance: Rise of Populism, Decline in Social Research.* Drawing upon a treasure trove of deeply embodied, immersive leadership experiences in social and public policy research over five decades, Dr Rao analyses India's experience, sparked historically by Nehruvian scientific fervour, tempered judiciously by institution-builders and public intellectuals like Homi Bhabha, Vikram Sarabhai, Sam Pitroda, and R.A. Mashelkar; and advocated and administered with mixed results in terms of relevance, salience, quality, influence, and impact by a plethora of governmental and non-governmental research councils, centres, institutes, and societies.

The book presents the contours—both wide and deep—of public and social research in India, including the forging of a historical report card, i.e., a critical appraisal of social research and public policy formulations through the seven-plus decades since India's independence, noting how social and public policy research in India, even though established initially with scientific temper, autonomy, and administrative independence, may not have been keeping up with the times, or perhaps even be in a state of decline. The book argues that in a country of 1.2 billion people, with tremendous social, cultural, regional, and linguistic diversity, divides, and disparities, high quality, mixed methods, and adaptive social research processes are needed to make informed public policy decisions, and for these to be subjected to the highest standards of transparency, reliability, and ethics. The book raises questions and dilemmas about the preponderance of populist public policy formulations, quick snapshot research outputs, including ratings and rankings, polling and voting, and the rising tide of market and consumer research—almost all geared toward those with expendable income.

I invite you to read this engaging book. It urges policy-makers to adopt the Lincolnian gaze as also the Gandhian praxis of being anchored in the common concerns of people, the importance of including diverse perspectives and viewpoints in assessing phenomenon, and above all a compassionate and humanistic approach to the ethical use of high office, and attention to ground-based data collection and research. That is the kind of research that Gandhi undertook in Bihar's Champaran District some 100 years ago upon his return to India from South Africa, patiently listening to the grievances of oppressed indigo farmers, collecting and analyzing thousands of documents over a dozen visits, systematizing and thematizing 12,000 farmer testimonies, and then presenting a research case to the Viceroy and local British administrators, leading to the passing of Champaran Agrarian Law of 1918. That is the kind of public-policy social research that is needed in India and elsewhere.

Whether Lincoln, or Gandhi, a policy-maker, or a social researcher, one should always ask: Research for whom, with what purpose, with what reliability, and with what humanity?

ARVIND SINGHAL[*]

---

[*]Singhal is the Samuel Shirley and Edna Holt Marston Endowed Professor of Communication, The University of Texas at El Paso, and was appointed the William J Clinton Distinguished Fellow at the Clinton School of Public Service, University of Arkansas, and Professor in the Inland School of Business and Social Sciences, Inland University of Applied Sciences, Norway.

INTRODUCTION

One of the missing links in India's 70 years' growth path has been much-needed research backup and a shared rationale—across governments—for public policies. As a result, our policy priorities, planning, and implementation at the district, state, and union levels have been uneven and development has remained unsustainable. This is despite us choosing the 'planned development' model in which research is central. With several new resources, databases, analytics and infrastructure, the scenario should, I hope, be different in the near future. But only if we are serious about bringing about change through high-level, independent and inclusive research and analysis.

When the Republic completes 100 years, our confidence levels have to be much higher regarding future prospects. That becomes feasible if the first years of the second decade of this century become landmark years in terms of initiatives and correctives to rejuvenate social science research in India. Will that happen? Do we see a paradigm shift in the rational support for our public policies? It will mean ensuring appropriateness and compatibility of research and analysis methodologies, plus transparency in the process—how a research base is formed, and how data is reliably generated and utilised without bias.

This is an immediate challenge and an opportunity. Can we face this without an introspection of where we stand today in terms of research pursuit? The scope and structure of social science research in the country reflects the direction in which the country is moving, the state of our democracy, the scope of development, and the inclusiveness of governance. It is with these concerns that I wrote this book. But this book can only be a 'work-in-progress'.

It was exactly 60 years ago that I had my first brush with survey research as a part of my master's degree (1961) at Andhra university. It was a socio-economic field survey on the living conditions of the Harijan settlement part of my village, Mudunuru, Andhra Pradesh. In 1962, I conducted an organisational study of Anakapalli cooperative jaggery market, India's largest jaggery source. In 1964–65, I was part of Osmania University's project to identify awareness about public affairs (which showed that a number of people outside Hyderabad did not know even about Mahatma Gandhi and Jawaharlal Nehru). As a part of my rural development course, I critically reviewed two master sources of social research at that time, M.N. Srinivas's* *India's Villages* and S.C. Dube's** *Indian Village* on caste and change. Both books were based on pioneering anthropological research. This research continues to be a reference, benchmark, and model research even today. On my return to India in 1970 after completing my PhD in the US, I was an advisor to the Ministry of Health and Family Welfare, as a resource person of the Ford Foundation, New Delhi, and gained first-hand experience in applied research through work conducted in Hubli, West Bengal and rural Punjab, which formed the basis for 'social marketing' of India's family planning policy and campaigns over the next decade. Two years after that stint in policy planning and programme strategy in the Ministry, Dr Vikram Sarabhai took me to Baroda (1971–72) where I got the opportunity to dabble in a range of research tasks and assignments and engage in a constant endeavour to improve accuracy, reliability, timeliness, and transparency in survey research.

Constant efforts to improve and make research applicable or useful in improving practices or changing behaviours

---

*Srinivas, M.N. (ed.) 1955, *India's Villages*, Asia Publishing House, New Delhi

**Dube S.C., 1955, *Indian Village*, Routledge, London

have helped me sharpen methodologies for analysis and field research. That, in turn, increased my curiosity for larger national issues. It was around this time that, working with Prof. Everett M. Rogers (of *Diffusion of Innovation* fame), experiences at India's premier academic institutes sharpened my quest for research and public policies. That was when I was sought out to set up a Directorate of Evaluation in the Ministry of I & B and a Department of Research and Evaluation at the Indian Institute of Mass Communication (IIMC). Two decades later, at the request of the Ministry of Communication, I experimented with a new methodology of social auditing for two years and repeated the same at the Ministry of Environment. Before completing my PhD at the University of Iowa, USA, I benefited as a fellow at the Upland School of Social Change, founded by Dr Martin Luther King Jr, where major US government policies were appraised for evolving citizen-led strategies.

In India, however, I have observed that despite pioneering research in academics, the results and insights have rarely been used for framing public policies, especially since the 1970s. For example, faculties of agriculture extension and economics in premier institutes were being set up during my early years as a researcher—1965–75—and they were to provide research support and a framework for policies. However, taking vacuum as an opportunity, rather than original methodologies suited to Indian realities, foreign methodologies, such as ratings, rankings and such other quantitative indices, were adopted in such endeavours, devised and pushed mostly by profit-driven multinational research corporates. Over the years these methodologies penetrated into the Indian market and academics, gaining monopoly by 2010. The Indian authorities not only allowed such 'intrusion' but also preferred foreign outfits for research, unconcerned whether their models and methods were of relevance here, or in other democracies similar to ours. Such foreign research outfits are mostly market-oriented and concerned more with the 'consumer' and the 'voter' than with the 'citizen' and the 'society'.

Will research in the next couple of decades become more

rigorous, more focused and informed by our particular realities? Will it become a more reliable tool for proactive initiatives and enhance the chances of government policies becoming inclusive and responsive to our society and citizens—and to all citizens equally? Research should not become a tool for manipulative initiatives or persuasive strategies of the powers of the time and thus promote bias or centralisation and monopolies. Instead, it should reflect and ensure grass root concerns. It is important to develop independent research capabilities and methodologies for our academic networks. In the recent decades, research has been of increasing help mainly to corporates, markets, advertising, and electoral politics, rather than to people.

A fundamental civilizational feature and strength of India has been its quest, its constant search, for truth. That being the heritage of India, independent research should have been a natural quest at different levels, including our public policy apparatus and strategies. If mathematics and physics were the source for inventions and development earlier, today analytics and feedback tools from anthropology and from sociological and psychological studies are also crucial. Today, we have technologies, databases, and methodologies to optimise human endeavour, and yet, one finds that what is sought or encouraged is only 'supportive research', and that too with a 'control and command' view of decision makers.

As an independent researcher with 50 years of experience, I have been concerned with policy formulation at the Centre and in the States, especially over the last decade, regarding the rationale of policies and their assessment. I believe that no country or party can expect to remain democratic, sustain its development, and offer good governance without believing in and conducting independent research. Yet, I see no professional research body or voice presently akin to people like P.C. Mahalanobis, VKRV Rao, Rajni Kothari, and Vikram Sarabhai, as it is difficult now to debate, discuss, assess in a transparent and an independent manner without being debunked by the powers the be. This is why I thought I should share my own thoughts and experiences as a researcher in this book. It is clear that the space for independent research has been shrinking, but without critical appraisal, we cannot expect public policies to become pro people and genuinely democratic and help accomplish the grand development and social goals envisioned in the Constitution of India.

I have witnessed the twists and turns social science research has gone through in India over the last six decades (1960-2020). I have seen the kind of importance—or otherwise—that universities have given to the disciplines of economics, sociology, psychology, social work, and anthropology. I have also seen how the governments have been proactive in seeking ideas or snubbing them, in making good and enlightened use of research insights for the greater common good or in misusing them for their own agendas. India has shown to the world how statistics can be used for change, creating development plans, and supporting public policies, but India has also shown the opposite in the last couple of decades. I am concerned that India is not unleashing its potential and I hope this publication helps to regroup and rejuvenate social sciences towards a trajectory of good governance, development and democracy. I also hope that social research can take us towards a citizen-centric, society-sensitive future than one focused on just the market and the consumer.

The 'melting pot' idea of American society in the mid-20th century was studied closely and evaluated by sociologists and contributed to the assimilation process that changed the course of American social progress by changing the mindset of the American nation. In India, however, 70 years after Nehru's idea of assimilation, people are more divided and development has not reached a large number. Part of the reason for this is that for much of our post-Independence history—up to the present—there has been hardly any critical research and independent appraisal of policies and plans.

There was great promise in the first couple of decades after Independence, and for a few years after that. In the mid-1960s, the pioneering physicist, Dr Vikram Sarabhai, whose interests also included the arts, sports and statistics, founded the

Operations Research Group (ORG), the first market research organization in the country. Research was also central in the success of the Green Revolution of the 1960s. The idea was based on the research and initiatives of, among others, the pioneering American agronomist Dr Norman Borlaug and the sociologist Everett M. Rogers of Michigan State University who studied how new ideas and practices are spread and adopted in different societies. In India, this revolution was spearheaded by a team involving C. Subramaniam, a senior politician; B. Sivaraman, a senior bureaucrat; and, perhaps most notably, by Dr M.S. Swaminathan, an agricultural scientist and researcher who had a grass-roots and holistic view of the society. (I happened to have played a small role in this movement during 1963–65 by popularising nitrogen fertilisers.) There were

As prime minister of a newly independent country, Jawaharlal Nehru had realized from the very outset, through insights gained from research on and analyses of democracies, that people's participation and decentralisation is essential for sustaining development and reinforcing democracy. This was also his approach to the 'public cooperation' division (1955) in the Planning Commission, which prompted several citizen-led organizations to become stakeholders in government schemes. The advice he gave me in 1960 significantly influenced me. He said, 'Young man, when you complete your degree, you should not look for a government job, but work for the country.' He had recognized then that education and a job, or employment, must be viewed independently, and that a country is shaped not just by governments and bureaucracies but also by skilled and committed citizens. Nehru believed that research is a catalyst for change, that it has a great impact on development as it helps involve people in the process. India's Green Revolution and the family planning campaign were breakthrough consequences of rigorous, scientific research. Both these programmes also proved that research influences policies.

Some development themes echoed by the present Indian prime minister, Narendra Modi, have the potential to change the face of the country if they are backed by high-quality independent and unbiased research. Some of his slogans and themes—such as 'Sabka Saath, Sabka Vikas' and 'Minimum Government, Maximum Governance,'—and ideas—like the one which stresses that 'politics should not override public policy'—deserve to be followed up far more seriously, consistently, and critically. But there is a gap between stated intention and actual practice. Sometimes, there is a contradiction between the two. For instance, despite PM Modi reminding the nation and scientists in 2018 of the 'scientific temper' and the idea of 'lab to land', there was a clear setback to this spirit in the 2019 National Education Policy.

This book aims to understand the history, successes and failures of research and the spirit of research in India since Independence. I hope it will be of some use to research professionals, students and policy-makers. I have done my best to share what I have learned and observed during my personal experience of over five decades at India's premier research organisations, the Operations Research group (ORG) and the Centre for Media Studies (CMS), and a few ministries; and through my association with remarkable people such as Dr Martin Luther King Jr, Dr Vikram Sarabhai, D. V. N. Sharma, Jamal Kidwai, Dr M. S. Swaminathan, Durgabai Deshmukh, Inder Gujral, B. G. Deshmukh, Justice P. N. Bhagwati, Abid Hussain, Everett Rogers and R. A. Mashelkar, who have all inspired me.

DR N. BHASKARA RAO
New Delhi

CHAPTER ONE

Planned Development

India is a country of contradictions. For many years, it was known by many almost entirely for its poverty, snake charmers, famines and beggars, while its many unique, thousands of years' old features related to philosophies of ahimsa, pluralism and sustainability remained mere curiosities. India has a long and rich heritage, but since Independence, it has also emerged as a modern state of stature and substance.

From being a country of poverty, illiteracy, communal violence and shortages in 1947, today, over 70 years later, India has come a long way. It is now a country of surpluses, with an indomitable manufacturing sector, an unparalleled educational base, state-of-the-art communication and health infrastructure, and a global competitive soft power. There may be many shortcomings, but this country is in many ways a remarkable success story. How was all this possible? A major factor behind this was the Constitution that was developed after lengthy deliberations by wise men and women from around the country. It intended to provide for the passions and aspirations of people while addressing the fundamental issues such as plurality, equity, inclusiveness, to give the framework to ensure that a democratic setup was adopted at different levels. A second factor is the way the Parliament and the State Assemblies were developed and structured to represent the people of the country. A third factor is the way these legislative bodies, full of elected representatives, made public policies. And a fourth factor is the way the pillars of the state—the legislature, the judiciary, and the civil service—functioned in a checks-and-balances manner to strengthen democracy. Credit also goes to a majority of the political leadership, political parties, civil society, and the news media since Independence for being part of the country's larger pursuit and accomplishments.

Universal franchise, rule of law, parliamentary democracy—where a simple majority decides the course of the country—and certain institutions to safeguard democracy, such as the Supreme Court, are at the heart of the Constitution. This, and the rare achievement of 17 rounds of general elections—the largest and most complex in the world—in 72 years, and a change in political regimes seven times, all largely peaceful, makes India a unique country where citizens and their rights continue to be the core concerns.

In this process, however, political parties have emerged as the final arbiters of policies and priorities at the federal level and in the states—often overriding the citizen, the community, and civil society, despite the fact that the parties are expected to represent the people and their interests, which are supreme in a democracy.

The balance of power among the pillars of the state has of late tilted toward the political parties. As if foreseeing such a situation, 60 years ago, the Nehru-Mahalanobis team developed the idea of field surveys, feedback, data, and analysis as some kind of an interlocutor. They even wanted scientists, technocrats, and economists to work independently rather than on the terms of the politicians and bureaucrats. They even believed that data from within—that is, from the same people who are responsible for the execution of policies (i.e., ministers and bureaucrats)—is not always reliable for framing public policies. That was how they created capabilities and institutions for research, data gathering, surveys and statistics, with an emphasis on autonomy and independence. They realised the significance of independent and rigorous research not only for economic development but also for social development, which includes citizen participation. This realisation and understanding of research capabilities helped in building a momentum for socio-economic transformation and development. This was during the first 20 to 25 years of India's independence.

But there were some shortcomings in those decades, though it was after that time that such research was neglected or undermined. This is one reason why India has not accomplished more and has not met the minimum development and sustainability goals established by the United Nations recently (for 2005–2030).

It is important to understand this downward trend after the first two decades of Independent India, so that the country can catch up and adopt models appropriate for the situation in the country today. This book will try to examine how or why this situation has arisen and discuss ways to enable institutions to truly aid development, rather than being stuck in the syndrome or 'trap' of ratings and rankings.

Research as an Essential Element for Socio-economic Transformation

India reflects a unique trend in its journey toward development, growth, modernity, and becoming a 'super power'. The US became a super power within 100 years of its constitution. Israel emerged as a superpower in less than four decades, despite being an entirely new country, very small in size, and with a population comprising people who were barely emerging from the unimaginable trauma of the Holocaust. Japan rose to superpower status within a few decades of the Hiroshima and Nagasaki bombings. Modern-day Malaysia is another impressive example of transformation to prosperity. A common factor in these four nations becoming visibly developed and prosperous is that they implemented a sound research system; of course, in conjunction with hard work and visionary leadership. Moreover, all of these countries learnt from and used another country's practices as a shortcut to transformation and growth.

The story of India as it approaches its 75th year of independence is no less a wonder. In fact, its story is even more unique. Although India continues to be a country of divides, plurality, and multiplicities, considering what its people have accomplished and demonstrated outside the country as technologists, doctors, scientists, researchers, innovators, and leaders in software, it leads to more questions. Why do the Indian youth excel and emerge at the top outside their own country? Don't they get an opportunity to unleash their creative talent within India? Is something missing in the nation's priorities? Indians are hardworking, perhaps more than most. Taking into account the growth in educational infrastructure, particularly in science, technology, and communication infrastructure, India has been able to quickly catch up and even excel in these fields. Why are we then not in the foreground in terms of socio-economic development, eradicating poverty, reducing inequalities, and emerging as a global power in research and development (R&D)0? It is the R&D leaderships that differentiate countries and their global status. All this, despite the first Prime Minister of India calling for scientific temper in all the early national endeavours as well as establishing pioneering institutes that could ensure the development of a knowledge-driven country.

Whither Scientific Temper?

First Prime Minister Jawaharlal Nehru talked about 'scientific temper' and reiterated the idea of scientific outlook among the people of the country. He was also responsible for establishing several special institutes and academic centres and intended for poor people, in particular, to benefit from public policies based on scientific outlook, rational practices, and discourses and logic. He hoped that science and technology, two sides of modernity, would help equity, eliminate poverty, and bring people together. He expected India to make leaps in socio-economic development. Has that happened, and who has benefited more from public policies? Why are inequalities increasing? Nehru expected that 'science, research, and technology' would not only scale up opportunities but also address the problems that the country was facing. Have they?

Taking the idea of scientific temper further, the Parliament had passed a 'scientific policy resolution' in as early as March 1958. Realising that scientific outlook in the country was not on ascent but on decline, in 1975, Indira Gandhi included the concept as part of the fundamental duties of citizens. 'To develop scientific temper, humanism and spirit of enquiry' was included in the fundamental duties. A decade later, in 1987, the education policy laid emphasis on the 'development of scientific temper'. And yet the idea was pursued neither with any seriousness in the education stream nor in the public media or in the government's pursuit. The political parties and leaders too did not endorse or reiterate it.[1]

Prime Minister Modi should be credited for reminding the nation in 2018 of the idea of 'scientific temper' and calling for scientists to nurture it. Modi promoted scientists to reach out to the youth of the country by spending 100 hours a year to nurture scientific temper. Of course, his focus was on 'implementing technologies' by extending the 'lab to land' idea. He exhorted scientists in March 2018 while inaugurating the 105th Indian Science Congress at Imphal. Modi pointed out that scientific temper assures the nation of its 'rightful place among the front line nations'. Consequently, the government took certain initiatives such as fellowships, although not exactly in line with what was suggested by the Prime Minister. It needs to be seen whether the proposed National Research Foundation in the 2019–20 budget reverses the declining trend of research in the country, as outlined in the 2020 National Education policy drafted by Dr Kasturirangan's panel.[2]

I have spent more than 50 years working with applied social research in New Delhi, Vadodara, Hyderabad, and Vijayawada without losing my roots and links with the grass roots. I can thus say that it is the priorities of successive governments and the preoccupation of political parties with populist policies that has hindered India from emerging as a country of innovations and R&D. Why has research and development not become a national priority, a serious and sustained pursuit? On the contrary, it has been more like one step forward and two backward. One reason could be the mixing up of political parties with the government, not differentiating between the government of the day from governance, and placing an individual leader above the governing political party. The government has also failed to realize the difference between job or employment and skills. Another reason could be that those in government have not yet acknowledged the difference between feedback from those responsible for implementation and from independent sources. They are also unable to differentiate between data and analysis, assessment and appraisal, impact and evaluation, development and prosperity, achievement and benefit, and macro view and citizen-centric view. However, neither the educational system nor the leadership in the country has prioritized these dilemmas that are the underlying reasons hindering the country from becoming a power house, a country of opportunities, and a beacon of knowledge that it once was.

Origins of Applied Research

The Planning Commission was a brilliant idea put forth by Jawaharlal Nehru and several other builders of modern India even before the Constitution of the country was unveiled in 1950. By any count, it was a visionary initiative and a turning point for the future of the Republic India. This was not only Nehru's vision but also of a host of visionary leaders like Sir Mokshagundam Visvesvaraya,[3] Subhas Chandra Bose, Sardar Vallabhbhai Patel, Ram Manohar Lohia, Shriman Narayan Agarwal;[4] civil service luminaries like JC Kumarappa; academic professionals such as PC Mahalanobis and VKRV Rao; entrepreneurs like JRD Tata; scientists such as CV Raman, Homi J. Bhabha, and S D Kothari; and educationists like Zakir Hussain and Ramachandran of Gandhi Gram. They were all thinkers inspired by great leaders like Gopal Krishna Gokhale, Bal Gangadhar Tilak, Lala Lajpat Rai, Mahatma Gandhi, and other such stalwarts.

Plans for a modern India were envisioned and outlined in the Planning Commission which, at the very outset, was independent of the Cabinet as the Cabinet and the government were busy coping with calamities facing the country, including the immediate ones resulting from the partition, issues of consolidation of the states, and forming the civil service, judiciary, and legislatures. The Planning Commission recognised that data and analysis were necessary for 'nation building' and for gaining a perspective into the future, including the Five Year Plans adopted for 'planned development'. By 1953, the Planning Commission was ready with the Research Programme Committee (RPC) that aimed to identify research support and generate measures to execute the national development plans.

This resulted in a foundation being laid out for institutional support with numerous research bodies within the government during 1955–65. It was Dr DS Kothari's commission on education in 1964 that suggested Dr VKRV Rao to look into promoting social science research. His recommendation for an Indian Council for Social Science Research (ICSSR) in 1965–69 kick-started research in the context of public policies and national pursuits. To guide these efforts, a number of forums, institutes, and societies were initiated outside the government, including the Indian Council for Historical Research (1972), Indian Council for Philosophical Research (1977), Indian Institute of Advanced Studies (1965), Indian Institute of Social Welfare & Business Management (1953), and the various state-level Tribal Research Institutes. None of these, however, had taken any initiative in their early years to explore new opportunities, perhaps because their organisational structure (state-funded and based on nominations) did not allow them to take on the challenges. Other similar agencies created during this period remained merely as forums. The National Council of Economic and Applied Research (NCEAR, 1956), Indian Institute of Public Administration (1954), National Council for Educational Research and Training (1961), National Institute of Nutrition, Hyderabad (1958), and All India Institute of Local Self Government (AIILSG), Pune, however, were structured as independent professional bodies. These are only a few examples that showcased the opportunities for private or independent initiatives which took proactive measures.

Simultaneously, voluntary initiatives were being undertaken outside the government to develop training, research, and experimentation. Within the first 10–15 years of independence, a few such proactive initiatives had been established in different regions of the country. These efforts included traditional ways of assessment, enquiry, and experimentation. They were truly Indian in scope. Rabindranath Tagore's Shantiniketan and Rukmini Devi Arundale's Kalakshetra, for example, had their own ways of conducting research. But Western research models had soon taken over the academics of the country. There were, of course, exceptions. G. Ramachandran's Gandhigram Institute (1956–62), Nanaji Deshmukh's Deendayal Research Institute (1969), Bunkar Roy's Barefoot College (1972), Jiddu Krishnamurti's Rishi Valley School (1978), Albert Mayor's extension methods (1954–56), Welthy Fisher's Literacy House in Lucknow (1956), and Bhartiya Gram Udyog, Pune were examples of original, indigenous centres and initiatives of learning and research. However, with some of these centres coming under the UGC and others becoming dependent on government funding in later years, their uniqueness was marginalised.

Curiously enough, despite the potential of decennial census data, even post-independence data of 1951 and 1961, none of the national agencies included anything apart from the formal composition to for further desegregate analysis in the context of national plans. They merely used aggregate data of the census. The least some of these research councils could have done was reorient census objectives and methodologies according to the new requirements of independent India. Even decades later, why should the census remain part of the Union Home Ministry? Law and order outlook dictated census more than they did developmental needs. Not only that, having spent more than Rs 1600 crores in 2010–12 to conduct census operation, the government or its departments' expenditure on earnestly using the census data and the demographic trends is not commensurate to the efforts. This effort remained limited to New Delhi. It was much later, in the '70s, that a more serious churning of the census data was conducted, such as by Ashish Bose with his symbolic 'BIMARU' analysis of development disparities.

A second wave of socio-economic research took place during 1965–75 when a series of initiatives that, although taken outside the government, were inspired by the momentum of the government. These initiatives prioritized logic, future plans, the interrelationship of sectors (number of schools needed, etc.), methods of data generation, data analysis, and sampling. Some such early initiatives are indeed noteworthy. Those in the public domain include the Indian Institute of Management (IIM), Ahmedabad and Calcutta (1961), while the private ones are Operations Research Group (ORG, 1966), Centre for Policy Research (CPR, 1973), Centre for the Study of Developing Societies (CSDS, 1963), and Council for Social Development (CSD, 1962). These are only some of the examples known to me.

The third wave in social research included independent academic and professional institutes such as the Indira Gandhi Institute of Development Research (1987), Mumbai; the Institute of Economic and Social Change (1972), Hyderabad; and certain institutes aimed at development studies as well as some ICSSR affiliated institutes.

In recent years, two types of research interests led to a shift in the scope of public domain research. Today, these two types of preoccupation have overtaken other concerns. For many, research means either pre- and post-poll surveys or rating and ranking surveys. Both of these have shifted concern and priorities of researchers in the country and changed the scope and potential of methodologies. They have also led to a shift in the research interest from behavioural change, impact, and evaluation to outcome and influence. Today, the new concern and priority is more on populism, image building, influence, and control over key sections. The interest is for *outcome* or *ends* rather than the *processes* or *means*.

Survey research in the context of elections has been prioritized over the years. These surveys are intended more to keep voters engaged in a guessing game. There is no evidence of these surveys adding to the basic knowledge or making any difference in behaviours or outcomes, such as the representative character of those being elected and encouraging citizens to become active participants. In recent years, pre- and post-election poll surveys have gained ground. Today, a social researcher is reduced to someone who conducts sample surveys focusing only on who wins or loses in an electoral context.

But, both poll time surveys and rating and ranking type studies suit political interests and are often marred by populist concerns and competitive compulsions. Under the impression of encouraging competition in order to promote public interest and 'good practices', rating and ranking research not only inhibits creative initiatives but also hampers 'think beyond' potential opportunities. The new technologies and the way they are being adopted are no longer in singular terms. The plurality in values, beliefs, and regional differences being what they are, rating and ranking approaches promote repetitive and 'common denominator' practices. An example of this is CSDS (1963). Rajni Kothari pioneered CSDS to help understand voting behaviour, deepen the democratic process, and sensitise stakeholders, but it is now known more as a poll survey agency. Of course, it is better than many mushroomed fly-by-night operators. One consequence of this trend is that public policies of consequence do not receive the much-needed research support. The government too has fallen victim to this trend as 'global mentors' seem to be behind promoting such a culture or phenomena. Assessing how different prime ministers over 70 years perceived research as a window for public interests and policies is quite revealing.

Dr M.S. Swaminathan, Dr R.A. Mashelkar, N. Vital, and Dr Vijay Kelkar are only a few exceptional examples of scientists and civil servants playing a proactive role. Dr Mashelkar chaired more than a dozen crucial national committees on policies as a member of the Science Advisory Council of the Prime Minister of India for three decades. He also chaired the Mashelkar Committee to guide the destiny of the nation based on research and analysis of technology and policy options. The

Pune International Centre (PIC) has also set a new example for how the civil society can play a proactively positive role in enlightening decision-makers about contentious issues using their insights based on years of hands-on expertise. In the last decade, they developed two dozen papers on policies and influenced the designing of policies at the national and state level.

R.A. Mashelkar and Ravi Pandit, in their book *Leapfrogging to Pole-vaulting: Creating the Magic of Radical Yet Sustainable Transformation* (Penguin Viking, January 2019), presented the idea of 'four levers' of public policy making which included technology, policy, social engineering, and economic model to make a lasting difference in the affairs of the nation. They pointed out that these four levels have 'interactive, strong coupling'.

Public Policies, Relevance of Research

Between 1970 and 2020, there has been a shift in the scope of research and priorities based on the changing concerns of policy makers at different points of the country's growth path. Similar to the decision-makers' priorities in public policies, their concerns regarding data and research took different routes, with several twists and turns over the years. As focus on concerns changed over the years, the scope of research and data too changed. These concerns and changes over the years can be traced to certain broad trends that influenced research priorities.

Regional Differences and Disparities

Without data and research, it is not possible to gauge the extent of differences between regions in their development and the needs of different sections of people. Secondary data, including the decadal census, was useful for the governments. However, establishing the Indian Institute of Statistics in Calcutta, the Planning Commission's Programme Evaluation Organisation, and the National Sample Survey Organisation reflected the need for reliable research data beyond the census.

Development Indicators (Agriculture, Health, Education, Infrastructure)

Development strategies and perspective plans require desegregated data beyond regions, states, and even districts. This data was obtained from within the existing administrative channels that were time-consuming, not reliable, and not compatible across the states. Studies conducted on the poverty level and what that poverty may comprise such as nutrition intake or daily income impacted public policies. This urgency also led to the development of district handbooks that listed village-wise infrastructure facilities including economic and infrastructure indicators. Such indicators were based on the type of data available and the reliability with which they could be updated.

KAP Studies

By the late-sixties, it was known that inadequate awareness and knowledge was a major hurdle and people's cooperation was required for pursuing public policies to assess awareness, for which field surveys were conducted. It was also understood that some people were hesitant to accept the kind of change that governments were trying to usher in. Concern for population growth, for example, prompted the first National Family Planning Survey (1971–72). Similarly, the first National Readership Survey (1970–72) was conducted to understand the reach and access of the general public to mass media. Such studies provided the basis and rationale for public policies, and their reach (1979–80).

Demographic Disparities and Inequalities

Once political parties and leaders began expressing the interests of their communities, the need for desegregated data concerning specific development indicators was acknowledged, for which new research requirements were needed. This led to collecting primary data, analysing it, and integrating it with the census data. Following the Mandal Commission controversy and agitation for reservations, state governments started collecting caste-specific data after 2000. That was the beginning of data collection for political ends.

Socio-economic, Behavioural Change, and Influence

Research indicated that awareness is not enough and that knowledge or merely launching a scheme is not enough; how they are understood by the concerned people and how they are availed is critical for strategies. Devising public policies in a targeted manner requires desegregated database. However, there was no social, anthropological, and psychological research (1990–2000) available.

Efficiency of Public Service Systems, Corruption, and Grievance Redressal

The realization, made public very dramatically by Rajiv Gandhi over 25 years ago, that hardly twenty paisa of a rupee reaches the intended target of welfare schemes, led to my concern for tracking efficiency in distribution or delivery channels. Also of concern is the fact that there is too much reliance on instant recall-based data. For example, ASER research on school outcomes resulted in a new concern from *outlays* to *outcomes* (2000–2005) in schools. This research reminded policy makers of the concern about quality of education policies. And yet, what initiatives have been taken in that direction? Will NITI Aayog's ranking of states make the much-needed change? While small unrepresentative ratings of Transparency International were taken more seriously, the large-scale, specific-to-public service representative studies by Indian research agencies was not considered despite them offering focused correctives for much-needed process changes.

Rural Distress, Control, and Command Aspects of the Government

Rating and ranking orientation had changed the scope of research and data. Transparency International's ranking of countries' corruption based on perceptions has changed the scope of research and methodology. Even NITI Aayog has taken to ranking the states as a priority. The realisation that India's social development was not in tune with the growth in GDP has revived interest in social research. Monitoring indicators for social growth has become a priority. Monitoring, Sustainable Development Goals (SDG), Management Development Programmes (MDP), and Management Information System (MIS) have become a routine (2005–10) at the cost of impact and evaluation studies.

Competitive Politics becoming Electoral or External Compulsions

With political parties dominating policies, there has been greater emphasis on winning elections. This concern has become the priority for research. This obviously meant conducting studies that cater to the populist appeal which included election studies and poll surveys meant to influence voters while change measurement and long-term implications became secondary (2010–20). But this has not yet sensitised the political leaders nor the concerned agencies in the government.

Good Governance and Populism

The government's recent campaigns such as Swachh Bharat or Smart Cities has brought about a new kind of research. 'Endorsement research' or supportive research or justifying studies has garnered more preference recently. Whether research is independent is no longer the preferred criteria. Even the credibility of independent institutions, which have been the primary sources for the country's statistics, have come under questioning. There has been more reliance on audit-based methodology than evaluative research (2015–20).

Despite 'national policy' becoming the latest craze among leaders in power, primary or independent research remains ignored. Instead, there is more reliance on the 'consultation route'. Although the consultation process is overall effective for policies, it is necessary to question whether this process should be used to get 'endorsement'. Today, every ministry claims to be developing a 'national policy'. In fact, every time there is a new minister, there is a call for a new policy. I recall how some ministries like the I & B were against a national policy until a few years ago as it also meant restrains, controls, and centralisation.

These trends are not distinct points as there is an overlap in their implications. They also reflect what the country is prioritizing in its public policies and research opportunities.

A retrospective analysis or reverse tracking of these developments indicates two trends with implications on the kind of research being conducted in the country. First, the idea of 'public policies' is getting diluted in the extent of concern for the 'public'. As these policies focus more on voters, they are becoming increasingly politically oriented. Second, public policies are being driven more by fewer groups or individuals. This trend is becoming more evident with every election. Third, as populism suits the rhetoric, a populist scheme has become the pursuit, even in research. One result of this trend is 'supportive research' or endorsement.

Is Populism a Safer Bet?

Populism is an outlook of leaders, and a methodology and strategy of those in power to control, command, and exert their authority. What we are witnessing today is an altogether new populism where ideology has little importance. The new instruments of communication and network have changed the course to such an extent that populism is being made to appear or sound synonymous to democracy and development, when in fact it can turn out to be a countervailing phenomenon. What is being regarded as a boom may turn out to be a bubble. This depends on the leaders' grip or control over the instruments of administrative authority or political power. In populism, the difference between ends and means becomes blurred.

The new wave of populism sweeping across the nation is rhetoric-centred. That is, it purports people as masses but is led by a few who are masters of rhetoric. Here, institutions matter less, as do future implications and research and feedback. Populism depends on revisiting the past rather than focusing on the future beyond three–five years. Polarising people through destabilization is part of the strategy. Perpetuating hate, anger, and resentment form the core of populism and help sustain the phenomena. Doubletalk also comes handy in this process.

Citizen activism, debates, deliberations, and checks and balances are no longer virtues, and may even be snubbed. Populism does not care so much for self-correctives or plurality. Populism needs an imaginary or a virtual villain or an enemy to prompt realignments. It submits a polarisation that thrives in terms of 'We of now and They of the past'.

Populism implies making people dependent on the government and reducing them to being 'beneficiary citizens'. Introducing new tools (Aadhar, bank account, etc.) provides an even easier grip over the masses. Homogenising people with other emotional issues also maintains populism (one nation, one language; or one nation, one election; or one nation, one market; or one nation, one policy). Political leaders think such methods are far more reliable to control and command than transparency, feedback, and research. (The National Register of Citizens is a new found measure along these lines.)

When concern for consequences is no longer a priority, the scope for feedback and research, scientific basis, or logical rationale gets marginalised. As do ethical responsibilities. In fact, even public opinions become less important while surveys matter more. Populism propels new alignments that surpass ideologies. Increased income in equalities has added to populism and added support to populist parties. Economic insecurity is another aspect that drives voters to populist parties and sustains populism.

Fantasy of Populism, Perils of Over-promising

Populism is a global phenomenon today. As a political phenomenon, it includes two streams. The first stream is economic that is based more on the anxieties and expectations of people, including jobs and means to fulfil basic needs, as well as the lure of attractive-sounding schemes and sops which may exist only on paper. Shortages and crisis situations become the stimulus for, and sustain, populism. More often, this stream is based on positive inducements. The second stream is emotional populism which is euphoria and rhetoric-based, often giving negative signals. Emotional populism often promotes and exploits majoritarian prejudice and has no concern for long-term consequences at all.

Both these streams of populism are short-sighted, cynical, and not really concerned with sustaining fair governance, democracy, or even development.

Populism is a fantasy, a mirage. It does not necessarily imply welfare, as is being claimed across the world today, particularly by those in political power. A common belief is that populism wins votes, and hence the power to govern. It is a mirage because it has no end. Populism is not the same as being popular or being liked or making oneself interesting to people. It has different meanings in different contexts. In India, populism refers to the phenomena of appealing to the base interests or emotions or the lower instincts of people. It is not an ideology of any political party. There cannot be one consistent view of populism. In recent years, however, populism in terms of elections has become all-pervasive and has been driven more by competitive compulsions for polls.

Populism often involves promises unconcerned with budget or their feasibility. For example, despite the Supreme Court striking caste/community-based reservations, promises continue to be made. Populism is believing something that is temporary and is not an honourable or ethical way of seeking support for a productive or sustainable cause. Populism is a lure, a bait for short-term advantage. Such populism has become a tactful strategy intended to induce or tempt people to support a leader or the government. Politics has become an art in populism, as an election-time tact. In this process, populism can very well be deceptive.

Considerable research has been undertaken on how or what should be done to create a populist course or to sustain support. Populism may also work as a trap when promises are not kept and cannot be explained to the concerned public. Populism is a tricky affair. It can sometimes be rewarding in temporarily and sometimes in a lasting manner.

Someone concerned with long-term interest may not find populism the preferred method despite its immediate benefits. There are examples where populist moves by governments have not found popular support. A 2016 referendum in Switzerland that granted basic income to every family was a populist move, but the motion was rejected by an overwhelming majority as people were against dependence on the government and were concerned about the government's sustainability and productivity. But such examples are rare. Recently, in Telangana as well as Andhra Pradesh, there were demands that every household be given one million rupees for their household expense. It should not be a surprise if this demand becomes a manifesto promise of parties just before the next elections in 2023.

That populism is becoming the norm in India has been too obvious in recent decades. The more this trend grows, the bleaker the chances for evaluative research and independent data and statistics.

Populism can also cause a boomerang effect by backfiring and reversing the intended outcome. Populism always involves a risk factor. Sometimes such unintended outcomes can be managed depending on the credibility, oratory powers, or dramatization skills of the political leader.

Populism in India is considered an irresponsible style of political parties. In fact, populism is viewed in many quarters as an unfair practice and a threat to economy and democracy. And yet, populism is sweeping not only in India but across continents.

Control and command of the public opinion-manufacturing machinery may be one reason for taking to populism. Depending on this confidence, political parties continue to live by populism wherever economic disparities are increasing.

Political parties, political leaders, and governments tend to thrive on populism. In fact, this tribe engages in populism in an electoral context. Party leaders tend to believe that populism wins them power. That is how populism has become a strategy and why election manifestoes are full of promises of populism.

It is also why parties are engaged in 'competitive populism'. The belief is that whoever is populist and offers more lures has better chances of winning. Surveys have also spread such perceptions. A rhetoric-oriented campaign sustains populism. Once set in such course, it becomes an ongoing practice.

For justifying poll promises or lures in the manifesto, the political party in power tends to manipulate the numbers, data, statistics, and research findings. This is when the problem gets complicated as it can have long-term implications by eroding the credibility of national agencies created for research and data collection in the early decades after independence. Populism involves playing a numbers game. That is, when the numbers in an electoral context are no longer of advantage to a political party, the party uses populism to overcome such a situation.

Data, statistics, and research are manipulated to justify a populist claim. Political leaders consider this an easier way to claim their 'achievement' and get featured in the news media for their glorification with the help of surveys by research agencies. For news media, too, this route of supporting or criticising a political party or leader comes handy as they do not have to make any effort to critically appraise the claims of politicians. Politicising data and statistics erodes the very credibility of not just the party but the economy, democratic stature, and the governance of the day. And yet, poll-centric parties do not seem to care about the consequences of such short-sighted populist strategies.

'Achievements' vs. 'performance'. Once, in the thick of competitive politics (1972–75), Mrs Indira Gandhi's government was more concerned with projecting herself using 'achievements' and claim credit (1974–84). On the other hand, Rajiv Gandhi as Prime Minister was more concerned about 'performance', which is target- and recipient-orientated. With 'achievements', it is all about claims, intentions, administrative feedback, or budgetary allocations. PM Modi's regime focuses more on quantitative evidences to claim various successes. The concern in all these numbers is to showcase the 'impact' or differences made by the policies and schemes. Delivery of promises made in the poll manifesto and public utterances when wooing voters is what political leaders try to do with data and research findings. A relevant recent example of this is the promises of doubling farmer's income.

Another outlook that suffered a setback was the futuristic vision of our nation builders. Competitive politics and populist policies have dampened visionary, future studies. Futures studies in India took off through the efforts of the Department of Science and Technology (DST) in the early 1970s. Dr Abdul Kalam, Dr S. C. Seth, Dr Y. S. Rajan, Dr R. A. Mashelkar, among others (after 1970), should be thanked for their pioneering initiatives. Their focus was, of course, on technology. But it was the implications on public policy formulation that Dr S. C. Seth campaigned about in different ways to sustain futures studies. He even talked of data generation, analysis, information retrieval, and information processing. By 2000, nobody was concerned with futures studies, and it never gained ground. Instead, 'poll predictions' or promoting populism became the model despite the fact that a rise in populism would lead to the decline in futures studies that require reliable research methodologies.

Despite India's long history of research, governments have not invested sincere time and effort to further develop this field. How else in January 2019, in response to a US submission to the WTO that India is no longer a 'developing' country but a developed nation, did India claim that not only is its per capita very low but it also has a 'very low research and development capacity'?[5]

CHAPTER TWO

Significance of Research

> **Four lakh female out-patients of AIIMS missed in 2016?**
>
> Gender discrimination or ignorance or apathy in access to healthcare is known to those who are familiar with public policies in India. But nothing has ever been initiated to correct this anomaly. For example, in Bihar, the ratio of female patients who visit a hospital is the lowest. This ratio is also low in New Delhi's All India Institute of Medical Sciences (AIIMS). In an analysis by experts including of Indian Statistical Institute (ISI) of out-patients from Delhi, Haryana, UP, and Bihar who visited AIIMS in 2016 revealed that nearly half of female out-patents were 'missing'. They concluded, three years later in a research paper, that little over four lakh female patients in AIIMS in 2016 were 'missing'. This was determined by analysing the gender of patients from OPD outpatient register. Was this finding followed up?
>
> How was such an analysis not conducted before? Why was a statistician required to bring out such a vital data from already existing outpatient registers? Sources for public health policies are all around, yet how many of them are based on data?[1]

No country in today's complex world can expect to remain democratic as it remains on the course of development while offering 'good governance' if it does not have constant support of data and research, both primary and secondary.

Independent research, reliable data, and analytics are essential elements to ensure efficient planned development, deepen democracy, and sustain responsible governance. Independent research can guarantee a country's growth, level the playing field, provide inclusive opportunities, reduce inequalities, and ensure government accountability as well as decentralisation of governance. It should also be noted, however, that research can help bind people or divide them. When used consciously, research facilitates inclusive development. Data, analysis, and research should not be the cause of divides and conflicts; rather, it should heal or contribute for the resolution of issues and proactively help to prevent undesirable trends. All this is possible when research evolves from being a mere formality and becomes a national concern. Public should, in fact, become sensitive to research methods and findings. More schools should introduce courses on the role of research and methodologies at the high school level itself instead of the postgraduate level.

Public policies remain relevant and yield desired objectives when they are based on research, data, and analysis, from within as well as from independent sources and on an ongoing basis. To identify peoples' pulse in a democracy is a recurring requirement. How does a country the size of a continent keep itself together despite its innumerable contradictions, which are natural in a nation that is a complex mosaic of cultures, castes, communities, socio-economic classes, and climate zones? It can only be done through enlightened policies and programmes that are inclusive and respond to people's needs without pandering to anyone, and which can avoid populism and are far-sighted. Research is crucial for such policies, and it is extremely important that it is seen as rigorous and scientific and is respected. In a diverse country with many points of view and competing interests, data simply has to be reliable, objective, and representative.

Public policies depend on the type of data available and the sensitivity with which they are initiated. Data is generated from research and analysis and provides feedback, evaluates efficiencies, identifies correctives, and indicates the impact of ongoing policies and programmes on different objectives and targets concerning different segments of society. Not only does research offer a perspective, facilitate new initiatives, and help formulate public policies to achieve the desired immediate as well as long-term objectives, but it also lends credibility and acceptability to policies and programmes. Independent and transparently conducted research makes this process easier. No country, no political party, and no leader can expect to formulate plans or strategies without basic data analysis and field research. More so when the country is full of complexities, contradictions, inequalities, and uncertainties. No other indicator reflects the course and direction of a country or people as its research pursuit. Thus, a 'developing country' must conduct research and rely on data. Those who are in power and those who are outside, both require research equally to present their arguments logically and convincingly.

It is no surprise then the origins of independent India show our early leaders pursuing data to frame policies, perspectives, and strategic plans for attaining national goals, development plans, and aspirations. An individual is the focus of the Constitution, beyond creed, community, caste, socio-economic class, gender, and region. The primary concern of the Constitution is equity, justice, and empowerment of people. This has dictated the priorities, including research endeavours. This pursuit would not have been possible without realising the need for data as the basis for perspective plans, implementation of strategies, and concern for delivering public services to people.

Even before Independence, for example, Netaji Subhas Chandra Bose envisioned implementing population planning based on the population growth as per the 1941 census, while Sriman Narayana Agarwal developed an economic plan for India with what was known about the people and regions. Later, after Independence, Babasaheb Ambedkar put forth his concerns and knowledge based on the available data on demographics and distribution of population on socio-culture-economic lines. Moreover, while J. C. Kumarappa advocated a plan for a self-reliant India, Jawaharlal Nehru created development plans, Five Year Plans, and presented a perspective for a future based on his analyses of the socio-economic and cultural trends, and all this much before Mokshagundam Visvesvaraya envisioned urban infrastructure and developed irrigation plans. All these ideas, approaches, and perspectives were based on whatever data was then publicly available. But these pioneer leaders' recognition of the importance of more reliable and updated data goes beyond the census and demographics that paved the path for the Republic India. That determined the scope of research in the initial years. Such realisation also laid the foundation for the country's research infrastructure.

Tracing Research Origins

No country can offer a better tomorrow without availing basic demographic data on its people and resources to gain a more rounded perspective regarding public policies. These policies are formulated by governments after taking different priorities into account and proclaiming their objectives, scope, and expected benefits. These policies are then formalised through a parliamentary democracy process, with political parties and peoples' representatives driving the concerned agencies towards achieving the objectives envisaged in the public policies.

It is no surprise then that the national government of independent India has taken multiple initiatives to identify and organise sources for basic data, mobilise these resources, and compile capabilities to analyse and conduct primary research. That was how so many national institutions were launched in support of public concerns and policies. The Five Year Plans, too, augmented such capabilities. And the first Prime Minister Jawaharlal Nehru's idea of 'scientific temper' had given further momentum to this approach. That was decades ago. The idea of planning is based on gathering data and analysing primary and secondary sources. Today, we have access to many more databases and analytics. This means that Prime Minister Modi's reminder of a 'scientific temper' in March 2018 should have made a far more visible impact. So why has it not yet?

In 1970, realising the limitations of decennial census of India, the Planning Commission opted for independent research and brought the National Sample Survey Office (NSSO) and the Programme Evaluation Organisation (PEO)—both with professional capabilities—under its purview, instead of relying on the bureaucracy. The initial national policies and schemes were based on sound data, analyses, and field research, apart from the wisdom and visionary outlook of individual leaders.

Much before August 1947, national leaders like Subhash Chandra Bose, Shriman Narayan Agarwal, Jawaharlal Nehru, K.M. Munshi, and Kumarappa, among many others, discussed their vision for an independent India. The idea of Five Year Plans promotes rational public policies. Agarwal's book *The Gandhian Plan of Economic Development for India* made leaders of the time aware of such an approach.[2] J.C. Kumarappa's *Gandhian Economic Thought* also provided development options.[3]

The Congress party, in fact, had formed a group almost a decade before Independence to explore how India should develop, plan, and go about with its development endeavours, starting with the 'self-sufficiency concern' for food and basic amenities. These initiatives were based on 'facts and figures' available mostly from the census of India. However, as the new government noticed the limitations of this source, it geared up the Planning Commission as well as other ministries to put together basic facts in quantitative terms. The agriculture ministry, for example, compiled data for various crops, soils, and yields and sources of irrigation. Even the Reserve Bank of India put together 'rural credit' scenario based on a field survey, which was the earliest primary research initiative in Independent India. New departments were also added in agriculture colleges and field research on farm practices became an ongoing activity. Initiatives on agriculture and family planning were based on primary and secondary data. There was no one-source documentation of this period as it was mostly anecdotal. Wherever foreign aid was involved for national schemes during these years, there was some kind of research, as in the case of agriculture (Green Revolution), family planning, rural electrification, and even community development. This research was based on field experiments in Nilokheri, Almora, and Kurukshetra.

The National Institute of Community Development in Mussoorie, now known as the National Institute of Rural Development in Rajendra Nagar, Hyderabad, was also established as a centre for training and research. Research and training were considered to be linked with the objectives of the institutes set up in the first 20 years of Republic India. They were viewed as essential for national policies and for empowering people and developing the country. Rockefeller Foundation, Ford Foundation, USAID, and other foreign agencies have funded some national institutes of research over the decades.

Initial interest in primary research received boost first from agriculture and rural development endeavours. The Delhi school of Economics, Institute of Economic Growth, Development Study Centre in Madras, Ahmedabad, and Trivandrum, and even the earlier Gokhale Institute in Pune began focusing on research and inputs for formulating public policies. At the same time, with departments of economics, sociology, statistics, psychology, anthropology, and social work cropping up in universities, research discipline became more sustained. Thus, in some universities like the Andhra University, the 'Applied Economics' outlook offered a theoretical base. I was one of the beneficiaries of this approach between 1960 and 1962. Professor Damle of Pune University and M. N. Srinivasan and S. C. Dube of Sagar University, for example, were early gurus who studied push and pull factors concerning 'change', 'behaviours', and 'influence' in qualitative terms and offered theoretical propositions from the perspective of India. They were mostly from sociology and anthropology disciplines.

The curriculum of a host of these departments included 'research methodology' as a key subject and a field project report as part of the academics. Stalwarts from the Indian

Institute of Statistics in Calcutta had become part of different public policy establishments across the country. These initial academic efforts promoted a research environment in India. They created concerns in national institutes and universities to usher in a data-based orientation and academic back-up for research tools like sampling, data analysis, and survey research. Prof. P. C. Mahalanobis also gave new hope to such endeavours by being close to Pandit Jawaharlal Nehru. He should perhaps be credited for planting the seed of the idea of institutes and institutionalising, like National Sample Survey (NSS) organisation, Programme Evaluation Organisation, Research Programme Committee, etc. A host of demographic centres were set up across the country as a part of premier universities.

With such initiatives intended to ensure authentic data, both primary and secondary, one could expect public policies to be based on rational and reliable inputs. The efficacy of policies was verified by regular monitoring including conducting field studies to achieve national objectives. All such efforts contributed towards independent India's growth and progress. But there was a dilemma—how to ensure 'growth' with 'equity'? How to adopt behaviours and policies for 'change' without discarding 'traditional' systems and values. This dilemma is what led to *quantitative* orientation rather than *qualitative* value orientation. This process also led to the inclusion of surrogate indicators for development, change, and growth—indicators such as GDP, rate of inflation, unemployment rate, household savings, the number of newspaper subscriptions in homes, TV sets per thousand populations, etc.

Had we strictly gone with such a quest to gain research support, we would have realised many of our public policies and achieved the goals outlined in the Constitution and envisioned in the Five Year Plans. Today, we would not have been left in the wilderness, with many of us wondering why, 70 years after gaining independence, we have not been able to accomplish, for example, universal literacy; why the divides and disparities in the country have increased; why nearly one-fifth of our people are in poverty, and why one-fifth of the youth, mostly educated, are without any work. Is this related to what is prioritised in our public policies or is it concerned with their implementation without sufficient backup? Adequate research support would have saved the situation from a 'half-glass-empty, half-glass-full' syndrome.

Dr V. M. Dandekar and Dr Patnaik (1965-1975) from Pune Institute of Development were continuously engaged in field research and secondary analysis of data of census, NSS, etc., to determine correctives in our war on poverty and measurement criteria for Below the Poverty Line (BPL) numbers.

Dr Ashish Bose, an eminent demographer, developed the concept of 'BIMARU' (Bihar, MP, Rajasthan, and UP) based on his years of field research and data analysis to examine why these 'Hindi" states' growth in various fields of development remained static or slow. It was Dr Bose's presentation to then Prime Minister Indira Gandhi that convinced the leaders to incorporate this concept into national policies and generate state-specific schemes.

In addition, Dr Amulya Reddy's research at Indian Institutes of Science, Bangalore, provided the basis for the country's energy policies from 1966 to 1991. The research by Dr Norman Borlaug, Dr M S Swaminathan, and many others on high yielding variety of rice also helped saved the nation from deprivation and food shortages. Dr Bhatnagar and Dr R.A. Mashelkar further led the industrial research in the country and have not only motivated many researchers but have also upheld the research culture in the country. Dr Mashelkar also pursued technology research with a future perspective.

In the early fifties, there were instances of the Parliament facing embarrassing situations as government did not have any facts or figures to back up its statements on policies. Panjabrao Deshmukh, the then Minister of Agriculture, was said to have given exaggerated figures for area under cropping and compost manure in the country, much to the embarrassment of the government. This, however, also reminded the nation of the necessity of reliable facts and figures regarding ground realities, thus expediting the process of building primary data.

But then, in the July 2019 session of the parliament, more than thrice in one week, the government was asked by members to substantiate its claims with data. This showed that the data on policies continues to be inadequate even today.

Initially, during 1950–60, it was research findings that led to a shift in concerns from *awareness* to *knowledge*, and then from *reach* to *behaviour change*. However, it should be noted that awareness alone is not enough and will not lead to action or adoption. A good example of this was family planning. Research on family planning had indicated that awareness was not enough but knowledge was required for married couples to make logical decisions. That was how concern shifted from awareness to extension and knowledge. And since knowledge also had not caused change, motivation and persuasion were acted on.

It was realised that *reach* is not enough and that exposure to messages and delivery of family planning services were critical. Reaching urban household was not what was needed but focus should have been more on 'hard core couple' (rural couple engaged in agriculture labour, and with both, or more usually the wife, being illiterate) for a breakthrough in the family planning programme in India (The first ever National Family Planning Survey in 1972, funded by the Ford Foundation and supported by the Ministry of Health and Family Welfare, was conducted by Operations Research Group (ORG) and I was involved in writing the report). Adoption, practice, and benefit of an idea or a scheme is not the same as knowing, reaching, and delivery of service to the needy. In the first two decades, the pursuit was of awareness and reach, but it was research that helped expedite the process of motivation to ensure behavioural change and streamlining of delivery strategies of the Public Distribution System (PDS). In the next decade, research became part of the development schemes and strategies. Many public schemes of the time included research as a support with baseline data, feedback, and post-evaluation. Programme Evaluation Organisation and National Sample Survey organisations within the Planning Commission were in fact mandated to include research. When the Five Year Plan idea was launched, the government soon realised the need to have an ongoing methodology and mechanism to monitor and evaluate efforts in that direction. This led to colleges and universities setting up special cells for research activities. Government organisations and public sector corporations also began to conduct research and field studies. For example, the Rural Electricity Corporation (REC) took to social research in the 1960s as it was an obligation of US AID for rural electrification and started a research department with Dr Lalit Sen, a sociologist, as its head. The REC's studies in 1960–70 established clearly that an electricity pole in a village does not necessarily mean that electricity has reached the residents of that village—that pole is for transmission lines stretching well above and past the village, with no local power connections.

By the 1980s, however, the concern had shifted to creating and managing the government's 'image'; the efficacy and efficiency of development schemes became secondary. Increasingly, political parties were preoccupied with *influencing* voters rather than motivating and engaging citizens on critical, grass roots issues. This change or shift from *service* to image-management and influencing, or more accurately, *manipulating* public opinion led to de-emphasis on research. Independent research, particularly to evaluative and impact research, almost became extinct. Instead, the emphasis shifted to monitoring activities. Monitoring is concerned more with outlays and operations than with the processes and outcomes, both physical and behavioural. The discipline and skills needed for impact and evaluation research are different from that of monitoring and awareness. While the latter is more concerned with implementers and public relations, the former focuses on benefits at the recipient end. This trend in later decades became more obvious with political parties becoming more poll-centric. That is why advertisements on universal massages (like 'smoking is bad for health') carry the Ministry's name even when it is not needed, thus undermining the credibility of the message. That is, the message loses its seriousness once the government, which usually means the ruling party, comes into the picture or becomes the source.

It is a sad irony that in a country of immense potential with a well-established academic base and sound traditions of governance and development beyond mere numbers, the leaders within just a couple of decades of Independence were on a reverse course, a control and command course. Public involvement and participation today are no longer our priorities; privatisation, corporatisation, and advertising are.

The foundations laid in the first two decades of India's independence were unparalleled among the new democracies. The quest for national and scientific base was unprecedented and the research spirit evident among the leaders. The recent *Mangalyaan* project, or GSAT pursuit, are an example of such a spirit. Disciplines such as science, technology, and management took off and led to the establishment of institutions such as ISRO. Considering the growth of these institutions, the earnestness of professionalism and research orientation was evident. All of this would lead one to expect India today to be at the top of the world in innovations, technology, and scientific outlook and in tackling socio-economic issues confronting the country. However, an analysis of policy initiatives in the first 25 years (1947–72) of independence and in the recent 25 years (1995–2020), particularly in the last decade (2010–20), do not show us to be availing instruments of change, specifically in research, training, extension, and the proliferation of mass media for scaling up and consolidating outcomes of public policies. We have come a long way, no doubt, but where do we stand on issues of social development and human development? Why do we seem to be on a 'reluctant course'? On issues like caste, sex preference, crimes against women, hate and prejudice between communities, quality of education, malnutrition, our record is deplorable.

Another dilemma is what is the 'modernity' pursuit that India is on now? Copycatting, more of the same view, temporal and political or corporate concerns appear to be dictating the national pursuit in recent years. The chase is after surrogate indicators rather than real-time concerns of people. We seem to have become a more parochial and personalised society that has blind beliefs despite talk of digital connectivity, competitiveness, artificial intelligence, and scientific accomplishments. Yes, in the last two decades, more people have become graduates than in the previous four decades, there is more competitiveness in the country, and more corporatisation and better infrastructure than ever before. And yet, rational outlook and research culture has not flourished. A missing element in all this is a rational outlook, particularly in the social sector. Immediate electoral compulsions and corporate interests are dictating public policies more than the long-term concerns and objective research inputs.

Scope of Research

An analysis of scope and structure of research over the decades indicates that it was the concern and commitment implied in public policies that dictates or determines the extent of research. Concern for the future of the country and commitment to the objectives outlined in the constitution should have determined the priorities of research. The first decade of Indian independence was one of shortage of availability and reliability of facts and figures about the country. The 1941 census was the only source for any base data at that point. A few years later, top line data of 1951 census became available and desegregated results much after 1955, when the country was engaged in formulating a Five Year Plan.

The political parties and leaders of the time were as concerned with making available basic needs, specifically food, health, and education, as the government's public policies. Increase in food production and supplies by bringing more acreage under irrigation was a necessity. The compulsions of electoral politics had not yet become a priority then. The states were being supplied with food grains (wheat and rice) as per the claims of Below the Poverty Line (BPL) population. However, as the states had given different estimates for the percent of BPL households, it led to largescale corruption as states diverted FCI supplies to open market and thus tempted cadres of the ruling party. This was possible as there was no reliable data based on a transparent methodology to determine the BPL population. Moreover, each state had its own way and were happy claiming a higher percent of BPL households.

Interestingly, it was the overflowing godowns of the Food Corporation of India (FCI) that lead to the 'food for work' scheme (1977) when the Union Government gave away food grains in lieu of wages for those employed in specially selected construction or development projects. Lack of reliable data and estimate of arrivals of new crop yields had caused a demand-supply-storage-distribution problem.

What Happens When a Public Policy Suffers from Lack of Data?

In 2017, in Madhya Pradesh, the police fired at farmers, killing ten of them, which in turn led to the party losing power in the state. The farmers were facing a crisis for producing more paddy per acre. Neither the state government procured the paddy at the declared minimum price as promised at the outset nor was there godown facility for farmers to store their bumper yields. As a result, the farmers became angry and agitated. This was not the story of shortages similar to that in the earlier decades, but one of lack of research back-up when creating a public policy. In fact, the scene of farmers in several states (in 2015–19) spilling milk, throwing fruits and vegetables on public roads was another indication that research back-up was missing for farm policies. This was not a need for complicated research but for envisioning, having reliable data inputs, and adequate research. This was an example of the government's failure in realising the significance of field research.

At ORG, we were engaged by the Hindustan Unilever Limited (HUL) (Hindustan Liver (HLL) (1974–80) to conduct innovative crop surveys to estimate acreage under cotton/groundnut, probable amount of yield, when the farmer is likely to dispose of the produce in the market, the expected price, and the produce that is likely to go into godowns. This research helped HLL save and make appropriate decisions regarding when to procure, how much, and at what price. Governments never took to such an exercise based on the voluminous data accumulated from every District Agriculture Office over the years. They did not even consider a secondary analysis for preventing farmer suicides. Many farmer suicides could have been prevented if some such field research and analysis had been taken into account and if databases had been pooled for proactive initiatives. We have analytic methodologies to foresee emerging or evolving situations to ensure proactive initiatives that can help prevent or minimise such disasters as farmer suicides or the need to fire at farmers who had produced more food for the country on their own.

Public Policies—Decentralised Governance?

Public policies are never a one-shot affair. They need to be carefully formulated and then fine-tuned and refined, always guided by reliable and impartial data accumulated over years through constant and evolving research. Unfortunately, each time a new government comes to power, it is likely to review and often junk the predecessor's policies. Sound data is valued and encouraged only when there is sincerity of intention and sincerity in the implementation of policies. This depends on how serious a government is about achieving genuine change for the benefit of all sections of the public. When 'public' policies are diluted to cater to the interests of a few, be it a political party or big corporations, it is bound to reflect on the type of research being done and the date that is gathered.

One contentious policy is the decentralisation of the government which was a concern during the freedom movement. Mahatma Gandhi aimed for decentralisation of the government. In fact, he had talked and written extensively on *Gram Swaraj*. This idea even figured in the Constituent Assembly deliberations. After the Avadi Congress of All India Congress Party, Prime Minister Nehru appointed a committee with Gujarat Chief Minister Balwant Rai Mehta in 1957 to suggest a model for decentralised governance. In 1959, this committee put forth a landmark suggestion for a three-tier system of governance for the country—at the village, block, and district level. This model was first adopted by Rajasthan and Andhra.

Almost twenty years later, in 1978, Prime Minister Morarji Desai appointed another committee called the Dantwala Committee, even though Morarji Desai already had a report delivered only a year earlier by Ashok Mehta (Member, Planning Commission). The Dantwala Committee suggested block-level planning and direct elections to be held to the village sarpanch. In 1984, Prime Minister Indira Gandhi appointed another committee that suggested a district level planning board where the district collector would play a key role. Then, in 1985, Prime Minister Rajiv Gandhi appointed GVK Rao Committee that suggested abolishing block level committees that were suggested earlier by Dantwala. This Committee also suggested a key role for the district collector but suggested devolution of finances to districts. Furthermore, despite this committee also suggesting regular elections at the district level, many states did not go for polls for years. In 1986, Rajiv Gandhi appointed the legal luminary L M Singhvi Committee to study the panchayat raj system. This committee recommended a Gram Sabha to be held with legal backing and suggested state finance commissions as well as devolution of funds to local panchayats. He also suggested regularity in local elections. Much earlier, in 1984, Andhra Pradesh Chief Minster N T Rama Rao had abolished the tehsil system from smaller districts that had a population below 75,000 and the Mandal system. His idea was to take the government to people's doorsteps instead of expecting people to go to some faraway district or the state headquarter. It was the 73rd Constitution Amendment Act of 1993, however, that finally assured representation and devolution of funds and granted decision-making rights to the village. (Twice before, once in the Lok Sabha in 1989 and then in the Rajya Sabha in 1990, the bill had failed to go through.) But have all these measures made India more representative? Is India on a centralisation path or heading down a decentralisation course? The fact that presiding legislative leaders took so long is evidence that research back-up was a significant missing feature—such research back-up could have ensured better debates and legislative decisions. It was only in August 2019 that the idea of a committee to discuss the research needs of Parliament and Assemblies was taken up.

Thus, despite recognising that decentralisation was a virtue and a foundation for democracy, we are yet to see a model, even after 75 years, that consolidates and sustains grass roots democracy and development. Despite most of those eight Committees (between 1956 and 93) recommending devolution of financial powers and constituting state finance commissions, it has still not been implemented across the country. Instead, centralisation is gaining.

Throughout these years, several studies have examined decentralisation, local self-government, panchayat raj system, rural development, and elected women representatives, but there is no evidence that this research was used as a resource for any of these committees. However, although there are so many institutes, independent and set up by the government itself, there are no comprehensive action plans. As a result, India continues to lag when availing the wisdom of our founding fathers and taking feedback from regional experiments and pilot projects over the decades. Today, the trend is to polarise as the centralised government has been taking to management information system, new technologies, and new legislations. This issue is a good example of not going for longitudinal research and taking a temporary view of research while falling short of the desired goals. This is also an example of unending committees causing delay or deferring an issue and is a reminder that action is more important.

As early as the late fifties, the Reserve Bank of India conducted a study on rural credit to determine the extent of farmer's indebtedness and how they borrow from local money lenders at high interest rates. This study had guided policies of the government of the time with initiatives. But, 70 years later, the rural distress and continued suicides of farmers have highlighted the lack of reliable research updates or the conditional respect it is given.

Regarding agriculture, research played a significant role in the first 25 years of the country's independence. In fact, many of the policies concerning seeds, fertilisers, cropping patterns, and extension methods were based on field research and experimentation in agriculture colleges and universities. The recent increase in food production is more because of increased acreage receiving assured water on completion of new irrigation projects like the Bhakra Nangal in Punjab, Narmada in Gujarat, Indira Nahar in Rajasthan, and Nagarjuna Sagar in Andhra Pradesh. This, in turn, prompted research to make the most out of these projects. Research in agriculture universities boomed, particularly between 1965 and 1975.

But the call given for a second green resolution in the last couple of years (after 2000) never took off. Can we expect to double farmer income by 2022–23 without research support, for example, of crop change practices? There has been no new focused research in recent years despite agriculture and farm sector being in turmoil (except the report by Dr M. S. Swaminathan Committee). The other reason involves changing priorities of the governments, agriculture universities, and the entry of private sector players including foreign corporations such as Monsanto. It was also alleged that findings of agriculture research were being availed more by private foreign corporates and that budgets for research were curtailed. Indian Agricultural Research Institute (IARI) and Indian Council for Agriculture Research (ICAR), agriculture universities, and many research centres around the country, all set up in the first 25 years, played a significant role in promoting research and taking the findings to farmers (lab to land). They have contributed in the post-green revolution years. It is also important to note that importing BT cotton (1997) and groundnut without any research has changed the atmosphere. Neither has local research been prioritised nor have appointments been made for the numerous vacancies in research positions across the country. Multinationals have even engaged retired senior faculties and researchers to support their own profit-centred pursuit. Even the government often seems to be interested in privatising or outsourcing research, extension, and training functions.

Idea of Experimental Research Is Yet to Gain Traction

In a country of contrasts, diversities, and inequalities including on socio economic parameters, no intervention or public policy can be uniform for the country. As such, experimenting with ideas for policies and schemes makes more sense than going national. But what has been the extent of experimentation or piloting even across the states? Such experimentation is even more relevant since most of these welfare interventions in particular are based on instinctual assumptions of politicians or bureaucrats, or a political ideology. They require field testing, verification, or validation to ensure their relevance. What works and what does not—how do our decision-makers weigh this question?

Had the planning commission taken to experimentation research in the earlier decades, the country would have been spared from the tyranny and fallacy of implementing one model or one scheme for the entire country, which most of our public policies continue to be based on while ignoring regional peculiarities. India's plurality character obviously requires unique research methodologies considering equity pursuit. However, despite PEO and extensive detour at its disposal, methods beyond field surveys have never been considered.

Experimental and pilot research has not yet gained traction in the country in terms of public policy making as it has in advertising, communication, and social media. Controlled research experiments are often the basis for communication strategies. As a result, certain programmes were adopted across the nation without concerns of relevance and outcomes. This despite the fact that the 'green revolution' movement was first experimented, not randomly but in select rice-growing districts of specific agro-climate regions. Experimental research also helped scale agriculture extension initiatives.

This was also the case for the midday meal programme in Tamil Nadu and in Orissa. It was the Cantors Associates of

U.S. and CSD's research in Orissa which established midday meal programmes as viable and scalable programmes much before other states implemented it after 1972. (The midday meal scheme in India had its origins in Tamil Nadu's Madurai district. The Sourashtra Secondary School there had been offering noon-meals to its students since 1911. Inspired by this, TN chief minister K. Kamaraj, a school dropout himself, introduced the scheme in government schools across the state in the late 1950s. Following the scheme's success, the central government began its first midday meal programme in a limited manner some years later.)

Even in the case of family planning, for example, mass vasectomy camps were conducted by enthusiastic officers in Ahmedabad and Ernakulam (1972–73) as experiments. The idea gained based on independent evaluation. This study was initiated by Ford Foundation and conducted by me at ORG. The population council's first research study (1973–74) initiated by its director, J.C. Kavoori, was on mass vasectomy camps, and the idea of 'social marketing' for family planning was adopted by the ministry after it was 'tested' in Hubli by Peter King along with IIM-Calcutta (1970–71).

On the other hand, pilots on crop insurance and e-medicine in the earlier years, for example, took considerably longer to be applied as there was no research available. Subsidies on solar is, of course, another example, about whether solar had helped or harmed, so that large scale adoption can be strategized. This was never researched.

Reservations to certain sections and subsidies on the numerous services are two of the oldest interventions being continued without systematic evaluation for establishing their role in level playing, equity and poverty reduction strategies, and for operational modifications.

As a policy tool, experimental research gained traction much later. It was academics from Harvard, MIT, and Johns Hopkins Universities in the US that promoted the idea more seriously. The MIT's J-PAL (Abdul Latif Jameel Poverty Action Lab) Project in Rajasthan, which was eventually awarded a

Nobel Prize in 2019, gave much needed positioning to social science research regarding public policies. Social audit is another idea that was not adopted on a large scale despite experimentation in a couple of public services for the same reason—it was not researched systematically. While Aruna Roy's grass roots people moment that led to the RTI Act did not reach beyond Rajasthan, many other initiatives like Bunker Roy's Barefoot idea in Rajasthan did not catch on, perhaps because of lack of international or foreign involvement or backing by a network of collaborations. Experimental research did not gain perhaps also because political leaders realised that 'promise" and 'performance' never match, whereas 'evidence' or proof of pudding is the bases for scaling up and adoption.

However, not all public policies require or are amenable for a controlled or any experimental research. But some type of evaluative exercise for outcome or tracking change in the phenomena is not only desired but can also save the country from wasteful efforts and boomerang effects.

Is a Research Culture Missing in Policy-making?

Research is a misunderstood idea. Research is a systematic way to objectively or reliably establish reality, linkages, and relationships that contribute or lead to certain outcomes. Research is availed to envisage future, analyse the past, and understand the present. Research can be in the context of or availing discipline of anthropology, economics, sociology, psychology, social work, etc. It helps in planning, reviewing, correcting, and accomplishing public policies, of course, when and if research findings are utilised. Thus, research has potential both to help and to harm the processes and formulate policies depending on the reliability of research or how seriously the research results are interpreted and availed. It is expected to make a difference to the decision-making process. Data makes a difference in logical or rational decision-making both at the macro and micro level.

One could also argue whether the decision of giving voting rights to 18-year-olds in India in 1984 was based on any specially conducted research or on insights of wise men. According to Dr Subhash C. Kashyap, a constitutional expert, whose persuasive suggestion to the then Prime Minister Rajiv Gandhi led to that landmark decision, it was based on an analysis of people between 18 and 21 years and a belief in their level of knowledge.

A similar public policy decision, approved by Parliament of India without a discussion (Select Committee had gone over), was the Right to Information Act (RTI) in 2005. This Act was facilitated by experiments in Rajasthan by Aruna Roy (a social activist), as recommended earlier by two committees, and based on experiments in two states (Maharashtra and Karnataka). Neither of the experiments were analysed to gain insights. This led to several members of the Parliament trying to dilute the Act within five years of RTI's implementation, despite the kind of impact the Act had made on ground. After more than a decade, the Act was diluted in 2019 with an amendment. Independent research and evaluating the Act's implementation would have helped avoid potential risks. It should have been a win-win opportunity, including for the government and the political parties who were reluctant to embrace transparency.

Better Research for Better Debates

Continued decline in the quality of debates and orderly conduct of legislatures in recent decades has reached such a pass that the speaker of Lok Sabha took initiative for a 'code of conduct' to MLAs and MPs. The presiding officers also acknowledged that lack of research had hampered legislative debates and that there was a need to 'gauge the research needs' of legislatures for better debates in the legislatures.[4] Better debates is bound to lead to better public policies, more participative policies, and an opportunity to consider social policies for the country.

The National Health (Protection) Ayushman Mission Insurance scheme of 2018 was launched with much hype and a budgetary allocation of Rs 6,400 crores (2019–2020).[5] This is a massive scheme, next only to MNREGS, in terms of budgetary commitment. The scheme was announced in a hurry, without analysing or ascertaining the viability and participation of corporate hospitals, simply due to electoral compulsions. Some relevant research would have saved the government from the embarrassment of postponing its implementation, but more importantly, would have saved the people from disappointment and despondency.

In 2017-18, there were ten national major schemes with over Rs 15,000 crores of budgetary allocations. Together, they accounted for Rs 2,00,000 lakh crores concerning the national roads (Rs 70,000 crores) or the Pradhan Mantri Awas Yojana (Rs 27,000 Crores). How many of those schemes were backed by research or some field-based assessment regarding their scope, implementation, strategy, and utilisation, beyond bureaucratic internal exercises?

Research Sensitivity of the Prime Ministers of India

As India nears 75 years as a Republic, it is interesting to take a retrospective view of the different political regimes and how Prime Ministers have distinguished themselves with their public policies. Although India has had fourteen Prime Ministers since 1947, only eight of them could be said to have distinguished themselves. They completed at least one term and made a mark with their outlooks and policies. These eight prime ministers had distinct approaches regarding formulating public policies for the country, depending on how intensely they were tuned into poll politics and populism.

Prime Minister Charan Singh, V.P. Singh, Chandra Shekhar, H. D. Deve Gowda, and I. K. Gujral did not complete more than a couple of years (1980-1998). During this period, the country witnessed uncertain years when poll surveys mushroomed and divisive politics and populism were taken to newer heights while research on reservation and caste politics received boost.

Foundational Years, Quest for Research

The 70 years of Independence can be broadly classified into three distinct periods of 20-25 years each. The first period from

1950 to 1970 was dominated by India's first Prime Minister, Jawaharlal Nehru. These years have been considered as glorious and truly foundational years that showed visible impact. Nehru continues to be remembered as an institutional builder and a true democrat who believed in citizen-centric policies and in the Fourth Estate as an essential independent institute of public opinion. Nehru believed in a modern outlook, rational thinking, and advocated scientific temper in people and policies. He viewed school, library, and irrigation projects as modern temples of India. Impressed by the then USSR model of planned economic development, he believed that to be the fastest path for the newly independent country. He respected public opinion, which was evident in the reversal of his and his party's decision (Avadi Congress approved) concerning cooperative farming at the last minute before it became an Act in the Parliament. All or most of the country's pioneering institutes in technology, science, and social research were the result of his initiative and visionary outlook. They are all approximately 60 years old now and have futuristic mandates in their concerns with a long-term perspective for the country. Public policies during this period were based on data, debate, and discussions within and outside formal policy framework, and all of this includes a rational outlook and surpasses party politics while continuing to aim for better outcomes and futures. For Nehru, processes were as important as outcomes. He believed in participatory and inclusive development, which formed the basis for his propagation of public policies. During this period, public policies were truly public-centred, rational, and inclusive. Improving data bases, their inclusiveness, and reliability remained a concern, and such an outlook was cultivated across the country in a visible and lasting way. Public policies were driven by data and research but research was also policy-driven.

No other Indian prime minister in 75 years has encouraged and supported so many scientists, researchers, and independent thinkers from diverse fields as Jawaharlal Nehru did. Nor have so many institutions been established in different fields. Many of them today are of global standards and have produced many world leaders of stature. While some of these institutions were set up with government support, many were encouraged to operate independently. All of them, however, enjoyed freedom, earned credibility, and became benchmarks. Some of them were for child development, some for tribal development, and there were institutes of higher education and technical education. He realised that children are the future and took to inspiring them as a mission. That was Chacha Nehru. Those institutions were looked upon as catalysts of change and development in economics, technology, science, humanities, and welfare, and harbingers of peace and prosperity. Many of those institutions continued subsequently undented regardless of who the Prime Minister was or which political party was in power. The credit goes to leaders of the country for not dragging them into a partisan view or politicising them. Nehru never succumbed to vote-bank politics and was known for saying that he would rather resign or even lose an election than do anything that he considered wrong or improper.

Distinctly Different Years (1970–95)

The second period had seen three Prime Ministers over the span of 25 years, each having his or her distinct impact, concerns, and priorities. Morarji Desai, Indira Gandhi, and Atal Bihari Vajpayee made their mark for different reasons and styles. Lal Bahadur Shastri's 'Jai Jawan, Jai Kisan' slogan in 1965, coined based on his wisdom and understanding of a crisis on the farm front and in the wake of war with Pakistan, is recalled and remains relevant even after 55 years. We could have expected more from his regime, had he not suddenly died while serving as the Prime Minister.

Indira Gandhi's regime was one of command and control. It was a period of politicised development, involving claims like 'Decade of Achievements'. That was also the beginning of an era of self-centric outlook and populism as an undercurrent of public policies. She considered public institutions (founded by her father as visionary initiatives) as 'instruments' of influence rather than something to sustain change. She nationalised banks without consultation, only to rebut a political competitor (Morarji Desai) and to cope with a split orchestrated in the ruling political party. A Nehru streak in her compelled her to end National Emergency (declared by her a year earlier to hold on to her power) and go to polls, bowing before public pressures. Or, was that a strategy to correct a hasty political instinct? (She went to polls based on an independent research which some of her cabinet colloquies debunked.) Her stint as the prime minister was overall one of centralisation, control, and command. She was accused of pursuing her goals at the cost of national institutions. In fact, there were examples of her using 'institutions' as 'instruments'. I do not remember her initiating or establishing important new national institutes. She did, however, expand radio and television networks and changed programme mix and priorities of state-owned radio and television. In those years, *popularity* had not been pursued through mass media. But Indira Gandhi was interested in knowing the *effects* and thus supported evaluative research of government programmes and initiatives, both for image-building and impact. She also supported innovations and social researchers, as in the case of SITE.[6]

Morarji Desai was a unique prime minister who was known for following the 'rule of law'. He had the benefit of being a deputy prime minister with an impressive track of 'going by the book' of the Constitution. He also set examples by forming committees to look into the pros and cons of contentious public policies. Morarji Desai was known as a disciplinarian and was never accused of politicising public policies or eroding the freedom and independence of national institutions. His support to the Centre for Policy Research (CPR), as an independent body of researchers that had critically evaluated public policies, was visionary. He also had a holistic outlook towards public policies. To his credit, as the deputy prime minister and finance minister, he realised that credit was an important instrument, even for gender equity, and saw the role of banking institutions in the larger context of development, thereby promoting research in that pursuit. He appointed a committee of researchers, academics, and hands-on experts to look into banking reforms as well as the population and health in 1978. His duration as the prime minister was short-lived (two years) and the government suffered from inter-party bickering as it was the first coalition government.

Atal Bihar Vajpayee was the first non-Congress prime minister of India. He completed the full five-year term. Like the first Prime Minister Nehru, Vajpayee too believed in freedom and independence and did not interfere in the workings of the national institutions. He was not a political party-centric prime minister. The poet in Vajpayee was ever-present in public-policy formulation. He also followed inclusive politics despite his distinct personality of a tall political leader and being in the opposition party for too long. He was never known to interfere with the independence of national institutes, including that of educational bodies. As a humanist, Vajpayee was also concerned about values and refrained from humiliating predecessors simply because they belonged to a different political party. On the contrary, he had praised his predecessors when they deserved, including Indira Gandhi.

Reforms, Not Destabilising Basics! (1995–2020)

There are four Prime Ministers between 1995 and 2020 who stand out for the distinct mark they made. First, P.V. Narasimha Rao served a full term of five years without having the majority in the Parliament and without taking to populist policies. Second, Rajiv Gandhi became the prime minister from outside party politics altogether. Third, Manmohan Singh served as the prime minister for full two terms despite not being in politics. He was an economist who became the prime minister after holding several key jobs and could pursue economic reforms initiated by Prime Minister Narasimha Rao. Fourth, Modi trooped onto the national scene after being a successful three-term chief minister of Gujarat. He was out-and-out party functionary who had risen from the bottom and, most importantly, was considered a man of humble origins and a self-made leader.

Narasimha Rao had become the prime minister not because he had fought and won an election, but because he was chosen by the party for his solo stand despite being a chief minister of a state, not by leading the party in the polls but because he could pursue reforms both in the state as the chief minister and as the prime minister as he was never election-centric.

On any criteria, Narasimha Rao's years (1991–1996) will continue to be regarded as the landmark period for reform initiatives. The reform process he introduced had never been ventured into by any prior governments even with full majority. He was warned by his own party of opposition in Tirupati Congress Party. Such was his conviction after he read about 'Perestroika' in Russia by *Mikhail Gorbachev* and was also aided by his Finance Minister, a non-political economist. In many other respects, too, he tried to bring in reforms. He was credited even by his political opponent for his skills to introspect and draw upon data and research reports for several other initiatives; for example, he took a holistic view of the Ministry of Education as Ministry of Human Resource Development (HRD). He was also credited for being a good listener, a rationalist, and an analyst. Dr Pai Panandiker, President of New Delhi's leading think-tank and who was familiar with every Prime Minister, described 'P V', as he was popularly known, as a good listener and an interactive prime minister who was always looking for new ideas and feedback inputs.

As an airlines pilot, Rajiv Gandhi knew the significance of data, updates, live inputs, and on-the-spot decision-making. He was open to independent ideas until he was taken over by the system. I was one of few individuals who were consulted regarding him joining politics. Having won the general election with considerable majority, Rajiv Gandhi was quick in making a mark on politics despite having no political background. That is how his speech involving research insights in Mumbai about how hardly 20% of the money sent from Delhi was reaching the targeted beneficiary awakened the nation to realise the pitfalls of government schemes' distribution or implementation and of middlemen corrupting the system. He reduced the voting age to 18 from 21 and was responsible for the 73 Amendment on Panchayat Raj (1993) that considered research inputs from independent sources. His initiative to form the Knowledge Commission with experts from different fields like *Sam Pitroda*, Dr Pushpa Bhargava, and Bhanu Pratap Mehta; his call to gear up for future challenges; and his use of new technologies were his contribution towards making public policies more accountable and research-oriented. He was also respectful of public opinion, just like his grandfather. He reversed his own government's decision by taking into account the public uproar in the case of Shah Bano and Keshvananad Bharati. He was not a political leader, yet he geared up to poll compulsions. He swept into power on a sympathy wave. While he served as the prime minister, research and evaluative feedback received a boost. With the influx of 'foreign research corporates', that are more oriented towards the markets, local research initiatives' potentials and priorities experienced some setbacks.

Dr Manmohan Singh had not become Prime Minister by winning an election. He was handpicked by the party for his impeccable credentials as an economist and a humble humanist. The National Advisory Council with the party chief as its chairperson and the push and pull of coalition partners had kept him as a performer, reformer, and a citizen-centric individual who focused on a series of initiatives that aimed to uphold citizen rights. He sought justification for public policies and often engaged in evaluative research while being sensitive to user-end parameters. It was his party winning the general election at the end of the first five years that got him into political compulsions, thus pushing him into troubled waters. He always looked for facts, figures, and justification for his initiatives.

Modi became the Prime Minister after fighting a Lok Sabha election on his own terms and using his own strategy. The 2014 election was preceded by his winning three state assembly elections in Gujarat. No other Prime Minister has such a consistent poll record. Even after 2014, assembly elections in several states were fought using his name and under his direction. The 2019 general election, too, was fought by Modi as if he was everything and everywhere in every state, every corner of the country.

Interestingly, none of these elections were won by Modi without internal supportive research and a meticulous research-based strategy. All this research, planning, and monitoring which Modi availed in 2014, and has continued to avail ever since, was done by 'back room boys' with no background in or any respect for procedures or precedents. Even Rajiv Gandhi had his 'wiz kids' initially. Such a strategy, especially Narendra Modi's, relied on destabilising or disowning formal data sources and invalidating the credibility of established institutions. The modus operandi of Prime Minister Modi was to devise supportive data for big political claims and for his command and control strategies. But he deserves credit for very effectively repackaging and broadcasting, or echoing, powerful ideas. I referred to five such ideas specifically as 'Modi Mantras' for good governance in my 2019 book *Sustainable Good Governance, Development and Democracy*—the five mantras being: Swaraj to Su-raj; Power, but not by luring voters; Politics should never override policy; Less government, more governance; and *Sab ka sath, Sabka Vikas*. Besides, accusations of politicising national institutes like the National Statistical Office (NSO), the Central Bureau of Investigation (CBI), the Election Commission of India (ECI), the Controller General of Accounts (CGA), and other research bodies are not limited to Modi. Such politicising and undermining of institutions happened in previous regimes, too, although perhaps not so pervasively. There is a history of independent institutes becoming 'instruments' for political interests.

Unlike most political leaders, Modi has ushered in numerous schemes of numbers, data, and analyses in a very short period of time. This is his preferred way and it perhaps explains his insensitivity to academic rigour, which he may consider time-consuming and elitist and without grassroots moorings. His government also exhibits impatience and discomfort with views that are not entirely in agreement with it. Being a quick learner, Modi has shown rare understanding of the importance of research. He particularly understands the potential of research and technology in today's complex and fast-changing context and in influencing opinion on contentious issues. But he seems to value research more to enforce control and command, to mould people's perceptions, and to manage his government's image.

Modi, unlike Nehru, won power by working on political and ideological divides and through populistic priorities. He used research far more than any of his predecessors for politics, particularly for electoral strategies and populist schemes. The schemes at least would have been far more successful if the research supporting them had been independent and rigorous.

Across the world, leaders who have been primarily interested in winning elections and thus concerned with their party and their individual image have mostly been control- and command-oriented. Election-centric prime ministers are more likely to take to image building, populist schemes, manipulation of news media, and to engage in centralisation and consolidating their party for competitive politics. They are more focused on the political agenda than public policies. Data, analysis, and field research may often not support the claims of such prime ministers and their regimes. When this happens, such regimes try to junk or discredit the data, particularly when the source of the data is independent and beyond the possibility of influence or moderation.

Election-oriented presidents and prime ministers are hardly concerned with long-term consequences. Leaders who have fought four or five elections tend to go for a win at any cost and focus on the victory more than the means they use to reach it. Leaders who are even a little less poll-centric have distinctly different styles and priorities, as can be seen in the performance—and the research involved in the public policies—of such prime ministers as Jawaharlal Nehru, Lal Bahadur Shastri, Morarji Desai, P.V. Narasimha Rao, Rajiv Gandhi, and even Manmohan Singh initially.

This retrospective view of elected leaders and their concern and approach about public policy initiatives indicate that those prime ministers who were less preoccupied with party politics and competitive compulsions were far more rational and put greater emphasis on professional data and research. Such leaders also acknowledged the role of rigorous research and supported evaluative and impactful research. They were also far more futuristic in the orientation of public policies.

With governments becoming too sensitive to independent research, it is no surprise that the potential of academic institutions for proactive research underwent a setback, as was indicated in the 2020 National Education Policy. Today, we can hardly name more than a couple research outfits with proactive initiatives. We have more foreign or foreign-dominated research and consultancy outfits functioning as 'supportive bodies'.

None of the Indian prime ministers in the last couple of decades have taken any initiatives to revive or strengthen research and training institutes or even effectively use their capabilities when formulating public policies. On the contrary, there have been too many instances of contracting an outside agency. More than 30 institutes are funded and controlled by one or the other ministry. There is hardly any example of any of them coming up with proactive initiatives concerning public policies, programmes, and governance.

Earlier, during the '80s, the Rajiv Gandhi Foundation in New Delhi held a series of workshops, debates, and discussions on public policies and sponsored reviews and research in a supportive manner. More recently, another organisation has emerged called the Vivekananda International Foundation (VIF) that holds regular workshops and seminars while coordinating research and reviews on contentious public policies. The Rajiv Gandhi Foundation is now forgotten as it has given way to the Vivekananda Institute. Could these institutes be considered independent? Or are they 'supportive' of the policies of the governing party? Both enjoyed substantial support of the government of the day. Not just organisations but even individuals who worked to promote the image and interests of the political party in power were given extraordinary support by the government.

Don't we have insights from the concerns and outlooks of our past prime ministers? Those leaders who give importance to logic, research, data, analysis, and professional, impartial feedback, and who invite outside evaluation, make better prime ministers in terms of making a positive difference for the country through public policies and future perspectives. Those who rely on populism may manage their image better in the short term but do little lasting good for their country.

CHAPTER THREE

What Steers Public Policies?

At the outset of independence, ideas concerning public policies were initiated more by individuals who were concerned, committed, and had a visionary view of the country. They were also aware and familiar of ground realities while being responsible for some of the landmark public policies. In fact, most leaders who spearheaded the freedom movement had contributed their ideas and were responsible for public policies. Even Mahatma Gandhi who was never part of the government or with any of the policy-making bodies was responsible for some of the public policies. Some of these policies continue, a few have gone into limbo, and a few others were abandoned. For example, Khadi continues to be a government policy and a national programme. Prohibition of liquor, which was a public policy, was abandoned in most states (Gujarat is an exception as it continues the policy), while leprosy eradication continues to be a national programme. Policies to do with, for example, untouchability that were put into legislation could not even be discouraged.

Baba Saheb Ambedkar's ideas and proposals were adopted as public policies. However, Prime Minister Jawaharlal Nehru's proposal for a cooperative farming could not be turned into a public policy as it was voluntarily withdrawn in the last stage to respect public response. Some of the women welfare and child development programmes became national policies because of the pursuit of women activists of the time such as Durgabhai (Deshmukh), Sarojini Varadarajan, and Sushila Nayyar. One such public policy was the minimum age for marriage of girls. Family planning programme had become a national policy as it was taken up by some women activists like Avabai Wadia. The Family Planning Association, founded by Wadia, pursued this issue until it became a national policy. It was then that JRD Tata took it up as a cause to pursue.

It was Aruna Roy's pursuit backed by a large section of women workers in villages and by experiments in a couple of states that helped freedom of information to become a public policy and Right to Information (RTI) legislation was adopted.

Poverty eradication continued to be a priority concern. Professor Dandekar and Dr Patnaik's research over the years made poverty eradication a national programme and made it a part of public policies.

Chandigarh Region Innovation and Knowledge Cluster (CRIKC) was a recent initiative that sought to enhance collaboration between research and industry and local community institutions. In 2019, the Union Government extended the project to six other cities including Bhubaneswar, Jodhpur, Pune, Ahmedabad, Hyderabad, and Chandigarh. This initiative mainly aimed to ensure that existing research and knowledge could be availed by local institutes and innovated.[1]

This idea was an initiative of the Principal Scientific Advisor. The scheme was announced after holding consulting meetings in each of the cities with local industries, academics, and other institutes. This project is expected to bring together various projects such as the Lab to Land project in the Green Revolution and make research relevant, need-based, and easier to adopt. The success of this scheme can only be assessed after a couple of years. In the meanwhile, monitoring and feedback research indicate that the project is moving in the expected direction, perhaps because it was not backed by political leaders.

The 2017 Sample Registration System (SRS) by Census Registrar indicated that infant death rates in 2017 was as high as 32 per 1000 in some states like Andhra Pradesh compared to 10 per 1000 in Kerala and 16 per 1000 in Tamil Nadu. It is important to examine why this number is so high in some states despite the recent increase in the percent of births in hospitals.

In the last couple of decades, there have been more policies by individual visionaries, political parties, and interested elements than the ones based on statistics, surveys, or any research.

But today, with increasing complications and the involvement of interested groups, public policies have had to rely on some kind of data, analyses, and field surveys. For example, ministries and governments tend to conduct their own 'surveys' to implement a programme or a predetermined policy. The AP Government in August 2019 announced that surveys will be conducted to determine the number of people who require a roof and the number of eligible farmers who will receive special benefit to ascertain the percentage of SC, BC, and other minorities who deserve special help and the number of families who need ration supplies. But the catch is that the government itself appointed 'volunteers' who conducted the survey and collected data from households. As these 'volunteers' were politically associated, the credibility of the numbers becomes questionable. States were already conducting their own surveys to come up with increased numbers to claim food supplies from the Union Government and subsides for BPL households. These surveys are a new way of collecting data from households for political reach out and electoral compulsions.

In a parliamentary democracy, the ultimate responsibility of public policies is holding the Cabinet of Ministers accountable to the parliament of elected representatives of people. These legislatures are expected to initiate proposals for policies and programmes. In the normal course, it is the constitution that forms the basis for initiating or adopting public policies. While the constitution remains a source or the basis, amendments can be adopted in the parliament to form new policies or change the old ones. Initially, it was leaders and the committees who were the sources for initiating public policies. Political parties and their committees or forums continue to suggest policy proposals to the government.

Thus, it is a combination of sources who play a role in formulating state public policies. These include formal and non-formal and institutions and individuals. In more recent years, the United Nations' resolutions have been adopted as national policies. For example, the Millennium Development Goals (MDGs) or Sustainable Development Goals (SDGs) with goals and targets have become national policies. Global rankings and indexes based on certain performance indicators have also prompted national policies at one time or the other.

The cabinet of ministers, in turn, is assisted by senior officials and specialists. The Parliament is assisted by various committees. Although there are no outside experts in these committees, they can invite experts or stakeholders for a discussion. NITI Aayog, the government's policy think-tank, although is a bureaucratic setup, holds consultations, analyses existing data, and conducts primary research. The policy ideas go through these various routes and channels. There is a chance that some of them are exposed to some data or research that guide or prompt certain stand to be taken on a public policy or initiate an idea to push forward as a public policy. But there is no specific example of any policy being recently pursued by the Cabinet based on a research.

Although NITI Aayog is expected to be a proactive outfit, it is more involved with endorsing or following up mode with an idea articulated by a political leader. It is busy analysing data sent by the states/departments to rate them in the name of promoting competitive politics and competitive performance in the country.

As the 'hold' of political parties and elected representatives in the legislatures has increased in recent years, it is not clear whether their 'grip' on policy making complements their presence. In fact, considering the profiles of the elected legislatures and the scope of discursions in the parliament and assemblies, their representation has been visibly dented and declined. It is a wonder then that the legislatures and the governments now claim 'achievements' in superlative terms and as if so many achievements have been made for the 'first time'.

The number of 'amendment bills' passed, for example, in the July 2019 session of the Parliament were around 35, more than ever before. Amendment bills are expected to be based on experience or on some appraisal of the initial legislation of the Act. The question is then whether any of those amendments were based on or backed by any new data, feedback, analysis, or research apart from routine formalities.

There are also recent examples of some states (such as AP in 2019) where public policies have neither been based on an ideology or an objective assessment or research but intended mostly to preserve the previous political leaders' or competitors' policies. More recently, 'vindictive politics' have also been responsible for the creation of public policies. This trend seems to be catching up of late. That is, vindictive politics may become a source for government policies at one time or other, or more often given the type of 'competitive politics' sweeping the country with populist policies.

But the early leaders had realised the need for the importance of reliable data to formulate public policies, for making decisions, and for planning the future. Earlier, it was religious gurus and missionaries who talked about peoples' destinies. Once the freedom movement gained momentum, it was the visionaries and then, after independence, the constitutional obligations became the guiding sources for public policies. Political ideologies also have shaped economic policies. Electoral compulsions and competitive politics, however, changed all that. Adding to this trend, the passivity of citizens led to the concentration of political power. The leaders in power have become preoccupied with gaining control and command. All such concerns over the decades have played a role in formulating public policies. Leaders' approach to data, analysis, and sensitivity to research depends on the kind of outlook and priorities of the government of the time.

India's journey of having a surplus of food in fifty years from being a country of famines and scarcity despite its growing population has been a fascinating story of transformation. What was written about India in its early years on becoming a free country included its hunger, scarcity, famines, and diseases. All that, of course, has changed not by religious gurus or spiritual sanyasis, but because of the visionary insights of wise men and women of the time. At one point, India had even gone for PL 480 agreement with USA for import of food (1954–1972). But in thirty years, its godowns were overflowing with paddy and wheat so much so that the government had to implement food-for-work programme and other schemes. It was research coupled with foresight of political leaders and agriculture scientists that helped this transformation. The research on motivating farmers involved extension methods using lab-to-land schemes, utilising fertilisers, high yielding variety of seeds, and more land under irrigation. All these efforts were labelled as 'green revolution', which was considered a pilot programme in one or two districts of Punjab, Andhra Pradesh, Tamil Nadu, and Orissa and was supported by research that helped to scale up the experiment. But today, as we are confronted with water shortage, farmers' suicides, and increasing disparities, there are still no research-based alternatives being explored. Although research has shown that crops such as rice and sugarcane require heavy water, we continue to rely on these crops.

Maternal Mortality Ratio (MMR) is another good example. Dr Srinath Reddy, an eminent personality with several distinguished initiatives to his credit, explained in his 2019 book, *Make Health in India: Reaching a Billion Plus*, how health policies have let down the country. He cited examples where significant results were achieved by reducing MMR from over 4 per 100 to less than 2 per 100 in 30 years. Dr Reddy also noted that the task ahead is extensive.

It could also be said that research has averted India from massive malnutrition and communicable diseases like cholera and TB. Although in terms of education, there is a long way to go, a lot has already been accomplished. Free schools for girls, midday meals, adult education, and campaigns such as 'Each

Make Health in India

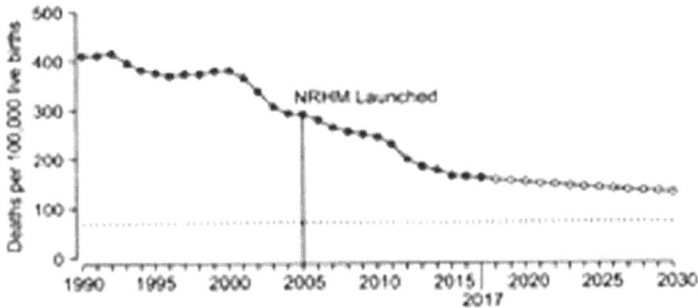

Figure 5.1: Trends in MMR in India

Source: Adapted by author from Vos et al. 2017 and additional data accessed from The Global Burden of Disease study (provided by the Institute of Health Metrics and Evaluation).

(Dr Srikanth Reddy, 2019, Make Health in India. Rural Health Mission)

One, Teach One' have all helped India come a long way. But no research was conducted to establish this confidently and scale the programme uniformly.

Early realisation of the significance of research, training, and extension, and establishing institutes as in the case of agriculture, health, and education with IARI, ICAR, ICMR, CHEB. NIHFW, NCERT should have been a research finding. Indian Agricultural Research Institute (IARI) and Indian Council of Agricultural Research (ICAR) have become model centres. On the other hand, like some other premier institutes, the National Institute of Community Development which was shifted from Mussoorie to Rajendra Nagar, Hyderabad, 50 years ago with research mandate and focus on rural development is not known for its contribution.

Visionary leaders like Kamaladevi Chattopadhya promoted research ideas 50 years ago. Avabai Wadia, pioneer in handicrafts and family planning, took to research in 1965 on pilot programmes. Avabai had launched All India Family Planning Association much before the government's schemes. Durgabai Deshmukh, in 1972, established the Council for Social Development (CSD) to undertake research to support her concerns regarding India's social development. Gandhi Gram Institutes of Development by Dr T.S. Soundaram and Dr G. Ramachandran in the mid-60s is yet another example. Many others of the time considered research an important requirement and even relied on it for initiating policy ideas and implementing them.

These visionaries looked for research support in four different ways or contexts. First, they compiled data to understand the dynamics of the issue and formulated a strategy to implement on a pilot basis. Second, they collected feedback once the project was under implementation. Third, they determined whether the desired objectives were being achieved and the types of mid-course correctives that were needed. Fourth, they assessed how the interventions were implemented, who benefited more and with what implications, and identified lessons for scaling up with regional modifications in the project.

With the influx of foreign aid agencies (Rockefeller, Ford Foundation, Gates, etc.) and foreign research corporates (Neilson, IPSOS, etc.) between 1965 and 1975, all that concern for the role and type of research changed. The focus has shifted to copying the foreign model in the last 25 years and implementing quick formulas and research tools to capture the most hyped trends and mood.

If news media themselves become predominantly supportive of the powers of the day, independent research and research findings not palatable to the government will have a difficult time getting coverage. Such occasions, which are frequent, are challenging opportunities in terms of how the government, researchers, and the media negotiate complex and contentious situations. Such situations strengthen the fundamentals of democracy and governance. This is what 'checks and balances' is all about. In the last two decades, however, the structure of news media has changed and their role is undergoing a dramatic turn in determining public agenda and policy priorities.

Public Opinion as Primary Source?

Public policies are sourced from public opinions, perceptions, and support. But this is never readily forthcoming. Public opinion must be mobilised, mustered, and managed or manufactured. The context and the issues determine the complexity of the process. No public policy can be expected to yield the desired outcomes without direct or indirect public cooperation.

With proliferation of mass media channels, social media, and communication technologies, the process of determining public opinion has become more complex than before. Nevertheless, these various outlets and channels continue to initiate, advocate, resurrect, or uphold public policies of the government. With foreign interests making inroads into these outlets of public opinion in India, their significance has increased, not declined, despite the decline in their credibility.

My personal encounter with the electoral politics was with the 1975–77 Lok Sabha and the 1986–91 State of Andhra Pradesh. I have seen how those in power, those concerned with elections, go about influencing the news media and use official information apparatus of the government in the interests of a party. My experience was with tracking the public standing of the government while considering the electoral opportunities and challenges. Based on a series of field surveys (1976–77) (case studies and field surveys), I indicated that the Indira Gandhi government had lost ten percent of votes and the poll outcome was a foregone conclusion. But on seeing my survey report, Minister V. C. Shukla debunked it as 'statistical scrap'. If citizens and the media are to respond to surveys more responsibly and intelligently, survey agencies should operate far more transparently, professionally, and impartially than they do at present.

Early on in my long research career, I witnessed sponsor bias, source bias, interview bias, and even more blatant bias at the analysis stage of interpreting and presenting the findings of a field survey. This is what made me a votary of 'independent research'. But how could people be aware of any such bias when they see or read about a survey in the news media? Public sensitivity to any such bias is the best bet in a 'checks and balances' based democracy. In a nutshell, the scope and structure of surveys must be understood better than we seem to today, particularly in terms of their potential impact on public policies and free and fair conduction of elections. In this process, the news media should be sensitive to the function of all surveys. The potential of poll surveys may only be unleashed when there is transparency in them being conducted and covered by the news media. There is a need for professional survey research agencies to operate with concern about credibility of everyone rather than taking an isolated and primarily commercial view. Today, agencies and especially news media must make special efforts to indicate that their surveys are neither manufactured nor manipulated. Not only voters but candidates and leaders must also know more about poll surveys and the way they are conducted and covered in the media. Editors, anchors, and studio commentators also need to be sensitive about surveys, their methodologies, analysis, and any limitations.

Public Policies: By Committees and Reports

Reports presented by committees that are appointed by the government itself in response to and as a way out of a pressing problem end up becoming a Pandora's box. But they continue to be relied on by the governments to initiate or amend a policy or consider a correction in the existing policy. Some decades ago, such reports of committees were promptly accepted by the government by and large. More recently, committees are being appointed more to differ or delay a contentious public issue from being addressed or resolved. Reports of several committees are still pending, in perpetual limbo. I know the chairman of three committees, each in a different context, since the last 15 years and am familiar with the kind of extensive analysis and research each one of them have conducted, such as the Justice Sachar committee on the status of Muslims in India, Dr M.S. Swaminathan's Report on farmers' unrest, and Shyam Benegal's report on film censorship. These three involved serious public policies.

In 2006, Justice Rajinder Sachar, a former Chief Justice of Delhi High Court, submitted his committee's report which included two social researchers (Dr Abusaleh Shariff and Prof. T.K. Oommen). The report remains an impressive reference for many vital facts, data, and statistics on the socio-economic and educational status of Muslims, which is necessary for formulating policy initiatives. Despite being set up by the then Prime Minister Dr Manmohan Singh, and supported by a range of research data, it did not get anywhere as it was politicised for being Muslim-biased and ignoring the interests of other communities.[2]

Dr M.S. Swaminathan, an eminent agricultural scientist of over 60 years of standing, is best known for his continuous endeavours towards India's development and is credited for his active role in India's Green Revolution and modernisation of crop varieties and farm practices. He holds special recognition globally. I am fortunate that I had the privilege of associating directly with him, first during 1963–65 when promoting nitrogenous fertilisers as part of the Green Revolution and then much later during 1996–98 as an expert member of India's first Population Committee of the government with Swaminathan as Chairman. He held a senior position as the Deputy Chairman of the Planning Commission, as the Director General of the Indian Institute of Agriculture Research, and as the Union Secretary of Agriculture and was held in high esteem across the country. He has nothing to do with politics. For over two decades, the M.S. Swaminathan Research Foundation in Chennai has been a premier research body, founded by him, that has conducted several pioneering studies. He is also the Chairman of the National Commission on Agriculture, Food and Nutrition Security of India. Despite the continuous farmers' agitations for more than two decades with an increasing number of farmer suicides, the government was not as anxious to avail this research-based report, as claimed otherwise by political leaders.

Dr M.S. Swaminathan's report remains the most quoted and most appreciated by leaders of parties across the country, and it has been the most sought-after framework concerning the unrest of the farming sector. *India Today* carried a story about this, with the headline 'Swaminathan report kept the battle between the government and farmers for 12 years'. This headline explains it all. But the Union Agriculture Minister maintained that the Swaminathan report was being implemented when the Economic Times noted that 'the Minister would not have read the Swaminathan report' despite farmers in state after state demanding the implementation of M.S. Swaminathan report.[3]

Shyam Benegal stands out as the most concerned nationalist film producer and director and a rationalist activist. His creations stand out as the best in India's film and TV history. The Shyam Benegal Committee was in charge of the certification and censorship of films. Appointed at the end of 2015, the report was submitted by June 2016.[4] The Committee suggested diluting CBFC power to demand cuts in a film subjectively against the background that censorship in India, the world's largest democracy, is at a high. The Ministry of I&B which appointed this committee held a series of discussions on the Benegal report but could not take it ahead. The Committee included another veteran, Kamal Haasan, advertising guru Piyush Pandey, and film critic Bhawana Somaaya. But the government took the excuse of discussing with the public to defer the Benegal report. The government did not approve of a change in the archaic cinematograph Act of 1952. What does this tell? The government does not want to give up subjective intervention and possible political advantage.

These examples clearly show that the possibility of analyses, data, and research being applied for public policy-making through Committee reports is no longer what it was in the early decades of the Republic. Such official reports of committees could be a valid source for policy becoming research-based. But those chances too have declined. The government tends to take decisions under 'pressure cooker situations', rather than based on considered committee reports involving analyses and participation of stakeholders.

Public Policies: By Independent Reports

Periodic report of independent bodies is another source for public policies. There are many such reports, some periodic, some annual, and/or few occasional. Some also originate from foreign sources.

National Family Health Survey (NFHS)[5] was initiated in 1990 as an independent survey that positively impacted the sensitivities of policy makers. This report is more elaborate than that of the first National Family Planning Survey in 1970–72 by ORG, with which I was associated. This NFHS is the most comprehensive largescale survey covering infant and child mortality and the practices of family planning, maternal and child health, reproductive health, nutrition, anaemia, and quality of health. This comprehensiveness and the extensive representative feature of NFHS led to the Ministry of Health taking interest in it and assigning its International Institute of Population Sciences, Mumbai, to coordinate the study. So far, four rounds of survey reports have come out. It is now funded by USAID, DFID, Bill & Melinda Gates foundation, UNICEF, UNFPA, and the Ministry of Health and Family Welfare. It is because of the participation of so many agencies that this survey has become a referral source for policies. For example, institutional delivery has become a priority because it was highlighted by this survey. The survey has become a source of essential data on health and family welfare needed by the Ministry and other agencies to obtain policy and programme feedback. The fifth round of NFHS is now underway (2019–20) and is expected to offer insights concerning the next couple of years for more policy interventions. This report may be attributed as a source for a few recent policies of the Ministry.

Annual Status of Education Report (ASER)[6] has become a referral point for the quality of school education in the country. This annual report by PRATHAM, a not-for-profit organisation, started this research more than a decade ago as an independent initiative. Unlike the reports by NCERT, which is based on formal within-the-system administrative reports, ASER is based on primary interviews with children as per household surveys spread across the country and with large sample sizes. These reports show how children are actually learning in school classrooms. It sensitised the nation regarding education quality. But there are no specific instances of considering ASER as the basis for policy correctives. The 2020 National Education Policy considered the wealth of primary data of ASER to be presented before the nation. NITI Aayog and Planning Commission had based their priorities on the ASER report.

India Corruption Survey (ICS), a non-profit outfit, has since 2002 been offering annual ICS reports as an independent service based on comprehensive research including field surveys across the country. These reports are the only ongoing source that point to the corruption that a citizen encounters when accessing basic public services. Each year, this report detects an additional dimension like citizen activism or the differences in the latest key government policy interventions in policies or in the delivery of public services.

Governments struggle to digest these reports as they keep claiming to have brought in corruption-free public services and improvements. One revelation of these reports, for example, was that two to four percent of targeted people fail to access public services meant for them as they are either unable to pay a bribe or have no 'contact' to help them as middle-men, including the elected representative. CMS created a trend in the last 15 years regarding the extent to which citizens avail key basic public services.

These are only a few examples of how the government hesitates or succumbs to interest groups having conflicts of interests or political interest when availing primary research-based independent reports. But the government is quick to take into account reports of international bodies, known and unknown. The Transparency International Report on corruption based on a small unrepresentative sample is one such example. This is because governments are more interested in the ratings and rankings of international agencies.

In all the three examples, it is clear that they viewed the deep-rooted problem in a desegregated way and indicated initiatives that could be taken up. In fact, that is the only sustainable way to address and bring much-needed relief. ICS was rechristened in 2019, after 16 years, as the 'Indian Public Services Study' (IPSS) with a hope of reflecting a positive outlook and garnering better attention. Although Pratham (of ASER) services are now sought by several other countries, India has not conducted significant studies to avail these insightful research reports, as in the case of NFHS backed by international agencies.

Besides, foreign agencies are expensive and tend to not have any local sensitivities. Milind Sohoni, professor at IIT, Bombay, and IIT, Goa, lamented when he wrote for the *Indian Express* that 'state agencies tend to call on expensive international consultants even in traditional areas as irrigation' even when the expertise of world-class is locally available.[7]

Foreign Agencies, Public Policies

The role and relevance of foreign agencies when making public policies is becoming more prominent. An issue that should be of concern is that while these foreign agencies are mostly research-based and research-led, the agencies within the country that are concerned and contribute to public policy formulation are not. A second factor that also should be of concern is that these foreign agencies are market-oriented rather than concerned with the society or the country's constitutional compulsions or peculiarities. A third factor to be concerned about is that most of these foreign agencies have a direct conflict of interest. In fact, these foreign agencies also dictate the country's research environment.

These factors must be viewed against the fact that India has more or less had an open-door policy country with limited restrictions for entry and operation of foreign concerns as if it is a 'free for all' country. Until 1970, domestic compulsions determined India's public policies. For example, the policy of food imports, as in the case of PL 480 (wheat imports from the US). After 1970, more specifically after India had adopted new economic policies in 1991, India became a market for products and services of developed economics. While some global corporates viewed India as a country to invest in, some countries like Japan viewed India as a nitrogenous fertiliser exporter, and the US looked at India as a major consumer market for its products and services instead of merely as a market to provide arms and aid.

This is relevant as it points to how social and market research is being used by some with telling outcomes, particularly for market inroads and influencing behaviours and lifestyles. The role of foreign advertising, market research, consulting and lobbying groups in India and their penetration in the last few decades presents telling insights. This would not have been possible without research being conducted in India. Their initiatives, policies, priorities, and strategies are all based on consumer, behavioural, industrial, and political research.

Overall, there are three types of foreign sources that influence Indian public policies and opinions. There are some that, based on their research, directly influence public policies and priorities while others that, also based on research, have an informal or indirect influence. The advertising, market research, media, and lobby groups try to directly and formally influence policies and even initiate them. They are also crucial in the electoral campaigns of political parties. The indirect ones are the consulting groups and aid agencies. The third category that influences public policies are the UN agencies and diplomatic missions. Research and analysis is a common factor on which they all rely.

Advertising agencies: Advertising is no longer limited to consumer and industry promotion, but most social policies and their promotion strategies are decided by advertisers, as in the case of political campaigns. Advertising profession and business in India is mostly controlled by foreign agencies. In fact, all top 20 agencies account for more than two-thirds of that business and are fully or mostly steered by foreign corporates with known and unknown interests. They base their concerns, priorities, and strategies based on their research conducted here and abroad. The research they conduct in India is again based on their own branded or promoted methodologies. Even the Ministries of the Union and States engage these advertising agencies for their policies and campaigns. In fact, they recommend not only media strategies but also promote content programme including using instruments like Television Rating Points (TRP).

Market research agencies: Market research prompts and promotes products, policies, services, and ideas and offers strategies to float policies and programmes. Initially, until 1970, market research was limited mostly to market-oriented corporates. It was with milk marketing and family planning that market research began being inclined towards behavioural and societal concerns. However, by tagging on to electoral politics in more recent years, their role in public policy promotion has become too obvious. Most top market research agencies in India are foreign or global affiliates. Foreign or global corporates have taken over or absorbed a couple of decades of old Indian market research firms. These foreign market research corporates that have vested interests in other businesses dominate the Indian scene to the extent of influencing public policies. They are able to do so because of having large-scale and critical data and research that they have accumulated on India.

Mass media and their contents: Because of government policies, news media has remained controlled in India. But the content model, both concerning the news media and entertainment media, is Western-oriented and is based on research nurtured by them. The TRP-dictated content priorities subdued local talent and potential and even local needs. Popularism can thus become a main concern of public policies. Media is often found supporting or opposing public policies and even proactively advocating policies.

Consulting groups: Consulting groups are the ones engaged in financial and management consultancy companies. Most that are in India are of foreign origin. Even a few small local groups are affiliated with a foreign firm or consultant. They undertake research proactively and evaluative studies in a client-specific manner so that they can offer consultation services and promote themselves. Many of them are engaged by the governments for assessing or advising on one or the other subject. They were initially limited to financial and management issues, but over the years, they have also been drafted into the social sector and public services assessment. Their criteria and considerations have of late been the basis for the design and assessment of national policies and programmes. I had experienced how a chief minister of a state can insist on roping in a foreign consulting group to formulate a vision document for the state, despite my arguing that it will send wrong signals. Thereafter, he involved this consultant in most of the state's policy initiatives and evaluative exercises on their terms and using their methodologies.

The government assigning all central and centrally sponsored schemes (over 125) in 10 different categories 'assessed' by four multinational consultants in September 2019 is a good example for how research and evaluation is viewed by the government. This 'assessment' cannot be considered as an evaluative appraisal nor an 'independent third party' exercise. Yet that is the impression that the government/NITI Aayog/DMEO tried to give.[8]

First, while these multinational consultants (KPMP, EY, Deloitte, and IPE Global) may be reputed consultants globally for their 'financial assessments', they do not have expertise about India. Second, this assessment is not based on specially devised methodology or independently collected data but was based on data provided by the concerned department themselves which is mostly 'administrative data' by the same people responsible for implementation (only a percentage is likely to be verified). Third, there is no transparency despite the criticality of the assignment, not just for these schemes or for these years but for the future of the country's developmental endeavours. Fourth, this selection of consultants was not based on an 'open bid' as was claimed. The ad seeking the bids by consultants itself indicated that only foreign consultants with an annual turnover of Rs 50 crore will qualify, which no Indian-specialised organisation will be able to meet. Fifth, this cannot be considered as an 'independent' exercise as these selected multinational corporates are present in India at the insistence of the government and were already engaged in advising various ministries. Sixth, the 'assessment' assignment was to help the rationalisation of the scheme in terms of available resources. It could be described neither as an evaluation nor could it be a study on the impact of these various schemes.

Engaging foreign consulting firms at what cost?

For more than a decade, a very interesting practice is being conducted in the country. Foreign consulting firms, belonging to multinational corporates with HQs somewhere abroad but having offices in India, are being engaged for undertaking research studies across Ministries, including social development departments. Several issues arise from this as they present threatening implications to India.

First, these consulting groups have entered India as 'managing or financial consultants'. They operate as market-driven and financial analyses experts using their global models and cater mostly to a foreign clientele. Their expertise is mostly concerning stock markets and financial dealings. Subsequently, on entrenching into Indian markets and into some ministries, these agencies begin claiming expertise on diverse subjects, wherever there is money and policy involved and access to vital data on the country.

Second, by deliberately preferring these foreign consulting groups, the Ministries snub Indian researchers who have a better realistic understanding and insights on particular subjects. This discouragement of Indian potential is done in different ways. First, by asking for a high annual turnover (Rs 50 to 100 crores for three years) to qualify for the bids, which only foreign agencies can show (as they show their foreign turnover also) and for high earnest bank deposit. This is outright and provocatively preferential.

Third, there is no specific provision of assigning projects to these foreign agencies on their use of primary data on and of India outside India and otherwise. The Indian government does not even know where and how the primary data acquired from such projects is being used by these foreign agencies.

Fourth, wherever field surveys are required, they are outsourced to local agencies who have more appropriate expertise and background. There is no bar that can explicitly transfer such primary field data and statistics that these foreign agencies derive from field studies and ministries.

Fifth, after obtaining projects in a preferential way from different Ministries, these foreign consultants are provided offices in the Ministries, which obviously means they have access to the Ministry beyond a specific project. In that process, they acquire contacts with the government policy-makers who has nothing to do with a specific project and are able to influence which studies are taken up and how or who should be assigned.

Sixth, these foreign consulting agencies monopolise research and data in India, including on social development. For example, how can the Home Ministry consider only foreign consulting firms as qualified 'to rank Indian police stations'? As if there is no one in India who can take up such a study with better understanding? These foreign firms, in turn, hire Indian experts to conduct the fieldwork. Similarly, how come only foreign consultants are preferred to study Swachh Bharat? Ministries of Drinking Water and Sanitation, Urban Development, Rural Development Health, and Environment and Climate Change engage foreign consultants regardless of their expertise, grassroots sensitivities, conflict of interest, and in the context of 'global rankings'.

Seventh, the financial bid of these foreign consultants generally is much higher than that of Indian researchers and yet Ministries prefer foreign consultants on 'technical grounds' and believe that 'foreign is better'.

Eighth, monitoring and evaluation of critical sectors and projects of the country today are mostly the monopoly of these profit-driven foreign consultants with no scrutiny.

Ninth, such a situation has arisen because these foreign consulting firms are hired as 'project monitoring' experts by the Ministries, and in that capacity, they also recommend the research agency and establish the procedures, parameters, and eligibility criteria for selecting the researcher. Is this not a conflict of interest? They are auditors, assessors, and evaluators simultaneously, while also dictating the rank and rate practices and projects.

Tenth, the chief minister (such as Chandrababu Naidu) pampers such foreign consultants by hiring them to 'guide' and set the criteria for 'performance' as well as giving 'achievement' and ranking certificates. A close scrutiny of these practices makes one wonder that even after 70 years of independence, the dependency syndrome continues even when Indian experts and organisations have made their name globally.

Eleventh, today India's education and professional strengths are among the best in the world. Global agencies abroad are being led by Indians, and yet, in India, we are in the clutches of these 'foreign management consultant'. (India abolished management consultancy system in companies' decades ago.)

Twelfth, some leaders such as the chief minister of AP were under the impression that these foreign consultants facilitate foreign investments. The first thing the new chief minister (2019) did in AP in 2019 was to cancel all foreign consultancies (almost Rs 400 crores of funding) and to remove foreign consultants, openly accusing them of doing nothing specific for the state. This is the story in one state. The status in some other states and at the Union Ministries is similar, if not even more blatant. My estimate of what these foreign consultant costs the country is much more than Rs 2000 crores annually.

J.P. Morgan was recently accused of making 'windfall revenues'. Earlier, it was PricewaterhouseCoopers (PwC) that was named by the Supreme Court in another controversy. Arthur Anderson and MacKenzie were also found to have conflict of interest. Deloitte, Earnest Young, KPMG, PWC, Grant are actively engaged in monitoring and evaluating critical programmes even of the social sector and conducting field research, including on behavioural aspects.

Lobbying by foreign firms: Most of the formal lobby agencies in India are foreign or affiliated and push the interests of a foreign corporate or foreign government, including on security, nuclear, or policy issues and on social development policies or programmes, such as the policy on 'polio eradication' programme. These are based on an analysis or research, not all of which is transparent. They use data and analysis far more actively.

Foreign aid agencies: Many foreign aid agencies have been set up in India over the years, some from the very outset of Independence. Initially, they focused on rehabilitation issues but soon moved on to agriculture, family planning, health, gender, drug abuse policies, and civil society movements. They also sponsored research on various policy issues and used the research reports to advocate policy interventions. The Rockefeller Foundation, Ford Foundation, and Gates Foundation are only some of the examples for policy intervention in agriculture, family planning, women's development, and health policies.

UN agencies: Agencies such as UNDP, UNESCO, UNICEF, and the WHO sponsor research in India and use the research reports to advocate and intervene on policies and even promote activism outside the government. UNICEF's policies are a particularly good example of using proactive research and innovation to sensitise countries and collaborate with them on critical issues concerning children and rural families. The programme to build toilets in all schools, the design of the Mark II hand pump in the 1970s, and educational content for television channels are only a few such examples.

Diplomatic missions: They too are engaged in conducting research in host countries. This research aims to determine the line of policy that should be implemented or where they should invest or advance their money, or what their stand should be on contentious global or bilateral issues. Japan, for example, like many other countries, frequently conducts such research through an independent survey research agency.

The purpose of this discussion is to indicate how research is relied on for influencing public policies by various foreign sources, whereas at home reliance on research for policies is declining. This obviously implies that foreign sources have an advantage in domestic affairs. With the proliferation of market-driven and research-based agencies influencing public opinions and priorities, there has been a decline in the role of citizens and the civic society as well as of elected representatives in public policy formulation in the last two decades.

What Steers Public Policies?

What is the role or relevance of research in formulating policies or in taking up public programmes and schemes, particularly concerning the larger public? One such role is a proactive one. The other, more frequent situation, is availing research while implementation, evaluating, justifying, or endorsing a public programme.

Research, a Missing Link

There have been several schemes and programmes in the country that were launched and persisted with without being evaluated at all, or being evaluated merely as a formality rather than through independent professional research. Some parliament-approved schemes require assessment by overseeing agencies like the CAG or require a formal audit, but this too is only for the use of money, not to assess efficacy an outcome. Most aid agencies like ADB, the World Bank, and USAID require that schemes funded by them are independently evaluated. But often such evaluation is done only for form's sake and is neither independent nor professional. For instance, the Envi-Centres scheme going on for years in the Ministry of Environment is assessed periodically by an 'expert committee' comprising junior officers of the same Ministry.

Some such examples are discussed here, each of a different nature and context. Some of these examples have been included to show how research would have made a certain difference.

Behavioural change on the roads: A presentation of statistics on road traffics accidents and deaths changed the scope of the Motor Vehicle Amendment Bill (August 2019) and paved the way for safer roads. After the Bill was passed in the Parliament, the Road Transport Minister congratulated the citizens and captured the attention of the larger public. This is another good example of how research leads to public policy. The 2017 report by the Transportation Research of Indian Institute of Technology, Delhi, concerned the cause behind accidents and deaths and revealed that a third of road accident fatalities involved pedestrians (because of no pavement, etc.) and gave new insights to those engaged in drafting the Bill. The minister should be credited for promptly recognising the problem and advocating change in behaviour. Inputs from behavioural research can help his Ministry in coming up with initiatives to effect such a change.

Jan Dhan: This is a pioneering initiative by the Modi Government that aims to level the playing field and aims to eradicate poverty. With 36 crore people (as of July 2019)[9] opening new bank accounts since 2014, an independent research would have shown the significance of this scheme, comparable to the globally recognized schemes pioneered by Bangladesh's Noble prize winner Muhammad Yunus's Grameen Bank. The Jan Dhan scheme certainly played a role in the Modi Government's return to power with a thumping majority in 2019, but the Modi regime's detractors as well as neutral observers will not take the government's own data highlighting this fact seriously. There is a credibility problem which can harm the remarkable scheme itself. An independent research on this scheme would have credibly shown its significance. Independent research would also have shown how Jan Dhan in conjunction with the direct benefit transfer and direct cash transfer schemes could greatly minimise the scope for corruption and public grievances.

Drug Price Control Order (DPCO): This was a landmark public policy by the Union Government in 1981–82 when drugs in drug stores were brought under price control. Vinod Vaish, IAS, who was the Joint Secretary in the Department of Chemicals, dealing with pharmaceuticals, was confronted with frequent questions and debates in the Parliament regarding the shortages of certain drugs and the hike in prices. He then came to know that ORG was conducting 'pharma audit' on a monthly basis with state-wise and city-wise compilation of data on drug sales. After having discussions with me, he proposed to the Minister the idea of utilising the ORG data as input and requested ORG to monitor the sales and prices of certain essential drugs. Soon prices and availability of drugs stabilised and independent field-level data was available to the government. Independent research saved the government from frequent embarrassment in the Parliament and the country from dangerous shortages.

Earlier, policies concerning poverty were based on particular research within the country conducted by prominent independent professionals like Dr V N Dandekar and Professor Patnaik, as well as a number of independent economists from academics who have been associated with state policies over the years. Dr Arjun Sen Gupta's research-based review of below poverty population is another example.[10] This report was acknowledged as the basis for public policies, including MNREGS.

The prime minister had an 'economic advisor' and an advisory council for economic policies, involving mostly academics and ex-World Bank experts. Social policies never had such benefit although many economic policies concerning social development and social security initiatives that were based on the propositions given by many of these economists whose research focused on development and growth, including anti-poverty programmes and employment guarantee schemes. Research by economists had more say in the formulation of social policies than any research by social scientists. There were, of course, exceptions as in the case of Ashish Bose, BIMARU finding.

National Education Policy: It was more than thirty years ago that a national education policy was first formulated. Since then, although there has been a rise in the enrolment level and several new schools and colleges have opened, there is no evidence of changes in the quality of education or a much-needed shift in priorities. Access to higher education remains limited. There is no evidence that education has evolved to provide knowledge to society or to upgrade vocational skills. The Indian education sector is the world's third largest, with over 300 million students, over 1.4 million schools, and over 5000 higher education institutes, and yet there is no new study on learning theories of children in India. There was no review ever of research methods course, its syllabus, and how it is being taught at different levels and with what kind of field work.

It was in 1986 that a formal National Education Policy was approved by the Parliament, and six years later, the policy was amended. Then came the Right to Education Act in 2009 as a part of the then government's drive to rights empowerment. This Act only made a marginal difference as it is being violated quite often in some states. With no breakthrough on the educational front, Narendra Modi promptly took to the idea of a national policy on education in 2019–20.

Nearly two years after coming to power, in 2016, the Modi Government appointed a committee of five members to formulate a new education policy including a former cabinet secretary as the chairman and a former director of NCERT as one of the other four members. This Committee report was cold-shouldered despite it suggesting urgent initiatives within six months. It was a well-structured and comprehensive report. However, the government was not willing to offer this report for public review, not even on the Ministry's website. In the meanwhile, a new Minister had formed another committee in June 2017 with a space scientist as its head and eight other members, mostly with higher education backgrounds. This committee submitted its draft policy in October 2018 and this report was provided to the public in June 2019 when the NDA returned to power. The Ministry of HRD has more than a couple of national research and training institutes which include UGC, NCERT, AICTE, NUEPA, ICSSR, and there are as many premier bodies engaged in educational research in the country with studies of significance, and neither of those institutes were involved nor any analysis or research was considered essential.

It is a wonder how a country that has been so concerned with education from the very outset, with a key aspiration of the Freedom Movement focusing on education, has not been able to come up with a national education policy for more than thirty years. Despite the numerous experiments being conducted, no insights have been scaled up. There are many such examples. They were never researched for assessing scalability.

It is also surprising that a number of national institutes for training and research were established decades ago and yet there is no evidence or insights from studies concerning formulating or amending public policies on education. In the early years of independent India, we were quick to come up with initiatives and experiment. With the dominance of political parties in policy-making and an increase in personality-led politics, we seem to have lost momentum to accomplish national goals. A conflict of interest has crept into our public domain, particularly in political representatives. This has led to double standards in governance and policies.

Social forestry: Social forestry was taken up on a massive scale across the states with a massive number of trees planted. Social forestry was initially taken by the government, funded by World Bank, as an aided project under which districts were asked to promote plantation. The tree suggested was Subabul, a foreign sourced variety, claiming that it yields better income after five years.

As this Subabul recommended by foreign experts did not need water, many farmers across the country planted it on a massive scale, despite some active farmers expressing doubts about the suitability of Subabul as it draws the ground water and leaves the soil barren after a few years. The point here is that policy makers neither verified the caution of our own farmers nor conducted a pilot research before promoting this tree plantation on a large scale. It was after a decade that Subabul was discouraged, but by then considerable damage had already been done. A simple verification could have averted this debacle.

Source credibility, wrong impressions: Several years ago (1970-75) when I was an advisor in the Ministry of Health and Family welfare, considering my research insights, I noted that it is better not to include every time on every advertisement that it was 'brought by the Ministry of Health and Family welfare' or the Ministry of Information and Broadcasting, or Ministry of Rural Development, etc., when promoting the particular messages which could be universal and presented by any well-wisher. Stating that the slogan and campaign 'Don't smoke cigarettes' was created by the Ministry of Health or 'Keep your city clean' was brought to you by the Ministry of Urban Development does not add to the seriousness or credibility of the message.

Despite taking up this with policy makers over the years, nothing has been changed. This is because the minister and the ministry wants to take every opportunity to mark its existence and take credit. That is why we see photographs of the concerned minister or/and of the chief minister/prime minister in the advertisements of ministries. It is clear that no research finding will be given any value by political leaders if it does not facilitate their own publicity and promotes their image.

Ayushman Bharat was launched in 2018 as a health scheme for the poor. Approximately 10.74 crores families were identified as potential beneficiaries of this scheme, to whom a two-page letter by the prime minister was mailed. (This was when the 2019 poll campaign took off.) A year later, the National Health Authority conducted a survey and found that hardly 20% of families in Bihar and Haryana knew of the scheme. It was this survey which revealed that the prime minister's letter was not even opened in some cases. It was this survey that helped the government take corrective measures. The survey was conducted in the wake of the outbreak of acute encephalitis syndrome (AES) when barely 20% patients knew about Ayushman Bharat Scheme and how to avail it. Only 36 patients overall had availed the scheme in Bihar in the first year. This research saved the scheme from the complacency of the letter that involved 10.7 crore families across the country.

This research should not remain an isolated example. Every other scheme of the government can benefit from adopting the appropriate research support; the more independent the research, the more potential it will have. The prime minister writing a letter on the eve of elections apparently was viewed more in a political context. What else can explain the fact that so many had not even read/opened the letter?[11]

The 2018 Global Nutrition Report

A good example of how research can help public policies is the 2018 December research report by UNICEF on malnutrition. The report showcased how malnutrition impacts the social and economic development of countries. It even estimated how much malnutrition costs ($3.5 trillion) a year, with overweight and obesity alone costing $500 billion per year. The report indicates the link between overweight and obesity. The research conducted by the Centre for Food Policy called for immediate action by countries and identified nine targets to be accomplished. Only 95 of 194 countries were tracked in that research. The research highlighted solutions that already existed. New data was viewed as a game changer that could drive more effective action. It suggested that local data and action drives change. In 2012, Amsterdam, for example, faced an obesity crisis among its youth. Targets were fixed based on local research and action initiatives were suggested that could help alleviate the problem (in six years) by 2018. The study helped to build multi-sectoral plans to achieve targets.

This research shared forward-looking steps for

strengthening the ability of national food systems to deliver nutrition. Research reports such as this are never an end in themselves but are means to save lives, change lifestyles, and ensure that nobody is left behind. This research offered insights for a research framework in terms of behavioural change. And yet, India went on an altogether different route in its research priorities in the last decade.

Between 2013 and 2016, Delhi recorded 244 deaths due to malnutrition in city hospitals, according to a response to an RTI by the Directorate of Economic and Statistics and the Office of the Chief Registrar of Births and Deaths. In India, 23% of women and 20% men are considered under-nourished and nearly as many overweight. It was based on such data that India adopted its policies.[12]

In 1989–91, the Canadian International Development Agency's (CIDA) India director, Dr Mira Aghi, a nutrition specialist assigned me at CMS to conduct a study in Maharashtra on nutrition supplement to school-going children. At that time, some consultants were advocating the distribution of fish and chicken as supplements. Based on our research point, we recommended 'chickpea candies' (made of local pulses with jaggery) which was popular even otherwise among children as well as elders but was never viewed as a nutrition supplement. Based on this research, CIDA had extended its aid to Maharashtra state government to include chickpeas as an alternative school supplement.

Water Policy

Drinking water shortage is experienced in many parts of the country for years, particularly in the summer months. Successive governments have announced projects and budgetary allocations to addressing this shortage. Even in 2019, there were various pockets that continued to face shortage. There is no evidence of the agencies that have come into being to address the problem ever conducting a comprehensive research to examine water problems locally. The extent of shortage, sources of water around the year, and how the problem was addressed in the earlier decades were addressed and records were also made available. This is because India has unique examples in different parts including in Rajasthan, Karnataka, and Telangana of how drought and scarcity of water challenge was dealt with by different Rajas and Maharajas with lasting solutions locally involving the use of storage facilities like lakes, wells, tanks of different sizes and designs, and storing rain water. Based on its analysis, the Centre for Environmental Studies (CES) claimed that the problem in 2019 was exactly the same as it was five years earlier, as was featured in their magazine *Down to Earth*. And yet, nothing made a difference, despite so much coverage by news media and rhetoric by political leaders.

Instead of conducting an internal research using our own previous models, the UP Government, for example, (2018) sought an Israeli firm to help improve the water shortage problem. The Israeli firm sent a team of experts who, after a few days of local survey, suggested that India has better solutions for water conservation than what Israeli experts could suggest. And indeed, examples of superior, homegrown solutions can be found all over the country—some of the best-known being the Jaisamand lake in Udaipur and the centuries-old bavadis or baolis (step wells) in northern India, like Agrasen ki Baoli in Delhi and Toorji ka Jhalra in Jodhpur. Traditional ways of storing and using water in the country should have helped local researchers come up with suitable and sustainable plans for our geography and climate. But it is fashionable to assign a 'foreign consultant' so that it gets some publicity over time. Sustainable solutions don't come from such consultants. Comprehensive and continuous field research offers feasible, reliable, and sustainable solutions.

Farmer Suicides

The number of farmer suicides has become a tragic phenomenon in the last two decades, with no end in sight. It astonishes me that the effort made is more in terms of first aid or consolation and the issue has become a ping-pong blame game between political parties and leaders. Despite technology and management skills sweeping across the country, no serious scientific approach has been made to address the farmer's distress and prevent suicides. Having conducted crop forecast (for cotton and groundnut) for the first time in India—in Gujarat during 1972–74—using a unique research methodology for Hindustan Lever, I can say that India has come a long way in terms of research skills and technologies to forecast farm-front phenomena. Identification of potential families in distress in disaster zones closer to the harvest season and other such relevant data should help reduce the suicide rate. Through analytics and data bases (Aadhar and application software packages), it should be possible today to zero in on preventive and pre-emptive initiatives. Why is it then that farmer suicide has not been taken as a research challenge? Today, we even have drones to help in such research. This is baffling and tragic when we consider that in the past there has been brilliant and very useful research-based intervention in similar situations. It is important to recall that the Reserve Bank of India displayed great foresight in conducting a rural credit survey decades ago which was responsible for specific initiatives like the National Bank for Agriculture and Rural Development (NABARD) that made local interventions to address rural distress.

Policy and politics go together, but independent research—which most politicians are hostile to because it limits their prerogative and discretionary powers and interferes with their image management—must not be influenced by either, especially the dominant politics of the day. Issues like farmers' suicide should have made researchers rise to the challenge of resisting political pressure, of not allowing their work to get mixed up with political priorities. Sadly, this has not happened.

What I am trying to point out through these numerous references is that we have forgotten that the true role of research is to guide genuine schemes to resolve or address serious issues. Research should offer detailed information and options for decision-makers in an objective way and facilitate effective policy framing rather than being dictated by political considerations and administrative conveniences. Having identified the 'scientific temper' as a crucial means to the end of rational policy making, we seemed to have moved far away from this idea in recent decades. For example, an analysis of the budgets of the Indian government's Directorate of Advertising and Visual Publicity (DAVP) and discussion with officials shows that not even 1% of campaign outlays are spent on research (as against 10% in the private sector). Policy and strategy decisions continue to be made based on the whims and hunches of ministers and bureaucrats.

Missing a Solar Revolution

Despite India being one of the foremost countries to realise the potential of solar energy and having taken it up as a national initiative in the early 1970s, in 2020, India is nowhere near adopting and cultivating solar energy. China, on the other hand, took to solar policy a decade later and yet is more than a decade ahead of India. How did India miss this opportunity? Being familiar with Energy Development Agencies of Gujarat and Maharashtra (1975–1985) and having being associated with the Department of Non-Conventional Energy (DNCE) (with Dr Mahesh Dayal, Secretary Scientist and Dr Guru Raja, Principle Scientist and KS Rao, Director GEDA) and Minister Vasant Sathe, I know first-hand how we missed a big leap. Having installed a solar water system on my jubilee Hills house in Hyderabad in 1984–85 (the solar system taken from Baroda), I know how local electrical fitters and contractors resisted and badmouthed solar system. I know the research was more on technical aspects than on adoption and behavioural aspects of solar energy for households, institutions, industry, and services. I did not recall any field research at that point. In the absence of such research insights, the government went by 'incentive' policy (by offering subsidies) to promote solar, instead of communicating the basic merits of solar as a source.

My analysis 20 years ago was that the government did not realise the necessity of behavioural change of people for adopting solar and scaling the programme. Rural Electricity

Corporation (REC), a government corporation, on the other hand, conducted a behavioural research (1965–75) on how to convince farmers and villagers to go for electricity (solar was not yet recognised then as a source of energy). REC took to field research on behavioural aspects as it was one of the activities for which foreign aid was specified. Lalit Sen was a director at REC who had just (1964–68) returned with a PhD in diffusion of innovations and took to research at REC. And yet, the Ministry could not recognise the importance of research to promote solar. The 'Lab to Land' approach taken to promote improved farm practices as a part of 'Green Revolution' (1965–75) was another example of how field research was used for public policy. It was much later that a couple of isolated micro level studies were conducted, but they were never taken seriously at the department. A desegregated analysis on diffusion and adoption of solar tools at the household, institutional and community levels should have helped scale up and speed up the process. Even after almost a decade of 'Solar Mission' and promotion of subsidies, perceptions have not changed, as in the case of television and telecom technologies.

Climate change has become a national and global concern because of research. It was field research and analytical time series studies that led to climate change getting considered as a serious global issue which compelled nations to focus on public policies and action plans in the last decade. Much before all this, based on my research in various fields, a programme called 'Vatavaran' using the visual media, had been initiated to sensitise school children, adult citizens and communities to environmental issues. But it was not sustained. It is not surprising, then, that climate change concerns do not inform the lifestyles of individuals and communities in India to any degree. Even at the various global meets on climate change that now take place, micro-level initiatives like 'Vatavaran' are not taken seriously.

Child Labour

How did child labour become a national issue and lead to a national legislation? It was not only because of NGOs and civil society movements but also because research had clearly shown governments and politicians that the issue of child labour had become a serious issue for almost all sections of Indian society. This was an example for how independent research could lead to public policy making.

Based on census figures, the government was claiming until 1970 that child labour numbers were below 15 million in the country. It never became a serious issue. At that point, based on a nationwide field study, ORG estimated in its 1973-74 report that child labour involved 42 million children and was covered by news media prominently all over the country, thus becoming a national agenda. That was when the issue was echoed by political leaders, including in the parliament. Questions such as what is child labour, whom to consider as child labourers, and what policies are required were debated on for the next few years. Some people even went to the courts—some asking the government to prevent child labour, others asking children to be kept in school. The Supreme Court even asked the states/district administrators to ascertain the statues of child labour by conducting field surveys. All this was triggered by an independent research by ORG and its coverage in the news media. That research and debate in turn led to a stream of initiatives by the governments. These included policies on making school enrolment compulsorily which addressed the school dropouts concern and lead to explanation of mid-day meal programmes in schools. Midday meal has become a serious programme with more programmes addressing child labour, and midday meal programmes need field studies on a continuous basis. The way the midday meal programme is implemented locally keeps changing with different compulsions that change the scope of the programme. For example, in Mirzapur district of UP, the midday meal programmes completed 25 years and the decline in its implementation threatens the very purpose of the scheme. As a policy, the government increased the amount per child per day to Rs 11 and prescribed pulses and protein, whereas children in some places were reportedly being given only a roti and salt. In the absence of credible field research, isolated news media reports get highlighted out of proportion. Such reposts need to be tracked.

School Dropouts

Nearly 40 years ago (1982–83), with repeated news reports on school dropouts, the Ministry of Education (as it was known then) took to research to know more about the phenomena and it rightly commissioned field studies. One of those studies was conducted by me in Madhya Pradesh. After extensive field work and systematic research methodology, ORG submitted its report to the Ministry. The officer concerned was furious about the report and felt that the report deviated from the scope by discussing about 'toilets in school' as he did not understand then the connection between the dropout rate (specifically of girls) and the existence and functionality of toilets in school. As a result, the research report was shelved without further consideration.

Four years later, UNICEF wanted me to make a presentation in their workshop in Baroda on social development in the Western States of India. I made a presentation of this study in MP on school dropouts. It was to the credit of UNESCO that it picked up the that study and followed up with the powers in Delhi. But by that time the government had wasted almost a decade in acting on an urgent finding. Sensitivity of officials and confidence in field research would have spared the country the tragedy of a million children, particularly girls, dropping out of school.

The government claimed coverage of 92% households on World Toilet Day in 2018, while *Down to Earth* magazine of CSE reported 355 million women and girls in India waiting for a toilet. This is another example of the focus being on 'number constructed', not so much on usage by members of the household and their behavioural aspects.[13]

POCSO (2012)

Instances of exploitation of girls and rapes in society are not a new or recent phenomenon. But the extent, frequency, and brutality of incidents of rape and how they are reported in news media has led to uproar, emotional outcry, and widespread demand for severe punishment of the culprits. Based on such public outcry, the Union Government came up in 2012 with The Protection of Children from Sexual Offences (POCSO) Act. But the lack of decline in the incidents of rapes and continued incidents led to life sentence of the convicts amending the POCSO Act. This, in turn, led to public debate about death sentence of prime age culprits in the wake of yet another gang rape causing another round of public outrage.

That is, each time there was an outrage and extensive media coverage, the government took to making policies and amendments. But they never took to field research to ensure durable and sustainable policies. A field research would suggest that upbringing of children and their exposure to news and social media involving provocative contents are as important as passing new legislations against the culprits.

Drug addiction among children below 12 years of age is yet another phenomenon that, despite media coverage, has not become a serious concern of parents and pursuit of the government agencies. Despite 'ban policies', the phenomenon continues. Outside civil society agencies like 'Save the Children' have come into active work based on micro-research or case reports in media. More such initiative could have made a dent on the phenomenon.

Demonetisation (2016) & GST (2017)

In 2017, the government made an overnight declaration (such decisions cannot be otherwise) of demonetisation of certain notes (of 1000, 500 denomination) and allowed people to exchange their cash with ceilings, curbs, and time limits. Overall, irrespective of the desirability of such a 'hard decision', the government could have saved many people from the ill-effects of this decision by availing field research without losing secrecy. Even after three years and public discourse, the apprehensions have not ended. Credible research which would have been possible through independent research would have helped the government.

GST (2017) was preceded with several rounds of meetings with finance ministers of the states over time. Its implications to small entrepreneurs and unorganised sector could have been independently assessed to avoid any adverse effects. Demand for consumables would not have declined or unemployment would not have increased (even temporarily), as indicated by two research-based books of Penguin (2017) and Oxford Press (2017) as well as widespread adverse discourse. Sectoral field studies would have minimised the pains of this public policy. Even Nobel Laureate of Economics Abhijit Banerjee referred to GST and demonetisation as contributing to the slowdown of the country's economy.

Scope of Public Opinion Surveys

Gallop polls are known globally. George Gallop, who founded Gallop Polls more than five decades ago in the US, is viewed as the father of public opinion surveys across the world, including in the context of the Presidential polls of that country. Since then, such specialist agencies that conduct poll eve surveys have proliferated, particularly in countries such as India where an electoral democracy is well-established, markets are dominant in the economy, and news media have a unique stature. George Gallop and I have one thing in common—both of us did our PhDs from the School of Communication, University of Iowa, USA. Of course, I completed mine several years later (1968–70). The reason I refer to this is that a senior researcher and editor with Gallop Polls, David Moore, in his books *The Opinion Makers* (2008) and *The Super Pollsters* (1995) described how poll surveys vitiate poll atmosphere and scuttle the same democratic processes for which they had come into being. He gives 'devastating insider account of their several limitations and misapplications'. The revelations in this book have several insights for India. I have been talking and writing about some of these aspects for a few years now. On 1 November 2008, I referred to critical ones at the Lok Sabha Speaker's Second Roundtable of eminent people in the Parliament House Annexe. Unlike in the US, I believed that the way poll surveys have proliferated, the way they are being covered by the news media and used by political parties/leaders should be viewed critically to derive a positive potential of surveys in the interest of free and fair polls in India. Also, despite such insights, the methodology of such surveys in India continues to be based on the same Western model.

In this section, I tried to present the opportunities and challenges, availed and missed, and the occasions where research was initiated but not availed in the last two decades. The examples given here are those with which I am familiar or about which I have first-hand knowledge. There are many more otherwise. Through these examples, I hope to give an idea of the different situations concerning public policies. This chapter suggests that research should be given a fresh position in our national development programmes. Research should be a key resource when implementing strategies regarding our public policies. The dependency syndrome in our research outlook and methods has deprived the nation from realising the best of its own talent and potential.

CHAPTER FOUR

Social Science Research in India

The discipline of social science research and applied social research has its origins in the Second World War and in postwar campaigns (1935–50). The concern was propaganda and influence. The research of Harold Lasswell, Paul Lazarsfeld, Willian McPhee, Robert Abelson, and other legendary social scientists has become part of early literature. The initial trigger for their research was war-time communication, but over time, premier US academies like MIT, Yale, and Johns Hopkins built on their work to shape persuasive research methodologies.

The next phase (1950–75) was a concern for productivity and motivation. The research thrust was awareness, aspirations, and motivation. Apart from academics, economic bodies like the IMF and the World Bank became interested in economics and investments. Simultaneously, aid agencies such as US AID, Rockefeller, and Ford Foundation became keen on entering countries under different stages of development, but mostly those seeking external guidance and aid. In this process, some of the existing criteria and models of those countries like the US and UK were introduced and adopted for research and development. Indian leaders were anxious to seek assistance in its endeavours to get over its era of shortages.

By that time (1950–60), the International Monitory Fund (IMF), World Bank, and UN along with its agencies such as UNDP, UNICEF, WHO, and UNESCO had taken roots and emerged as proponents of models for growth and development with their research-based consultations. The US and the UK as well Germany, France, and USSR took to the aid and guidance route as per priorities of the countries, and in the process, promoted their 'market models', to the extent that countries like India were tempted to adopt them without even assessing the local relevance of those models and without consultations in the country.

That was how a 'top down' approach has come to stay as a development model. That is, when 'development research' has become a specialised research sought by the governments, services, aid agencies, international bodies, and even by civil society organisations.

Then came the phase when people's participation in the implementation of developmental programmes became a motivation for research, but mostly by a few independent scholars whose motivations were not always known, but more often were academic- or activism-driven.

Since 1995, however, research has been wooed by voters and image building and has become publicity and propaganda driven. That is when priority shifted from implementation to information and image building. Use of information and its effects thus became a secondary concern. Instead, public relations became the priority. In this process, after 2015, fake, planted, and surrogate coverage has become a cause for research concern. Quid pro communication instead of motivational research has become a priority. *Perception* more than *experience* has become the 'top' concern.

Origins of Social Science Research

It is rather disappointing that despite social research in India being more than fifty years old, it can hardly claim foundations of India-centric fundamentals or reliable base line or benchmarks on vital data parameters regarding development, policies, social change, lifestyles, and governance. Social research seems to have lost its way midway despite several initiatives as a part of a quest for scientific temper that the first prime minister of India had spearheaded. Social science research, in my analysis, was a missing link in India's development growth pursuit. How did it happen?

Early origins may be traced to the Indian Institute of Science (IIS), Bangalore (1909), although it pioneered fundamental science research and established certain discipline and baseline for social science research in India. Its early directors (such as S. Bhagavantam) never lost Indian moorings while building IIS as a world class institute with several pioneering research pursuits. Industrialists JRD Tata, Vikram Sarabhai, T.A. Pai, and VKRV Rao, in particular, must be remembered for their visionary foundations. Although the Indian Institute of Advanced Studies (IIAS) was set up in Shimla by then, it hardly created an echo system.

Policy research in India can be traced to Prasanta Chandra Mahalanobis, starting with the Indian Statistical Institute and at Planning Commission and its Programme Evaluation Organisation (PEO) and as a founder of Indian Institute of Statistics (IIS), Calcutta, made foundational contribution. G. Parthasarathy, J P Naik, pioneer of Indian Council of Social Science Research (ICSSR), Rajini Kothari founder of Centre for the Study of Developing Societies (CSDS), National Council for Education Research and Training (NCERT), Centre for Policy Research (1973) with Pai Panandikar as its president, Institute of Defence Studies and Analyses with K. Subramanyam, Durgabai Deshmukh, founder of Council for Social Development (CSD), Shanti Swarup Bhatnagar of Council of Scientific & Industrial Research (CSIR), Indian Agricultural Research Institute (IARI), Indian Council for Research on International Economic Relations (ICRIER) are some of the early pioneers of 1960s. Then came the next wave of research outfits who also played pioneering role. These include Indian Council for Economic Research (ICER), Tata Institute Social Science, Bombay, and Tata Institute of Fundamental Research (PRL) Physical Research Laboratories, Ahmedabad, as well as others that, under various Ministries, were expected to conduct research studies like the National Institute of Community Development, Mussoorie, followed by the National Institute of Rural Development, Hyderabad, Indian Institute of Mass Communication, Indian Institute of Foreign Trade, Indian

Institute of Public Administration, Indian Council of Medical Research (ICMR), and National Institute of Health and Family Welfare (NIHFW).

Outside the government, Vikram Sarabhai's role in setting up the Operations Research Group (ORG), Baroda, in 1968 was a significant initiative. G Parthasarathy, the first vice chancellor, and Prof B.D. Nagchaudhury of Jawaharlal Nehru University, New Delhi, deserve special mention for promoting research faculties and helping to create an effective research environment. In the next wave of institutions which gave a fillip to research include Delhi School of Economics and its offspring Institutes of Developmental Studies in Madras, Ahmedabad, and Trivandrum along with Schools of Managements and Indian Institutes Technologies (some include social science faculties). VKRV Rao founded Institute for Social and Economic Change (ISEC), Bangalore, in 1972. Potla Sen of Administrative Staff College of India (ASCI) also took initiatives for policy analysis and evaluation. Gandhi Gram Institute of Development and Health of Soundar Ramachandran near Madurai and A N Sinha Institute in Patna implemented good research initiatives, clubbing mostly economics and development. Rajini Kothari's initiative, much earlier, deserves credit for promoting political research with Centre for Social and Development Research (CSDS).

Faculties of approximately 10 disciplines have been involved and engaged in social science research, including anthropology, sociology and social work, psychology, political science, economics, agriculture extension, economic and development studies, demographics and statistics, communication, and social change. Despite landmark studies by researchers like Radhakamal Mukerjee (Calcutta University), M.N. Srinivasan (Mysore University), S.C. Dube (Sagar University), and Professor Damle (Pune University) in the mid-50s, social anthropological research never took roots on its own or in convergence with other disciplines. Economic development and social work also lacked vision and remained narrowly focussed. Environment and ecology were not serious concerns for a long time. Demographic studies were limited only to population growth and family planning. Overall, fundamental research on change, both economic and social, received scant and disjointed interest. Even the Programme Evaluation Organisation (PEO) of the former Planning Commission could not impact studies as it was engaged primarily in monitoring. Social research has to be multidisciplinary, across disciplines, and inter disciplinary to make a difference.

The Lal Bahadur Shastri National Academy of Administration in Mussoorie is a reminder of missed opportunities. Despite its concern with policy analysis, it did not take the initiative to further research methodologies and adopt them to the unique Indian scene. For example, one would have expected the Academy to engage in research on implementing RTI and the difference it has made in decision making. Administrative Staff College of India (ASCI) is another example but in an ad hoc way of interests with no proactive initiatives and longitudinal studies. Although it was funded by the government and international agencies for several of its studies, what fundamental difference have those institutes made in the research paradigm in vogue? Neither of these institutes contributed to adopting or evolving India-centric research methodologies or in-programme evaluation approach, as made by private outfits like ORG, CSDS, and CSD.

The Planning Commission had set up a committee for social science research under the chair of VKRV Rao in 1968. Much earlier in 1953, it had established Research Programme Committee (RPC) to generate suitable schemes of research of social, economic, and administrative implications. The concerns then were regional development, land reforms, public corporation, and social welfare.

Facilitating Factor

VKRV Rao suggested that social science research is a 'facilitative factor for nation building' and that 'social knowledge is important to promote and regulate social change and to produce a dynamic and healthy society'. He expected that 'social science research will have far more effective and continuing impact'.

ICSSR was formed to promote social science research in the country, both in academics and public policy framework. I had the benefit of interacting briefly twice with J.P. Naik who had pioneered its operations as its first Member Secretary. I also reviewed its operations at the insistence of Professor M.L. Sondhi, its chairman, in 1998. Over the years, ICSSR has been sponsoring workshops and training programmes in research methodologies through one or the other of its sponsored institutes. These were conducted at different locations, mostly by its own sponsored (27) institutes. However, the difference these workshops have made in consolidating social science research in the larger context of policy and programme evaluation was never reviewed as each activity was viewed in isolation. Of course, these various institutes have been conducting CSDS field surveys but mostly in an electoral context, not on any public policy or social change research or basic issues facing the country. I am fortunate to have met many of these pioneers (1970-85). In the absence of India-specific research methodologies, methodologies that are not locally ingrained and foreign agencies (profit-driven and markets-oriented ones) have gained and expanded.

ICSSR started with four affiliate institutes, with its number increasing to 27 in 1993. Hardly half a dozen of these 27 could be considered viable even after 50 years, according to Prof. Partha Chatterjee of Centre for Studies of Social Sciences, Calcutta. That was why, S. L. Rao (a former Director General of NCEAR) suggested some of these institutions to be closed and some others to be merged. He pointed out that most sponsored research was limited to data collection.

Prof. A. Vaidyanathan's (Director of Madras Institute of Development Studies) 2007 review committee observed that 'social research is increasingly commercialised and driven by the interests of the sponsors as distinct from public interest. The ICSSR is unable to reverse that trend due to its organisational structure and lack of adequate resources. It never acquired capacities to accomplish its mission'. ICSSR could not even promote any data bases. V.K. Malhotra, member-secretary ICSSR (2019), expressed his concern for the performance of ICSSR institutes.

In his review of ICSSR, Professor Anjan Mukherji of Jawaharlal Nehru University lamented that social science researchers ignore their responsibility and accountability to the society at large. He further stated that even privately funded social science research *should go through public scrutiny* 'if the findings are put in public media or even if the findings of such research have implications to larger public'.

Initially, the ICSSR institutes took up studies on gender, health, and elections. But soon, the election studies shifted from post-electoral trend to pre- and poll-time predictive surveys which are hyped by news media and have temporal relevance. Prof. M V Nadkarni of ISEC, Bangalore, cautioned about doctored research that vitiates public opinion. Prof. Muhammad Yunus's research in Bangladesh won him the Nobel prize as it helped trigger the process of social change. Even the Literacy House in Lucknow, set up by a foreign lady (Wealthy Fisher), won UNESCO prize—not any of ICSSR institute for its initiative for literacy promotion (1955–65). None of them ever thought of looking into the role of mass media plays in triggering an economic and social change and development. Even the difference television was making on children or on family system was never the concern of these institutes, even on an ad hoc basis. And yet, these institutes resent reviews of their performance, even by ICSSR.[1]

Social science research in India, edited by M. V. Nadkarni and R. S. Deshpande and published by the Academic Foundation (New Delhi, 2012)[2] was a commemorative volume based on 13 conference papers and the only source to understand ICSSR's role. In his foreword, Javed Alam, reminded that ICSSR was meant to promote and stimulate research in social sciences. Dr TCA Anant of Delhi School of Economics, a former Secretary General of ICSSR, commented that papers at annual conferences of associations are indifferent and that professional associations are yet to improve their services. Both public and private domains with a source of funding could be in the public domain and open to public.

ICSSR has two regional centres and 29 affiliated institutions across the country. In addition, there are five ICSSR recognised institutions in Delhi, Kolkata, Patna, and Thiruvananthapuram. Why do the Ministries not engage ICSSR or its affiliates for their research requirement? They often engage an outside agency, preferably a foreign consultant or agency. There is a clear preference. There are, of course, a few institutes affiliated to ICSSR which are engaged by a state or international government, but not because of the ICSSR connection but on the institution's own merit or because of an association with a senior chairman or director. Perhaps, many ministers do not even know that they need social research that can guide them.

Despite a senior functionary (vice president) of the ruling party being the Chairman of ICSSR (2017–20), it has not become the nucleus of social science research in the country or any repositioning in its network. Earlier, when the chief of UGC was the chairman of ICSSR, it did not give any edge to social science research faculties in 300 universities.

Outside agencies such as ORG, Vadodara, had shown initiatives in terms of methodology as well as their utilisation. Institute of Social Studies (1985), New Delhi, and even Economic and Political Weekly (EPW) contributed far more in promoting social science research in India than most ICSSR institutes put together. In fact, they aided more than the university faculties over the decades could individually do regarding conducting experiments or critical engagement on interdisciplinary methodologies.

The Barefoot School of Bunkar Roy in Tilonia in Rajasthan and Grassroots Research and Advocacy Movement (GRAAM) in Mysore are two unique examples with which I am familiar. They took initiatives that deserve far greater and more serious support than they have received. These institutes were more concerned with grassroots perspective and voices. In 1975–76, Jamal Kidwai, former Secretary Ministry of Information and Broadcasting, and I wanted to adopt this Tilona model and prepare 'barefoot researchers' at Jamia Milia Centre for Communication Research (which later was named after Kidwai). I tried to revive that idea in 2012 by setting up the Institute of Communication and Convergence Studies at Noida. As it was a new approach, it could not appeal to both parents and students, and the institute had to be shut down in two years. Copycat courses attract more attention than new, experimental, particularly research-centric prototype development and module courses that I was trying to implement at that institute. Ten years earlier, I did experiment with the idea of research as an integrated or converged aspect of every course at (MICA) Mudra Institute of Communication. This was what A G Krishnamurty of Mudra Advertising and I tried along with Kiran Karnik and Pradeep Khandwalla, former Director of IIM, Ahmedabad. But since its main concern was advertising and public relations, research-driven programme in the larger context could not be retained as a key concern, whole MICA continued to be backed by a big corporate.

Census data has not contributed as much as National Sample Survey (NSS) rounds. More recently, the National Family Health Survey reports (four rounds by 2019) have revived both analytical and evaluative studies, as have the annual surveys of ASER of Pratham. Much earlier, the first National Readership Survey (1972) and first National Family Planning Survey (1973) as well as the first national survey on child labour and housing by ORG triggered social survey research at various levels and in the context of public policy research. Then came foreign funding agencies and sponsors like the Ford Foundation, USAID, UNICEF, and Bill Gates Foundation. That changed the course and priorities of special research in India. Most market research outfits in the country today are fully owned or controlled by foreign corporates, and not all of their origins are known. Meanwhile, it was a fully owned Indian organization (ORG) which developed a paradigm for market research, survey research, and applied social research catering to the private industry and the Ministries (1965–95).

It introduced the idea of 'syndicated research' so that findings would not remain the monopoly of any one, methodology would be dynamic, and survey research would be reliable. Now, foreign agencies control such organisations and methodologies, including those engaged in political and electoral studies.

How much do governments spend on research and evaluation? Obviously, this is indicative of how much importance governments give to research, particularly regarding policy and program evaluation, monitoring, and feedback. According to a guestimate of mine few years ago, this was an insignificant amount at 0.3% of project/scheme budgets. More recently, in 2017–18, I estimated that the Union Government and the state governments hardly spend 1.0% of project budgets. And this, according to my estimates for the years 2016–18, is barely one-third of what the governments spend on advertising and publicising their schemes. What is being spent on all kinds of research, monitoring, and evaluation activities by various governments (at Union and States) and their departments would hardly be Rs 5000 crores annually (2014–15). For example, ICSSR's annual budget to support 27 institutes was hardly Rs 100 crores in 2010 (now, in 2020, it is approximately Rs 200 crores).

In 1971, I accompanied Professor Everett Rogers of 'diffusion of innovations' fame to a dozen research institutes across the country. Based on discussions, Rogers concluded that hardly 20% of their research was ever utilised or taken into account in any decision-making at any level. I tried to update this estimate during Rajiv Gandhi's Prime Ministership (1983) as, at that time, research was being given some priority. But that estimate on use of research was within 30%. I could recount several specific examples. In early 1980, I did a research project from ORG on the dropout rate of girls in Madhya Pradesh for the Union HRD Ministry. On finding that my report had a chapter on toilets, the Ministry found an excuse to dump the report itself (it was a few years later that the report was revived by UNICEF). A few years before the Commonwealth Games in India, CMS did a research project for the HRD Ministry on the status of stadia in India and observed how the stadia were being misused by local bodies. The Ministry put the report under lock as the report did not endorse any of its initiatives. In 2016–17, the government, after a lengthy process of competitive bids, commissioned CMS to conduct a field assessment of toilet and sanitation initiatives in the states. CMS went all out to submit 29 reports within the given timeframe. In the meantime, the team in the Ministry had changed which led to independent reports being put on cold storage and another study being conducted. If a similar track is made of ICSSR research over the years, it would be as disappointing. The governments were also anxious about allowing the publication of these research reports. The exception in more recent years was concerning field surveys in electoral contexts. Even more concerning is that after decades of ICSSR initiatives, no database can be referred to regarding any of the social development issues.

The state of affairs with social research reflects the credibility of data, which in turn determines its utilisation. First, when the numbers and percentages become yardsticks for change, development, and performance, they need to be validated with transparency with an evident source, structure, and timeline. Basic data should have nothing to do with politics or the party in power or periodic elections. And data should never be accused or doubted on those counts. Numbers become deceptive if they are not credible. Moreover, media coverage should not be a factor in that process of data fixing. Survey research at one time was based on or sourced from considered views and recall, but today it is based on instant or top-of-the-mind recalls. Like instant news for news channels, data cannot be based only on perceptions. And like fake news, there is fake data and research. From data, we are now in ratings, rankings, and index environment. With frequently changing socio-economic parameters, the structure of data should be far more transparent.

With proliferation of news media and the way in which visual media covers new, viewers' perceptions become vitiated, thus influencing the response pattern in sample surveys.

Further, the more recent phenomena of social media and ease of 'retweeting' has complicated the responses to field interviews and opinion formation process. The planted, paid, fake, and quid-pro-quo news phenomena has become too pervasive to cope with in survey research. And yet, we continue to use the same old survey research methodologies. Everything is changing, except the survey research methodologies. Is anything being done in this context by our social science establishment?

India is fortunate that it has several researchers from all sorts of backgrounds including social, philosophical, spiritual, economic, and statistics. Many of them, as original thinkers, have contributed much before India became independent. Their ideas and propositions have enriched global thinking and provided a direction for future outlook, framework, perspective. Prasanta Mahalanobis (statistics and research), M.N. Srinivas and S.C. Dube (anthropology), Radhakamal Mukherjee and Nirmal Kumar Bose (sociology), and Amartya Sen and Jagdish Bhagwati (development economics) are only a few of the many who have set examples for original thinking in the last 50–70 years. They noted how India needs an interdisciplinary outlook and approach to research and offered models which many outside India have also adopted.

Dr P.C. Mahalanobis pioneered primary databases required to frame public policies and welfare measures which have set standards for global statistical systems. The tools he developed continue to be used all over the world. In fact, it was the UN that sought his guidance, after Mahalanobis offered to share the knowledge and experience gained from his pioneering work of applying statistical sampling in the areas of demography, agriculture, and other socio-economic fields to set newly independent India on its development growth path. He chaired the UN Statistical Commission in 1954 and 1956, making immense contribution to not only India's socio-economic development but also the world's. Mahalanobis had been inspired by those in the forefront of India's freedom movement and by philosophers of the earlier era.

With such a pioneering track record, where are we today in 2020? Have we come up with any new methodology to monitor, understand, and appraise the changes, the process of development and evolving public policies?

The competitive compulsions of news media and their ownership pattern has added to the public debate on research, use of data, and the way findings are reported and covered by news media. The way the GDP rate is indicated on a varied range by different agencies from time to time, even within a month, for example, casts confusion and doubts. The way poverty levels are indicated or how employment rates are claimed or even how inflation rates (without explaining) or the sex ratio trends are announced has complicated public perceptions about government performance and achievements. How then does social science research impact public sensitivity and make policy makers wiser? It is easy to say that research has complicated issues. Why are we in such a situation? Is it because research has become a tool to serve the interests of self-interested parties or groups or leaders? One cannot escape from this question.

Analytics has certainly sharpened the potential of data and research. But what are the contexts in which analytical tools are developed and used? To what extent are they used for public policy formulation? Is citizen more active or passive? With so much research around, are consumers more inclined to jump on a bandwagon or are they more discriminative today? Are public functionaries and policy makers making better choices in the larger interest? Is that not what research is ultimately expected to enable? Are we in a better position to independently and objectively measure change, particularly social change, citizen empowerment, social justice, and level playing opportunities? Are the methodologies facilitating such a concern? Whether economic change is being measured any better today at micro level is a different question.

Researchers should never forget that they are first citizens of the country and that they have a social responsibility and ethical concerns. How transparently is research undertaken? Are findings available in the public domain?

Research should not become a tool for manipulative initiatives and interests. Persuasive strategies should never lose concern for the grass roots and the interests of the poor, the deprived, and those outside the power system. Social science research never took off and took roots in the Indian context. As a result, research methodology and discipline has not flourished. While most premier institutes were launched during 1965–75 at the initiative of the government leaders of the time, in the following decade, research failed to become a sought-after input for sustaining democracy and development. Nor did it really make social justice and inclusive governance its goal. In the next decade, research became a tool primarily to explore the Indian markets. The new economic policy brought in a new perspective of research. There were no corrective initiatives like the J-PAL project at Seva Mandir (Udaipur) or the Barefoot experiment (Tilonia) or the GRAAM (Mysore) idea in the later years to ensure that research helps policies, planning, and strategies, as much as it has helped marketing, advertising, and the corporates. Thereafter, research was reduced to number-crunching for manipulation and influence with not much known about any conflict of interest. Independence, objectivity, transparency, and inclusiveness, which are essential features of research, have never become the concerns as much as they should be.

Academic Research, Public Policy Perspective

Tata Trust has been a key supporter of fundamental research in India in a number of ways. It has helped set up institutions like the Indian Institute of Science in Bangalore which, after 60 years of being established, remains a pioneer not only in fundamental research in science and technology but also in policy research. Tata Institute of Social Science Research (TISS), Mumbai, is another pioneer that, over these 60 years, has trained an army of researchers. These institutes are only two examples of the many ways in which the Tata Trust has been supporting fundamental and policy research. In 2018, a Tata Endowment of Rs 50 crore helped set up in the Indian

Institute of Technology, New Delhi, a school of public policy.[3] Under the guidance of a Department of Science and Technology (DST) of Government of India, Tata's set up five Centres of Policy Research. Over the years, senior bureaucrats have been deputed for short term courses in public policy institutes in the UK and US universities. Have they made a difference in ministries availing social science research knowledge or insights for rational policy initiatives, better implementation of schemes, and achieve better outcomes?

Centres of higher education, including universities, have traditionally been engaged in one or other research that is locally relevant. This is apart from PhD theses or other such requirement at post graduate level. In 1960–62, as part of my master's degree, I undertook two research studies. One was a socio-economic study of Harijan Wada of Mudunuru village, which was my native village. The second was a study of Asia's largest jaggery cooperative society of farmers in Anakapalli. Both these studies have laid the foundation for my interest in research and for pursuing it as my career. These topics were not suggested to me by professors in Andhra University, Waltair, but I chose this subjected after seeing the kind of discussion happening in news media at the time about how cooperative societies were getting involved in enterprises and how Harijan communities are decaying. These studies acquainted me with different research methodologies and concerns regarding how such studies can help formulate and assess public policies and public services. The faculty in the university, of course, guided me in conducting these studies with equal enthusiasm. That was the situation in academics 60 years ago. It was based on that study that I observed in 1967–68 that houses in Indian Harijanwada were much cleaner than the ones in American ghettos of Chester and that the residents were far more concerned with keeping their surroundings clean. I even noted that if educational facilities and basic infrastructure was provided to Harijanwada, they would be uplifted from their deprivation. From the second study in Anakapalli, I imbibed the idea that peoples' participation makes all the difference in the success of public schemes and helps cope with competition in the market.

In 2018, the Ministry of Human Resource Development (HRD) issued a directive to vice chancellors and directors of national institutes that PhD thesis topics should not be on 'irrelevant topics' and should be on topics of 'national priorities'. It implied that the Ministry has become the nodal point for all academic research pursuit in the country. Such directive cannot be ignored as it can end up in research fellowship being refused. Considering the implications of such directive on the freedom of students to choose their topics, this directive made news. As it was becoming a controversy, the Ministry issued a clarification against such intentions to curb academic freedom.[4] It was criticised for curbing students' right to choose their research topic and for cracking down on dissent in academic campuses. This, however, was not an isolated instance. Such efforts to suggest preferences existed even before, although not as a policy. In 2016, Jawaharlal Nehru University (JNU) was reported to discourage research on human rights, rights of Dalits, and on marginal communities. And even open seminars on campus on such themes were discouraged. What does this imply for the social science research environment?

There are two different examples described here, one from 1960-65 and the other from 2015-20, indicating the types of academic opportunities and environment and how politics spilling over into research and academics can change the priorities as well as research culture and architecture. Amitabha Bhattacharya, a retired IAS officer, wrote on the HRD circular in the *Hindustan Times* of 16 April 2019: 'It is against the spirit of free enquiry, the guiding motive is political, it would saffronize the campuses and incalculably damage India's knowledge ecosystem...and policing of research will dictate ideas and go against critical thinking that engages with plurality of ideas. In other words, the purported action will be grossly against national interest.'

After years of a lull in governments' concern for social science research, in October 2018, the Union Government developed web portals to build a 'research ecosystem' in the educational system. The government acknowledged that 'only by good research' could there be innovations and that such innovations are essential to sustain growth and productivity. The objective of the government's Impactful Policy Research in Social Science (IMPRESS) is to identify and fund research proposals in social sciences that impact governance and society. The scheme was allocated Rs 414 crores till March 2021 and ICSSR was made the implementing agency of this scheme.[5]

Has Our Academics Missed Challenges?

India's educational network is one of the world's largest in terms of the number of colleges, universities, and professional institutes. They are present in the public as well as private sector. Today, India is an impressive source globally for managers, scientists, engineers, researchers, and even as enterprisers. But if we look critically as to what has been the contribution of these higher-end academics in addressing the basic problems of the country, there is little to take note of. Where are we in terms of the knowledge of the society? Why we are not at the top in innovations? How have Indian scientists in the US earned laurels, patents, and developed new technologies and application software? With such a large network, impressive talent, and highly dedicated academicians, why are none of our institutions in the top hundred globally?

With recent initiatives, we should expect to make a visible difference in the next five years. Why, for example, are the University of Georgia and many Australian and Russian institutes being sought after by Indians? It should be the other way round.

For example, with over 500 management schools, including more than 25 IIMs, what kind of research has been done on India-specific concerns? Exceptions include IIM Ahmedabad or IIT-Delhi. Dr Anil Gupta's research for over two decades on India's innovations at the grass roots should have triggered and scaled interest. Dr Abdul Kalam also posed this dilemma. TIAFAC made no difference. The research by Dr Dinesh

Mohan at IIT, Delhi, on urban transportation did, however, make a difference and was motivational. Only a few of these higher-end institutes have taken to behavioural research, despite many of the basic issues confronting India having to do with attitude and behaviour creating stumbling blocks. Why has India missed a solar revolution despite establishing the policy more than a decade before China? Why, despite having made so much progress in telecom technology—including the rugged telephone exchanges of C-DOT forty years ago, and from there to 5G technology today—are we still at the mercy of technology options from the US and China?

There is not much effort to enable diffusion of innovation. Successful innovations remain islands—just isolated successes that don't spread to entire sectors across the country and lead to transformation. The research methods being employed are copied, not original, and often the models being pursued are foreign. This is one reason why our research institutes have not made much lasting difference nationally. The Indian Council of Social Science Research (ICSSR) has four or five institutes that for decades have focused on Indian Industry, but there is no indication of any of them making any difference to industry. If bringing research from labs to markets is very important, how many of our IITs, IIMs, or universities can claim credit over the years?

Initiatives announced by the prime minister in recent years remind us that the government recognises the importance of research to sustain the country's growth momentum. In its 2019 poll manifesto, the ruling party had aptly referred to R&D under the 'good governance' heading. But at the same time, there is no indication that there is a reversal in the overall research culture, neither is there assurance of space and scope for independent research. Some measures by the government include: a) revival of research in the academics by increasing the number of research scholarships and the scholarship amount, b) setting up IMPRESS with special funding (2018-22) and entrusting partial responsibility to ICSSR for social science research, c) recognising more than a dozen institutes as 'eminent and excellent' and providing them special support (including some private universities), d) endorsing the idea of 100 research universities in the next few years, as envisioned in the National Education Policy, e) announcing a National Research Foundation in the 2019–20 budget although with only a notional budgetary allocation, and f) social efforts to fill academic positions.

The research culture in the country would receive further encouragement and would have been revived if only the government a) restored independence of data and primary sources of data; b) did not dent the credibility of the data originating from institutions by diffusing their role and standing; c) revisit the ongoing practice of engaging foreign consulting agencies by the ministries in a preferential manner and at the cost of Indian talent and resources; d) restored evaluative research instead of supportive research and did not snub critical faculties and initiatives; and e) bring in transparency in conditionalities selectivity and pre-approval restrictions in research pursuit.

Further, following are some measures that are needed to give a push to social science research in the country:

a) Reposition ICSSR and UGC with budgets and nodal responsibility for National Research Foundation.
b) Some special drive is needed to fill in a number of vacancies for research scholars and research faculty.
c) The budget for social science research has to be specific and much higher than even before.
d) Research methodology should be part of the syllabus at graduate level, if not at the higher secondary level, as some schools are experimenting.
e) Explore the type of enquiry being availed and with what conclusions. And do not hesitate to question research methods. If you do not ask promptly, you end up with 'TRP'-like misleading and un-reversible consequences.
f) Ask for the outcome of public policies and for implications of those policies on immediate future. The art of 'questioning' should be part of nurturing critical faculties.

As I discussed in my book *Sustainable Good Governance, Development and Democracy* (SAGE 2018), Modi's messages could be the mantras that could pull India out of the traps of the past and move on to the high growth path. These ideas cannot be realised and achieved fully without social science research being implemented at different levels in the country. The ministries should realise this fact and take corrective measures to welcome independent research.

Politicisation of Public Policies, Decline in Social Research

Public policies are state or national policies. All state policies are expected to be Of, By, and For the public. Although the idea of a policy may be politically initiated and politically motivated, once it becomes a policy in a parliamentary democracy, it cannot be considered as belonging to a party. In fact, it becomes a policy applicable to all citizens. Prime Minister Narendra Modi had given a call to the members of the ruling party (4 August 2019) to serve all citizens across party lines and who voted for them. This one advice of the prime minister could change the face of Indian politics, scope of development, and democracy, if only his advice is taken with earnestness by all leaders and parties.

Over the years, public policies have become and continue to be politically motivated even after being formally adopted. Members of the ruling party today call the government 'BJP Government' or 'Modi Government', even inside the Parliament. Even the opposition party in the legislatures call the government as that of the party in power or that of the leader of that party who is today the prime minister. The government is 'of India' and 'of all people', and as such, policies are applicable to all in an inclusive way. But political polarisation is evident everywhere today. The Swachh Bharat policy, for example, is not of BJP Government's or Modi's, as is being presumed and talked about often. Why do researchers avoid reminding the public of this fact?

Politicisation of policies and the government is a deviation that the country has slipped into decades ago without realising what it implies and the disaster it is causing to the nation. Today, many problems concerning governance in the country are because of this fallacy. By believing so, the paradigm of democracy is being constrained and limited. This outlook is a stumbling block in our growth and development. As a result, the leaders and parties tend to view everything, including public policies, through such a prism. The research environment in the country also reflects this trend.

The research implies an endeavour or a pursuit of a larger cause, inclusive growth, and efficient outcomes. There appears an inherent friction or clash in the outlook of politicians and the idea of research, particularly independent research. This sensitivity is what differentiates between leaders, parties, and the governments. This is what politicisation of policies is all about. Research is a liberal concept that aims to change and make better sense of the world. Politics, on the other hand, inherently is a conservative pursuit of legitimisation in the guise of the opposites and for hegemony by rhetoric. It is time to re-evaluate such public notions, perceptions, and preferences.

In the initial 20 years (Nehru, 1950–70), it was consensus building, public participation, or public cooperation that was a concern for public policies and development plans. This approach surpassed the interests of political parties. Leaders in the initial years were far more futuristic and concerned with the consequences for a better future. The next 20 years (Indira Gandhi, 1970–90) were driven by ambitious parties and political leaders. Domination or influencing was the driving force. After that, the next 20 years (Rajiv, PVN 1990–2010) were reform-driven and of paradigm shifts, despite increasingly more short-term political compulsions. In the years between 2010 and 2020, public policies were driven more by electoral politics, control, and command interests, with image and impressions determining far more. Research preoccupation reflects such a trend.

In the early years, it was the institutions which were the concern and centre stage of governance. Politicisation and vote bank politics has made India individual-centric, both at the union and state levels. Despite the emergence of regional parties and leaders, individualisation in national politics has been visible and marked. People prefer a strong leader. A team or a cabinet form of government has not gained traction at any level.

This cult of 'one leader', the 'supreme leader', and this leader being centre stage at all times has deemphasised or discouraged independent research and given rise to 'supportive research' in the country. This trend has certain implications for the research methodology and research institutes. This has signalled a decline in the stature and credibility of research and the role of researchers. Research has come to be viewed as an ally more, or even as a 'third eye' which Lord Shiv was assumed to have used to destroy in order to regenerate.

Despite expansion in IITs, IIMs, and universities of higher learning with research as a discipline and many Indians making significant mark globally in academic and research in a range of subjects, there has been no escalation in research or its use. All that should have meant a much higher use of applied research in the country and should have helped create a far more vibrant civic society. It was Dr Kasturirangan, former Chairman of ISRO, appointed by the government to draft the education policy, who came up with the recommendation in 2019 that 100 universities should focus on research. But this was not included in the Economic Review of 2019 and hardly any budget was provided for it.

Being a political beneficiary of 'back room research', the prime minister apparently realised the vacuum in the academics. His government had established 'PM research fellowships' for 1000 students in 2017–18. The fact that only 300 scholars could avail the fellowship indicated that the idea needed further improvement. The Indian Council of Social Science Research (ICSSR) remained side-lined as the University Grants Commission (UGC) in reviving a research culture in the country.

But in 2019, the historic 2005 RTI Act, which had created a new hope among citizens of the country, enabling them to question the government and gave an opportunity to the government to offer transparency, was diluted significantly.

Research: National Policy on Education

The types of initiatives taken in the country to promote research in the first 20 years of the Republic remains unmatched to date. This research endeavour was not only in science and technology but ensured equal priority to the socio-economic and development sectors. That was how there were so many premier research institutes across the country. Most of them were established prior to the 1970s. Private research outfits sprang up thereafter, most of them with a profit motto. With the commercialisation of research, there was an influx of foreign research corporates. Research thus became a commodity in the market. Sponsor orientation and bias gained and became obvious. All of this created competition while there is no evidence that the influx and competition has improved the quality and relevance or promoted better appreciation of research. Of course, the overall opportunities for research have increased in the country. However, how much of it is being availed, particularly by the public systems, is not known.

As if in realisation of this vacuum in academics, Dr K Kasturirangan's report on new education policy in 2019 presented various recommendations. Kasturirangan is an eminent space scientist who has made pioneering contributions to space research. These include suggestions towards consolidating research as a discipline. This report recommended a National Research Foundation to be established as a nodal agency to promote research in the country. It's core aim included 'to seed, grow and facilitate research at academic institutions where research is currently at a nascent stage'.[6]

This panel came to the conclusion that 'there is no research in most universities and colleges and lacks transparency, and competitive peer reviewed research. This report also suggested creating 100 universities exclusively devoted to research by 2030. A UGC committee report (2019) too came up with an alarm on decline in research in the country since 1990 and in the quality and relevance of research.'

After more than 50 years, since the creation of the Indian Council of Social Science Research (ICSSR) based on Dr V.K.R.V. Rao's report, a government appointed committee (2019) reminded the nation of the criticality of research when pursuing knowledge. Neither the first national policy on education in 1968 or the second national policy in education in 1986 (revised in 1992) had referred to research as a discipline or addressed the need to cultivate it in different contexts.

Earlier in 2018, a University Grants Commission (UGC) panel, headed by Professor Balaram of Indian Institute of Science, suggested sweeping reforms to introduce discipline into research pursuit at PhD and MPhil levels. It brought to limelight the practice of publishing research articles in 'predatory' journals and as presentations in conferences organised by such groups.[7] This panel exposed fake research paper racket that was reported earlier by the Indian Express in 2018. The panel even suggested a board for social science research with separate allocation of funds, including funds for a dean for research in universities, in order to ensure quality.

For this, the government came up with a special scheme to select faculty members by providing them with a four-week exposure (three weeks in India and one week in a premier US university) and then appoint them as dean or head of the department.

But the 2019 union budget, although it accepted the idea of a National Research Foundation, did not provide any budget exclusively for it. Instead, it indicated that the foundation would coordinate among the various government ministries, assess the relevance of different research projects and allocate/reallocate funds from a common research budget. The 2019 budget also did not provide a budget for universities exclusively devoted to research. Also, the thrust areas of research of the foundation did not seem to include any social development goals. Its focus appeared to be more on technology, and bringing research *into* the country under the government's direction and control.

Professional Associations

The annual science congress in the first week of January has been a practice for decades since the Nehru years. It is organised on different academic campuses across the country. In January 2017, the science congress scheduled at Osmania University, Hyderabad, was cancelled because of alleged student unrest. There were others who alleged that it was cancelled as an anti-Modi campaign was at its height there at that time. Political reasons were made up. The Science Congress has always been inaugurated by the prime minister of the country with a key note address sending out the government's affirmative support to scientific research. It has become a forum to exchange new research and perspectives. This event remains an annual endorsement of the government's policy and support of scientific pursuit in the country. The Indian science academy has kept up its stature as an independent body and ensured that different viewpoints are allowed in its conferences. Most papers presented and discussed in this meet are research based. Every year, some papers are found to be based on Indian ethos and original methodologies.

The Indian Council of Social Science Research (ICSSR) was expected to make a difference to the extent, quality, and status of social research in the country. It is now more than 60 years old and has organised and sponsored a series of short-term programmes on research methodologies over these years. These were organised by its associate institutes like CSDS and CSD. It had never taken similar initiative as the science congress to bring together social science researchers.

A review of ICSSR's activities, priorities, and focus indicates the path and progress that social research had followed. First, the budget of ICSSR over the years has remained low or marginal. The scope of the educational system has increased several fold during the 60 years, and more importantly, ICSSR activities have neither expanded or intensified or undergone any strategic changes. Today, ICSSR is of no consequence. ICSSR has made no difference to any aspect of research or social research or its dynamism or utilisation or methodologies.

Has ICSSR activities brought any new enthusiasm in research methodologies or their reliability to study peculiarities of India? Why have so few studies explored the basic issues of the country such as illiteracy, farmers' distress, increased violence, and the impact of social media?

ICSSR should have taken interest by sponsoring or promoting studies on social impact of television as its proliferation and viewership had gone up significantly and changed the attitudes and lifestyles of people across socioeconomic divides. Two-thirds of viewership was children and women. No other intervention has changed the extent of criminal, matrimonial, and violence against women behaviours. This was not an overnight phenomenon, but it is something that has developed over the last 25 years. This trend was not studied by any academic or seriously considered from a social impact perspective. I, along with Professor G.N.S. Raghavan, tried to examine this issue in our book *Social Effects of Mass Media in India*.[8] As TRP research by TAM swayed policies and perceptions of people, along with the model of broadcasting, there was no study on what exactly the TRP was about and what this model of broadcasting meant to India, particularly because this TRP methodology had snubbed other research initiatives in the country.

ICSSR should have concerned itself with the priorities and methodologies being used in the country. There were so many books and studies on research methodologies by foreigners, and all of them have been echoing and reinforcing the same study methodologies.

Earlier, the concerns of social research included the impact and implications of intervening policies, programmes, and schemes. With foreign players (consultants and researchers) becoming dominant, the research methodology shifted to agenda setting and then to monitoring and feedback. By 2010, it again shifted to rating and ranking in the comparative global context.

The idea of a 'Report Card'

This was an idea developed by independent researchers in Bangalore based on primary data developed from field studies of stakeholders a few years earlier. The Ministry of Urban Development, which is the nodal Ministry for 'Smart City Mission', had directed these cities to rank the schemes based on cleanliness, water, economy, inclusion, and environment. This report card idea was not supposed to be based on data with the source providers in the city administration, as the directive implies. How is this 'rating' based report card idea any different from self-aggrandisement? Also, a report card should be created by an independent or outside agency.[9] Dr Samuel Paul, a former director of IIM, explored this idea as an independent professional exercise with methodology distinct from the prevailing methodology.

Where Is an Indian Model?

With the 'foreign research model' taking roots and becoming a standard, rating and ranking became the new yardstick of research methodologies by 2010. This is based on 'administrative data' from within and by the same people responsible for implantation. And the basis for rating is relative. In most cases, the rating model does not recognise the local peculiarities, initiatives, and innovations. Rather, it is 'more of the same' and 'macro concerns' that dictate the methodology priorities. It promotes a macho outlook and is based on such criteria. It goes more by 'indicators' not by 'experience' and process pattern. Rating and ranking suits populism, centralisation, control, and command.

Three examples show the misleading or limiting nature of rating and ranking research methodology. The social science model in vogue is report-oriented and not concerned with actions. Mahatma Gandhi was an applied social researcher. His model was never studied from this perspective. His ideas and concerns were first sounded with people around and with stakeholders on the receiving end, and then 'experimented' with at the micro level. This model was what Dr Martin

Luther King, Jr, too, followed. Only then was the initial idea modified and put through formal committees for further deliberation and application regionally. This was before social science methodology was formally positioned. In fact, Nanaji Deshmukh or Barefoot Proponent Bunker Roy, for example, advocated an Indian model of research.

We never explored our own models of enquiry and exploration. The Indian model is action-oriented and yet objective because of inherent sincerity (with no conflict of interest) in the model. The International Initiative for Impact Evaluation (IIIE in 2018–20) had this component built into its methodology model in which researchers go beyond to prompt behavioural change with knowledge, awareness, and practice (KAP) approach.[10]

Transparency International (TI) is one of the global agencies promoting and popularising rating and ranking research. In this case, it concerns corruption in countries. This ranking methodology is informally endorsed by organisations like the World Bank (TI is by ex-World Bank professionals) and is taken by countries seriously as a yardstick. The government's concern was more regarding how to enhance the ranking in TI rather than addressing the phenomena of corruption in all its complexity at the micro level. The measures implemented thus involved macro-level claims. The perceptions, experience, and estimates (PEE) model, on the other hand, with much higher reliability (than the TI) provides insights for intervention at multiple levels and can curb corruption. While TI is based solely on a small unrepresentative sample, the PEE methodology involves multiple methodologies (sample survey, past data analysis, observations, case studies, and discussions with key stakeholders). This methodology offers not only a better understanding of the phenomena with a larger perspective but provides action suggestions for lasting initiatives to minimise the scope for corruption—unlike in the case of rating or ranking model. Corruption in India cannot be approached with an instant model or surface scratching initiatives. Corruption also involves a socio-psychological behaviour. This perspective cannot be explored in a rating or ranking approach.

Citizen report card, social audit, and indexing are some examples for locally developed alternate methodologies. Dr Samuel Paul, a former Director of IIM, Ahmedabad, on his retirement to Bangalore, initiated the Citizen Report Card (1990) at his Public Affairs Centre. This report card methodology is well-demonstrated across countries to help accountability of public services delivery. The Social Audit methodology was developed and demonstrated by Dr N Bhaskara Rao (1993-98). Both these methodologies engage citizens, involves them, and activates them for availing basic public services. Going beyond feedback, these methodologies, unlike in survey research, reflects the undercurrents for taking initiatives. These methodologies promote a collective feeling. Further, indexes are neutral. All these do not depend on any one primary or secondary source but on collective reflections that overshadow and generate trust and understanding.

Ranking 'water crisis': In 2015–16, NITI Aayog ranked states based on certain parameters on which Aayog had some administrative and monitoring based data. In 2016–17, for example, it rated Kerala at 43, which is less than 50%, for a 'safe level' of water crisis. What new initiatives could be taken in the last couple of years by the government to cope with such a threat as indicated in the ratings. For example, Aayog claimed in August 2019 that it had indicated the crisis by indicating a 43% in its ranking in 2015–16. But the moot question is what purpose does such a rating serve, apart from a 'certificate value' and coverage in newspapers? Rating or ranking makes sense in India only when it provides insights for specific interventions. This rating model promotes copy-catting and more of the same approach, which is easier, quicker, and is status view-oriented with no lasting guidance. What the prime minister had outlined on 15 August 2019 from the Red Fort as the mission of 'Jal Jeevan Abhiyan' with as 3.5 lakh crores can make no difference without the support of regional sociological studies.[11]

Ranking police stations: This observation also applies to the ranking of police stations which the Home Ministry is looking for from foreign consulting agencies (2019). Although the Ministry thought of conducting such research for police stations, it failed to understand the significance of this rating. Competition between police stations, the purpose that such ranking serves, is not good enough to ensure corrective initiatives for improving the standing of all police stations. Instead, it could undertake a three-phased research. First, an analytical study can be made of police stations to identify the features of stations that matter locally and then conduct a qualitative study of at least four categories of stakeholders (staff, clients of at least three categories including victims, complainants, and those who suffered, and with a local community of leaders, particularly women). Only such an in-depth and holistic study can help the police service improve.

TRP: On a series of complaints by law makers in the Parliament and outside, particularly women, the then Minister for Information and Broadcasting, Jaipal Reddy, called me to find out what this TRP was all about and who was responsible for such a system that had caused such an uproar. After explaining to him the limitations and irrelevance of TRPs, the Minister wanted to explore alternatives. He thus called a meeting of 40 activists from different backgrounds and sought their views on TV viewing. The first conclusion he reached was that an hourly or even a daily or weekly rating of TV viewing is misleading and gives a hasty perspective that adds to the problem. He could not pursue it further as he was shifted out of that Ministry. But he understood how misleading the TRP was.[12]

Indexing is a better tool to measure and track change, performance, and implementation or accomplishment, far more comprehensively than ranking and rating. Index offers better insights to stake holders. Index is also based on a range of indicators that are far more linked based on prior research. 'India child-well-being index' that was recently presented (August 2019) by a non-profit agency is one such example. Based on 24 indicators, it provides insights on health, nutrition, education, sanitation, and child protection. When releasing this report, NITI Aayog CEO, Amitabh Kant noted that the index offers an opportunity for states to develop new initiatives and interventions that can help improve the current situation and that it takes forward academic and policy related issues. Indicators in the index can be questioned for their relevance so that they can be improved in the next round. For example, this index by World Vision India has 'mobile phone usage' and 'digital access' as indicators. But this may be questioned considering what the global tech gurus have noted about the ill-effects of such new mobile gadgets on children. This perhaps needs further research.[13]

The National Crime Research Bureau has been generating an annual report for some years now with data on a range of deviant or out of the ordinary behaviours in the country. This report offers a wealth of data for social science researchers to help them explore trends, causes and consequences. With social researchers' support, this report can become a vital source for the government in dealing with crime and in devising social initiatives to address issues like farmers' suicides.

Tribal Research Institutes

There are 25 tribal research institutes in the country, some of which have existed since 1952–55, and some from 2016–18. A few of these state level ones are known as Tribal Research and Training Institutes, a couple of them as Tribal Cultural Research & Training Institute (West Bengal, Telangana), and others are Tribal Research Institute. Most of them operate as a government department. Their main objective is conducting research, promoting development, identifying needs and problems, and conducting evaluation and ethnographic studies. Activities of these institutes are limited to occasional seminars, publishing newsletters, and having a documentation centre and a library.

Perhaps no other example is required to conclude that 'research' exists only in name. There is hardly any basic or functional or applied research in these tribal research institutes despite their existence of well over 50 years. There is no indication of any of the policies or programmes or development interventions being implemented over the years based on these institutes' studies—despite the state government allocating budgets year after year and filling up posts in these institutes. Half of the sanctioned posts in many of these TRIs were vacant as of January 2019, according to the data given in the Rajya Sabha. An outlay of Rs 100 crore was made for these TRIs in the 2018–19 budget.[14]

The idea of a tribal research institute was presented by pioneers of India who realised at the very outset that we need to study and pay special attention to our tribal culture and attend to their special needs. Some of these institutes were initially independent and then were brought under a government department. A few were attached to a local university with a hope of generating research methodologies for anthropological research and guiding the institutes. But, overall, despite their long existence, not much has come out of these institutes. Most of them use the same research methodologies that were developed elsewhere. ICSSR has not made any effort to initiate policy studies or develop appropriate research methodologies specific to tribal pockets and populations. Even a separate Union Ministry of Tribal Affairs in 1999 created for a focussed approach towards tribal development did not activate these TRIs. It is no wonder then that the languages of many tribes like the Gonds are either already extinct or on the brink of extinction.

In 2019, the Ministry announced four new TRIs and indicated plans to launch a National Tribal Research Institute to coordinate the activities of state level tribal research institutes and take up national level studies. It remains to be seen if this will improve the situation, or indeed if this initiative too will remain only a grand announcement.

CHAPTER FIVE

How Serious Are We about Research for Public Policies?

How much is budgeted and spent on research in the country in support of public policies? This is a direct indicator of how much the nation is concerned about the future and the effectiveness of its policies and governance. A budgetary allocation is an indication that research is viewed as an essential and on-going activity of the state and as an on-going support service to development plans and schemes. But there is no way to know how much exactly is being spent on research, even in the case of social and economic ministries.

In the private sector, entrepreneurs provide anywhere upwards of 3–5% of their outlays for research. Depending on the targets, time schedules, and the task involved, the scope of research and the amount spent for research is decided.

Conventionally, 'research and development' have been viewed together as it has been a 'discover and develop' relationship in the physical sense. But now, research includes finding better options and alternatives. That is, innovation and training should be involved with a new idea. Today, in the government, 'research and training' are viewed together for budgetary allocations. In a democracy and a competitive scenario, research indicates a strategy to optimise governance, public policies, development, and growth. Research is not always shown, if at all, separately in the annual budgets and outlays of the ministries. How much is budgeted for 'research' is not easy to determine as it is not given separately in any of the published reports. As such, specific allocations and expenditure on research in the context of public policies can only be an estimation. Further, knowing how much of research concerns social research is not always possible as 'research' has become a generalised term. In some cases, research includes promotional activities like seminars and conferences, as in the case of Ministry of Culture.

Despite being one of the world's largest education system and a heterogeneous character of the country with divides and disparities, India spends much less than 1% of its GDP on research and development. Moreover, only half of it is spent by the government. With such little importance given to research, can India become a world power? How can it compete with the US, Japan, China, Israel, or South Korea, countries that spend anywhere between 2% and 4.5% of their GDP?

Percentage of GDP spent on Research and Development (2018)

Country	GDP (%)
US	2.74
China	2.10
Japan	3.14
South Korea	4.29
India	0.69
Israel	4.3
Sweden	3.16
Switzerland	2.96
Austria	3.1

Source: Wikipedia, the free encyclopedia[1]

The recent (2019) National Education Policy suggested that Rs 20,000 crores is spent on research. Although the government went ahead with the National Research Foundation's suggestion, no funds were committed for it in the 2019–20 budget. Nor was the suggestion of a hundred research universities included.

But to develop so many universities, a meagre Rs 400 crores was provided in this budget, with most of it going for civil works and establishment.

As the government's priorities concern its 'public image' more than evaluating the development strategies, money is spent accordingly. What else explains the fact that the governments, both Union and States, spend much more on 'publicity and advertising' than on research needed for policy strategies and programme planning. This despite no evidence of advertising contributing to the success of the government's schemes and even of its political fortunes, as in the case of branded consumer products. That there is such myth among political leaders is a different issue.

In 1972–80, I was one of the early trackers of the country's advertising expenditure in various media and would consider from ORG annual estimates for a few years in a desegregated manner to analyse the trend. This enabled me to estimate, in 2017–18, what the governments (both at the Union and in States) spend on advertising in news media, including on television channels. It works out to be much more than Rs 10,000 crores annually. This expenditure has been increasing each year. On the other hand, what is being spent on research for governance and development is either only marginally increased or has even been declining—despite the allocations being insufficient or paltry to begin with. The government, however, spends much more on advertising and publicity than what is provided for in the annual budget. In the case of research, more often what is being spent is less than what was provided for in the budgets.

Social science research and applied social research in India is supported or sponsored not only by the government but also by some multinational and private or volunteer sectors. In fact, only half of 0.69% GDP shown for R&D is by the government. But what percent of this 0.69% is for research in the context of public policies can only be an estimate. This is not available in any of the published reports. What is spent for this is shown differently at different levels in different ministries. This could be shown as research, monitoring, consultancy, feedback, surveys, or evaluation.

Sometimes, NITI Aayog spends on research required by the ministries. For example, the Ministry of Women and Child Development now proposes to collate data on six parameters from several ministries/developments and other sources. This information is available from four different sources, each varying from the other. Hence, a new study has been proposed. Similarly, on employment, more than one ministry conducts studies, some of which are given below.

Union Government
- Ministries/Departments
- Councils/ Agencies

State Governments

Multi National Agencies
- UN/Funding/foundations

Others
- Media/Private funding

Trusts/Lobbies/Civil Society

Apart from what the Ministries spend on research directly or what is built into project costs, University Grants Commission (UGC) and Indian Council for Social Science Research (ICSSR) are two major funding agencies of the government regarding research, primarily in the academics. UGC is the only grant-giving agency for research at higher education, for PhDs through fellowships. While UGC supports selected research proposals of researchers and empanelled organisations, ICSSR annually supports 27 institutes, including their overhead costs.

The two funding agencies of the government, UGC and ICSSR, were having uncertain allocation of studies between 2008 and 2014. Less than 30% of UGC fund was intended for research in social sciences. But, of what was allocated to UGC, hardly one-fourth was actually dispersed to universities. This is an important finding of this analysis. With such lack of priority and seriousness, what kind of attention can be expected?

The UGC Act is being amended after 70 years (in 2020) to change the scope and structure of UGC in terms of the Higher Education Commission of India (HECI). Under this change, the responsibility of funding universities is being shifted to the Ministry of HRD. The new HECI will be its singular regulator. In this scheme, the funding of research endeavours is also likely to be shifted to the Ministry of HRD along with promotion and support to research. What kind of support will be available for social science research is any one's guess, when there are increased chances of research priorities becoming political.

UGC Funds for Social Science: Allocation and Release

Year	UGC Grants to Social Science Research Allocation (in Crore)	Funds Released to Universities (in Crore)
2008–09	71.03	28
2009–10	89.21	20.7
2010–11	84.61	24.3
2011–12	51.21	11.2
2012–13	74.09	47.5
2013–14	39.06	—

Source: Sukhadeo Thorat and Samar Verma, *Social Science Research in India*, 2017

ICSSR: Nearly two-thirds of the ICSSR budget (Rs 150 crores) was given out as grants to approximately 27 research institutes in 2016-17. Almost five or six of these institutes did not even provide details. There was no pattern or any basis for the grants given to the institutes annually. Some were given over Rs 10 crores and other were given less than Rs 4 crores (in 2016-17). More than six institutes are running in deficit with high establishment expenditure. A review of the activities of these institutes for the previous two years (2016–17 and 2017–18) indicates a total irrelevance of public policy framework or governance concerns of the country. Whether they are adding to anyone's wisdom or efficiency or knowledge base is not clear.

In 2012–13, hardly 25% of expenditure of ICSSR institutes, for example, was spent on research projects. Around half of ICSSR budget goes towards the salaries and establishment, and this component has been increasing. This also shows that ICSSR and UGC is more concerned with bureaucracy.

But a significant part of ICSSR budget in more recent years has been allocated to political and election-oriented research. Since 2008–09, funds released by UGC for social science have been less than Rs 30 crores, except in 2013–14 when it was Rs 47.5 crores. UGC never actually released one-third of what was provided for as grant for social science research.

Neither ICSSR nor its institutes were involved in monitoring or evaluating any of the government's flagship programmes, including the ones that have been continuing for five or more years like MNREGs, Swachh Bharat, RTI, or those regarding any of the basic problems of the country involving mind-set and behaviours like corruption, preventive health, or governance issues like citizen participation, citizen pessimism–activism, etc.

Even more disappointing is that over these 50 years, there has been no indication of any initiative to allocate funds to develop India-specific research methodologies or a framework. For example, in place of primarily survey research involving a question–answer format, no one experimented with any other methodology. Anthropologists attempts in the earlier years had yielded better understanding of the process of change. Instead, all endeavours have been to recycle or copy Western models indiscriminately. Also, none of the projects supported have an action component in the research study, even in an experimental way.

Most of the ICSSR institutes are already in decline. They are not in any position to take new initiatives—which is not surprising as salaries and administrative costs alone constitute

75–90% of their total expenditure. A third of the institutes are already running on deficit while others are trying somehow to cope with the increase in overhead costs. They are functioning on a year-to-year basis. Mere survival is their priority, rather than long-term initiatives and plans.

Thus, both exclusive sources (UGC and ICSSR) of government funding for social science research in the country have been drying up in the last decade. And with an ever-increasing administrative and establishment expense, what is actually available for promoting research has been on decline. This was also because ICSSR institutes' staff are entitled for pay revisions. Moreover, many of these 27 ICSSR institutes continue to depend on the government for funding even after more than 25 years. Apart from two or three institutes (like CSDS and CESS), they have not emerged as independent organisations or have developed any specialisation including data collection and analysis. For decades, one-third of ICSSR-sponsored institutes have been on a deficit course (spending more than what was provided because of increased establishment expenditure).

That social science research in India is on decline course is too obvious. None of the recent measures by the government have made any difference to reverse the trend or relieve this situation. Whether the newly announced India Research Foundation can generate any specific initiatives to revive social science research remains to be seen. The implications of this decline will be on governance, the efficiency of the government, and on the overall social development and economic growth.

Tribal Research Institutes: The Ministry of Tribal Affairs funds 26 Tribal Research Institutes. What this Ministry spends for these research institutes and monitoring and evaluation put together has been on decline as the overall allocation for economic development and skill development of tribal affairs was reduced marginally in 2019–20. What is allocated for research and evaluation is mostly for salaries, overheads, and infrastructure. Further, 45% of tribal population is below poverty line, and their population is spread across more than

10 states. What was allocated for monitoring and evaluation of this ministry was Rs 1.27 crores in 2017–18. For 2018–19, the amount was increased to Rs 5 crores but was then brought down to Rs 2.50 crores in the revised budget. In the 2019–20 budget, however, this was kept at the same level of Rs 2.50 crores. Even what was budgeted for Tribal Research Institutes was the same Rs 99 crores in 2018–19 and 2019–20. This hardly works to approximately 2% of total outlays of the Ministry of Tribal Affairs, most of it going for maintenance and overhead costs.

Most of research expenditure has been in the context of 'programme implementation'. This was mostly to Indian Statistical Institute and for census, NSS, and statistics collection (which is mostly administrative data). There is no indication of any priority for policy related research, assessment, or appraisal.

The paradigm of research in the country is lopsided. Almost half of the total outlay is given by the Union Ministry of HRD and only about 25% by other Union Ministries. The state governments too account for only 25% of the total public spend on social research. Interestingly, what the foreign (aid) agencies, including the UN agencies (e.g., UNICEF), spend on and for research in India has been multiplying every two years over the last decade. This is also because the Indian government ministries themselves expect these agencies to spend on social research.

As is evident from the table on three Ministries, the percent of Ministry's total expenditure for research (of all kinds) has been declining since 2005. Ministries with outreach tasks and schemes like the Women and Child Development or those concerning the environment, forest, or climate hardly spend 1% on research.

Share of Research in the Ministry's Total Expenditure (Rs crore)

Ministry	2004–05			2008–09			2012–13		
	Research Exp.	Ministry's Total Exp.	% to TE	Research Exp.	Ministry's Total Exp.	% to TE	Research Exp.	Ministry's Total Exp.	% to TE
Culture	34.80	604.46	5.76	48.05	1046.72	4.59	32.31	1387.63	2.33
Women & Child Development	10.20	2447.94	0.42	25.50	6741.23	0.37	26.50	17035.72	0.16
Environment, Forest, and Climate Change	26.50	1145.21	2.31	13.03	1710.00	0.76	13.94	1753.00	0.80

Source: Union Budget of India, outcome budget, demand for grants, annual reports of respective ministries and 2004–05 data taken from ICSSR 2007.

Unlike other expenditures, like for advertising, the actual amount allocated or spent even by funding agencies for research at various times is not available to the public, or is inconsistent, if available. Only bits and pieces of information is available for some ministries. More pertinent is what is being spent on research in the context of public policies and public schemes is not indicated.

Ministries spend more on data collection and processing than on primary research to evaluate or ascertain the difference that was made by the schemes, including the flagships. With such voluminous data over the years, basic research, including analytics, on alternative strategies and efficient plans should have received a boost. For census operations, more than Rs 1500 crores is being spent every 10 years (2011). But no further research on policies with census data is being undertaken outside the ministries on a serious and ongoing basis. Whatever is there is more academic and conducted two or three years after the census data is available and in an ad hoc way.

A few years ago, what the states had spent on social research was estimated to be less than Rs 300 crores by Professors Sukhadeo Thorat and Samar Verma in their book *Social Science Research in India*.[2] This book provided some allocation details for a couple of years up to 2011–12.

Whether any of these agencies or ministries spend on experimental research for formulating policies or/and strategies is also not known. UNICEF in India is a good example of experimental research. Over the years, it has been a research-and-analysis-based policy and programme formulation agency. In 2019, for example, UNICEF implemented experimented research using television channels (2019–20) on 'gender discrimination'. Once it assesses this research action experiment after a couple of years, the insights can be availed in the context of other behavioural tasks.

Among the ministries, HRD, Labour and Employment, and Health and Family Welfare spent more on research than other ministries. But there is no trend regarding how much the ministries are spending each year. The Ministry of Culture

Data Collection Expenditure by Union Ministries

Ministries	Budget Head	Current Prices (Rs Crore)			
		2004–05*	2008–09	2010–11	2012–13
Agriculture	Agricultural Census	7.7	18	0	5.95
Agriculture	Cost of Cultivation Surveys	15.4	NA	0	NA
DARE	Economics, Statistics, and Management	14	32.4	89.28	41.97
Home	Census & Statistics	126	132.67	460	1050
Programme Implementation	Indian Statistical Institute	47.5	83.18	135	158.46
Programme Implementation	National Sample Survey	86.9	140.37	181	204.9
Programme Implementation	Economic Advise & Statistics	16.3	26.47	154	218.18
Environment, Forest, and Climate Change	Forest Survey of India	10.7	12.3	8.15	17.35
Micro, Small, and Medium Enterprises (MSME)	Update of Database	NA	10.65	5.8	13.22
Micro, Small, and Medium Enterprises (MSME)	Collection of Statistics of Small Scale Industries	NA	18.1	0	NA
Micro, Small, and Medium Enterprises (MSME)	Survey Studies and Policy Scheme	NA	NA	0	0.56
Women and Child Development	Gender Budgeting & Gender disaggregated Data	NA	2.7	0.9	0.64
Total		324.5	476.84	1034.13	1711.83

Source: Ministry of Finance, Government of India (2007 to 2012); Annual reports of respective Ministries.

Funding for Social Science Research by Different Union Ministries (Excluding MHRD) (in Crores)

Ministries	Current Prices (Rs Crore)			
	2004–05*	2008–09	2010–11	2012–13
Commerce	1.7	9.48	8	40
Finance	3.1	10.06	8.47	12.84
Labour	4.6	7.84	3.4	5.1
Planning	11.6	9.8	1.18	9.82
Water	10.8	39.81	41.3	NA
Environment, Forest, and Climate Change	26.5	13.03	18.7	13.94
Culture	34.8	48.05	76.85	32.31
Rural Development	NA	4.81	4.44	1.85
Panchayati Raj	NA	2	1.55	1.8
Women and Child Development	10.2	25.5	NA	26.5

Source: Ministry of Finance, Government of India (2007 to 2012); Annual Reports of Respective Ministries. Taken from Thorat and Verma's Social Science Research in India.

spends a relatively higher percent of their total outlays on 'research' (which includes seminars and conferences). Even the Ministries of Environment and Forest and the Ministry of Women and Child Development's expenditure on research of their total outlays has been declining. This reflects that even the ministers expected to take to research a lot more have been spending less and less.

Among the states, Assam, West Bengal, Andhra Pradesh, Bihar, and Kerala spent more than half of what the states had spent on social research in 2012–13. What the Ministry of Human Resource Development allocates, of course, can be identified in the budget.

In addition to how much the ministry formally spends on research, there are others that also spend on research concerning the schemes or concerns of the ministry. For example, on health-related issues, WHO and UNICEF, the Bill Gates Foundation spend prominently. Private agencies also spend significantly on research. What Indian Council of Medical Research (ICMR) spends on social research out of its Rs 1900 crores total budget for 2019–20 is not indicated.

Share of Research in Ministry's Expenditure

The expenditure on research was obtained only for three ministries, and only for three years (taken from ICSSR reports). This shows that a higher percent was shown for research by the Ministry of Culture than for Ministries of Women and Child Development and Environment, Forests and Climate Change. This was the trend for all the three years. Moreover, what was spent on research declined in these three years, including for the Ministry of Environment, despite its overall annual expenditure having increased, as shown in the table.

While presenting the budget, the Finance Minister asserted that the specific allocation in the case of core schemes was 'to make living better'. How can this be verified without specially designed research? For example, Swachh Bharat has been a flagship programme, but what effort has been made to determine the difference this programme has made? An analysis of three years—2017–18, 2018–19, and 2019-20—shows the kind of importance given to research, monitoring, and evaluation and also to IEC. Obviously, this scheme requires massive efforts for promoting and communicating it. But it is also pertinent to know what the communication, education, and publicity efforts are actually achieving, beyond just raising awareness levels. This can only be ascertained thorough research. How can the prime minister's idea of making 'living easier' be achieved in the next couple of years?

The Case of Swachh Bharat—Overall Allocations, for Research and IEC

				(in crores)
Allocation for	2017–18 Actual	2018–19 Estimate	2018–19 Revised	2019–20 Budget Est.
Swachh Bharat outlay	19427	17843	16978	12644
Monitory & Evaluation	1.74	2.04	6.0	2.0
Research	-	1.0	-	1.0
IEC	266	300	120	190

Source: Union Budget& Accountability Initiative. CPR

This table shows that not even 1% of what was spent for IEC was allocated for research, monitoring, and evaluation, which works out actually to hardly 0.01% of what was budgeted and allocated for Swachh Bharat overall during 2017–18, 2018-19, and 2019–2020. This scheme being five years old as a flagship programme of the government must be evaluated as it continues to gain substantial allocation.

This example of Swachh Bharat confirms the trend observed for the 2004–05 to 2012–13 period. What is allocated/spent for research, even in the context of flagship schemes of the government, was too low and has been declining. With whatever little 0.01% (or 1% of IEC) was indicated, it would not be possible to undertake even one round of impact or evaluative research. That may hardly be enough to monitor the scheme as it is extensive, nation-wide, and continuous. This scheme has implications at the community, household, and individual level. Today, a 'nationwide evaluative study' covering all states, for a scheme like Swachh Bharat, involves an expenditure upwards of Rs 1 crore. A rating or opinion survey, on the other hand, perhaps costs around Rs 10–20 lakhs, if it is exclusive.

In addition to what the governments and their agencies spend, a considerable amount is spent by multinational agencies, aid agencies, and trusts. UNICEF, UNESCO, UNDP, UNFPA, World Bank, Asian Development Bank, Gates Foundation, Ford Foundation, MacArthur Foundation, USAID, CIDA, British Aid, German Foundations, IDRC, japan International Cooperation Agency, etc. fund the government agencies as well as private agencies as well as directly commission research. No updated information on this expenditure for research by foreign agencies is available in the public channels. The Gates Foundation has spent (in 2018–20) about half of all research on social development in the country. This works out to nearly Rs 800–1000 crore on an annual basis. But an estimate of a couple of years ago of this expenditure on social research shows that this was nearly as much as what the government and their agencies spend put together. This expenditure on research in 2012–13 can be estimated to be in the range of only Rs 2000–3000 crores. Even assuming the same proportion of the budget, what should be allocated for social and evaluation research in 2020? Today, there are many more flagships schemes, most of which are more than five years old.

Some Flagship Schemes Allocations (in Crores)

S.No.	Schemes	2017–18	2018–19	2019–20
1.	MGNREGA	55,166	61,084	60,000
2.	Jobs & Skill Development	2,722	6,830	7,260
3.	National Livelihood Mission	4,925	6,293	9,779
4.	PM-Kisan Samman Nidhi	-	20,000	75,000
5.	PM Awas Yojana	31,163	26405	25,853

These flagship schemes require considerable research both in designing, operating, and monitoring its implementation, and for evaluating the scheme and its outcomes. In the case of MGNREGA, some research in all these respects has been conducted. In the case of Awas Yojana or skill development or even in the case of Kisan Samman Nidhi, research has to be an essential requirement. But there is no evidence of any budgetary provision being made for research, monitoring, or evaluation to expect serious research. For example, for Kisan Samman Nidhi, the allocation was increased from Rs 20,000 in 2018–19 to Rs 75,000 crores in 2019–20. What was the basis for this?[3] Has research support been provided for in support of such enthusiasm?

Even if 1% of these outlays was provided for research, it would have meant a substantial research support for each of the flagships. This would have meant a budgetary allocation of Rs 4000 to 5000 crores for research (monitoring, information, feedback, assessment, or evaluation). There is no indication in the 2019–20 budget that even half of this amount was allotted for research of any kind for any of the flagship schemes. (That is around Rs 400–500 crore per year for only the flagships.)

There are also some others (like the Family Planning Association of India or Vivekananda Foundation) that have conducted social and appraisal research, about which not much is known or is public knowledge. Even some trusts and industry lobbies spend on research. Tata Trust has been a pioneer in funding research. Wipro and Infosys Foundation are other recent examples. Some news media agencies also conduct occasional research. Research studies are also conducted by higher education faculties on their own as part of the PhD thesis requirement (not all get research fellowships).

This is a macro view of social science research in the country. If we take a more specific view in the context of public policies and the extent to which research is actually availed, the situation is more disappointing in terms of funding and its utilisation. An analysis indicates that hardly a couple of major recent policies were based on research or that research has evolved and is used to monitor and evaluate flagship schemes. In a couple of instances, as in the case of Swachh Bharat, the research tends to be supportive or endorsive of public utterances or claims of leaders or the official reports.

The government is hardly spending on 'independent research' even when research is outsourced. There is no evidence of governments taking critical findings of research studies seriously, even when commissioned or sponsored. Some years ago, 'independent research' or a 'third party' assessment was considered a virtue and, in fact, aid agencies indicated preference for such research as a part of the (loan or grant) agreement with the government.

The Bureau of Outreach and Communication, formally Directorate of Advertising and Visual Publicity (DAVP), is a division of the Ministry of Information & Broadcasting. This Ministry is responsible for the government's communications and handles the schedules of all paid advertising on all media. Even in the case of flagship programmes of the government, the creative part of the campaign is outsourced. Earlier research on the impact of campaigns was also handled by DAVP. It no longer conducts any research on the campaigns it handles. The concerned ministers themselves undertake research, including on the reach and effectiveness of the campaign. But the bureau does undertake research on behalf of the ministry, for campaigns undertaken by the Ministry of Information and Broadcasting. This bureau is expected to conduct basic research, which DAVP used to do earlier, so that outsourcing becomes more rational. A quick review of DAVP and the Bureau in the last couple of years shows that hardly any research has been conducted even today to identify the effectiveness of the IEC campaigns. There is no indication that the concerned ministries are conducting any such research to ascertain the impact or effectives of the campaign. Perhaps, the concern is more about the 'image' of the minister or the government than awareness or behaviour change aspects, as only such finding is made available.

In the 2019 election, one private 'polling agency', with a track record of a couple of general elections that predicted the highest number of seats for the incumbent party, won the praise of the ruling party. In no time after that, this psephologist was awarded the highest ever consultancy in the entire government. There was no track record of this agency doing any other social or evaluative research (other than poll-context surveys) for the campaigns of flagship schemes or of any other public policies. This shows the concern and priority of 'political communication' and supportive research.

Ministry of Rural Development

Providing financial assistance to States/UTs for conducting the BPL Census is not a regular scheme as BPL Census is conducted only once in five years. The nature of the activity is such that the bulk of the expenditure occurs in a short span of time and particularly when actual census takes place.

For conducting the combined Socio-economic Classification Census (SECC) in 2011, the EFC approved an amount of Rs 3543.29 crore. Out this approved amount, Rs 3543 crores was provided for SECC 2011 between 2009–2010 and 2013–14. For 2014–15, an amount of Rs 365 crores was allocated compared with Rs 350 crores in 2015–16. Details of the funds provided for the SECC are given below.

Year	Funds Allocated (Rs in Crore) for SECC
2009–10	150
2010–11	112
2011–12	2600 (field survey)
2012–13	375
2013–14	306
2014–15	365
2015–16	350

Source: Outcome Budget 2016–17, GOI

Another large-scale survey conducted for National Register of Citizens (NRC) was in Assam. An estimated Rs 1200 crore was claimed to have been spent in Assam for this exercise, including for verification of name.[4] Now some other states also are planning to implement NRC. Another research exercise contemplated was by the Ministry of Women and Child Development on sex ratio in coordination with a couple of other Ministries. The point is that Ministries tend to collect data or subscribe to secondary data or take up research projects that are of no consequence to the efficiency, efficacy, or evaluative aspect of special schemes. And yet, they opt for such surveys or census because it allows the leaders to claim what they want to.

Four specific trends in availing or benefiting from research must be noted. First is how research is used for proactive policy initiatives as well as for appraisal and evaluation of schemes, particularly flagship schemes that are hyped and raise people's expectations. Second is the extent of 'independent research' which is encouraged and the extent of critical feedback or correctives formed through research is seriously considered, even if it is outside the government. Third is the kind of seriousness with which research, researchers, and the findings are considered or taken into account when formulating policies or appraising programmes. And fourth is that independent researchers or/and research agencies should not be considered as being 'roped-in' or 'inducted in' or induced. The ultimate loser of such a trend is the system.

Is Research a Concern?

Budget/outlays of four Ministries (Science & Technology, Human Resource Development (HRD), Health, and Agriculture) are expected to indicate how much priority is given to research in general.

The Ministry of Science and Technology is a nodal ministry with several endeavours concerning research and innovation in the country. Its primary concern is science and technology. The budgets of the ministry's Department of Science and Technology do not earmark any support for social science research directly. Rather, some components are expected to be devoted to social research. So, for example, under the head 'Research and Development', allocations include nanoscience, climate change programme, capacity building, computing facilities, etc. These also involve behavioural research. The indirect allocation for research by the Department of Science and Technology for three financial years beginning from 2017–18 was as below:

Year	Budget (in Crores)
2017–18	595.50
2018–19	609.00
2019–20	481.00

Source: DST, annual report 2019[5]

The average budget/expenditure for the Department Science and Technology has been Rs 5000 crores a year for this period.

The average annual budget of the Department of Higher Education of the HRD Ministry budget over the same three-year period was around Rs 35,000 crores. And how much of it was allocated to 'Research and Innovation'? Here are the figures from the ministry's own records:

Year	Budget (in Crores)
2017–18	–
2018–19	350.23
2019–20	608.87

Source: Ministry of Human Resource Development, Department of Higher Education

In the case of both these ministries, what was actually spent on research was barely 60% of even the tiny fraction that was allocated in the total budgets. For example, Rs 75 crores were allocated for 'PM Research Fellowships' in 2018–19, but what was spent was hardly Rs 20 crores.

Even the Council of Scientific and Industrial Research (CSIR), which promotes national laboratories, spends hardly 5% of its total budget on capacity building and human resource development. Of Rs 300 crore budgeted in 2018–19, only 250 crores could be spent and only 300 crores were budgeted for 2019–20. The budget of the Department of Science and Industrial Research and the Department of Science and Technology together is around Rs 85,000 crores, and yet there is no specific provision in either for social or behavioural or even market research. Neither of the departments or their laboratories or institutes or schemes have any professional capabilities for such research.

The Department of Agricultural Research & Education is another body that is engaged in a very critical activity with annual budgets of around Rs 8000 crores. It provides a negligible percentage of this for 'need-based' research support. And even here, of the Rs 32.54 crores budgeted in 2018–19 for this purpose, only Rs 27.66 crores were spent.[7]

The Indian Council of Medical Research (ICMR) of the Department of Health Research is the apex body that promotes, coordinates, and formulates biomedical and health research. This is the only research body that utilised all the allocated budget for 2018–19. The ICMR budget is around Rs 1400 crores annually and it has remained almost static in the last three years (2017, 2019, and 2020).[8]

There is no indication that any of the nodal departments that are concerned with agriculture, health, social development, and technology have conducted social or behavioural or impact research for the schemes of their respective ministries. Nor have they engaged the services of social science institutes outside the government to do such research for them. It is sad and shocking that such rigorous and independent research and assessment is not seen as an essential responsibility — indeed, as a national duty.

CHAPTER SIX

Impact of Social Research on Public Policy Making?

How can we assess the impact of social science research on public policy making at any given time and over time? Some critical ways of doing that, which are immediately traceable, can be identified. These factors depend on time and the context. Some common criteria for understanding the role of social science include the following seven criteria.

First is research studies commissioned by the government or a ministry that are engaged in public policy making and in implementing. This may occur in two different streams. First is research-driven policy and the second is policy-driven research. One could find both types of studies. An example for the first type is that on finding that a significant percent of children below 14 years of age are engaged in labour, the government initiates policies to curb child labour. One could find many examples for the second type of research, like the study on the use of sports stadia that the government had sponsored or assessing Swachh Bharat programme. An important element in both instances is how transparent and fair the research was and how independent and professional it was in terms of methodology and concepts.

Second is the extent of data on performance indicators or and on related phenomena being accumulated in a systematic manner. And such data is analysed professionally for implications or consequences. This could be done by the ministry itself or by its institute or assigned to an outside agency drawn from open sources so that the policy-maker or the implementer knows overtime what is happening.

Third is that social researchers or academicians can be connected with government initiatives through funding an expert, an agency, or a university, or assigning certain responsibilities to certain institutes or researchers on an ongoing basis. This can also be achieved by being on the executive committee of an outside social research institute or by appointing a key functionary of an outside research body on the government bodies.

Fourth is that social scientists from outside the government can also be appointed as chair or member or advisor of an important policy-making forum or working group or technical committee or assign an evaluation responsibility to a researcher.

Fifth is that senior government officials engaged in policy formulation or their execution can be deputed to outside specialised social research and training institutes or academics for certain periods with an expectation that, on return, the officers will be more rational or sensitive in their functioning.

Sixth is the extent to which the policy maker or the implementer acknowledges that a study or analysis can be availed by a social scientist or an institute on a particular issue. This can occur through citing references to such analysis or data in official statements, review documents, or reports. Government leaders can also quote a research or an analysis justifying or negating a policy initiative (as Rajiv Gandhi did in Mumbai).

Finally, seventh is that there have been instances when research was ignored or shelved as it did not support or endorse the official claims of the day, even when such studies were sponsored by the Ministry itself.

Such an analysis or review on the above seven criteria can be conducted by the Ministry or by a scheme or programme. For example, it may be conducted for the Ministry of Rural Development or for Swachh Bharat as a programme.

The role and scope of research can also he considered in terms of the priorities of the leader heading the government.

For example, an analysis of how research flourished during the terms of different prime ministers of India can indicate the trend tellingly. Eight times during the 70 years of the Republic, the party in government changed. A review of these regimes reveals their research sensitivity (discussed in Chapter 1).

There could be other ways of assessing the role or contribution of social research, independent as well as sponsored. More importantly, all such research need not be in support of or as an endorsement, as they can also be critiquing or even opposing a policy or its implementation. In fact, the more such critical references are sited in the research reports, the better it is in a parliamentary democracy. Estimates of employment or even GDP cannot always be perfect. There cannot be success or failure of certain schemes as they are ongoing and the *process* may be far more important than the *outcome* in quantitative terms. Pros and cons are equally pertinent for overall efficiencies of schemes. It is always a good idea to implement corrections and ensure that reflections are open ended. A democratic spirit is essential for the vibrancy of systems and policies. This is possible only in a systematic research.

Involvement or association of a social scientist or a researcher or an institute is expected to make a difference or providing a perspective that has not otherwise been envisioned in the Ministry or in a project proposal, as in the case of Swatch Bharat, for example.

An analysis of NITI Aayog's annual reports of the last two-three years for any references given in the footnotes as well as in the texts to outside research studies or data or analysis is a good indication of inclusiveness. A similar analysis can be considered for Social Development Ministries and the Ministry of Information and Broadcasting as their annual reports may be revealing.[1]

Impact of Research, Research Methodologies

Today, the criteria for impact are no longer what they were decades ago. It is more about the 'image' or top of the mind or 'yes or no' responses that are viewed as influence of complex schemes with linkages, ripple, and spill over effects. Today, we rely on surrogate indicators as yardsticks for impact. The types of research methodologies used are limited in their scope of capturing change behaviours and perceptions. These methodologies were mostly borrowed from different cultures and markets and are often copycats, thus having limited sensitivity to capture the implications or consequences of policy interventions, particularly those of social reforms and life style paradigms. The impact of Jan Dhan Yojana, for example, is not simply related to the number of accounts opened or the amount of balance present or saved at a point of time. Similarly, the impact of Swachh Bharat does not concern the number of toilets sanctioned or build but the lifestyle changes related to the toilet users and other changes that have occurred in the families and their health, as well as the quality of life and the mindsets of the residents and their standing in the society. This is also the case for Ujjawala Yojana, Awas Yojana, or Ayushman Bharat. The way these programmes are reviewed undermines their significance and is an injustice to the kind of paradigm shift taking place that is not visible initially. These are *process-*based interventions that are not amenable to a time point quantitative assessment. A 'snapshot view' of these schemes or programmes does not explain the impact, or may even be misleading or indicate a larger impact.

This phenomenon is because there is no longer a concern for the future beyond now (this year, this election). This shift is because of change in the outlook of political leaders and also of the bureaucracy. This trend has its effect on concerns of research, research methodologies, and research objectives, and on the kind of outcomes that are chased.

The kind of research methodology availed depends on the concerns of policy makers and stakeholders. If the concern is not merely immediate but also for the future, and if the concern includes effects or consequences, then the research tends to be more behavioural and longitudinal, preferably much beyond the top of the mind images and perceptions. A frozen scenario based study never reflects the deep rooted dynamics. A 'process view' along with the 'outcome' makes more sense than the 'top of the mind' approach that is being chased these days.

The concern for voter and media coverage had changed the research paradigm significantly in India. Political interest and indulgence control has further created a shift in research priorities.

One reason for the recent trend of not opting for more reliable field surveys is the attraction for instant findings, top-of-the-mind responses, and not opting for behavioural changes which require time, experimentation, and pre- and post-intervention rounds of field study, which is what control experiment involves. In such studies, the respondents are selected random or on purpose depending on the way intervention is proposed and the kind of strategy options being considered.

There is no one research method that can claim to be good enough for the ground reality. It all depends on the type of reliability and the intended use of the results or findings. In some instances of measuring or identify outcome of a policy or programme intervention, a combination of research methodologies care needed. Even controlled randomised methodology stands out when supplemented with other methodologies.

Field surveys are based on a sample of respondents selected according to the context and objectives of the survey. It also depends on whether the concern is household or individual or even community-based. In terms of the household, the individuals in the household such as wife, husband, or both, form the focus of the survey. Or, it may be random while being 'proportionate to the population' concerned or respondents selected purposively. Whether a survey is part of an evaluation, impact, reach, awareness, or knowledge and behaviour aspects determines the basis for the sample characteristics, selection, and size of the sample.

Over the years, I followed two basic instincts based on my initial grounding in field research. First, a bigger sample **size** is not always more reliable as is often believed. Second, the *selection* procedure of the respondent is more important. In many cases, the *spread* of a sample is critical for the reliability of representative character. That is, the three S's—Size, Spread, and Selection—procedure of sample together determine the reliability. The selection procedure may also be random or selective. And, of course, the study could be a pre-test or post-test based experiment. Each method has its limitation. The precision or reliability that is required determines the nature of these features. It should be noted that not all surveys require 100% accuracy, which may not be practicable anyway. Whether reliability is above 80%, 60%, or 50% is preferred is something that the research user must determine. This, in turn, concerns the cost, time, and resources available for the study.

What else explains the change in research methodologies from impact to perceptions or image? Researchers are determined to capture the top of the mind recalls. This has led to a shift in methodologies from time-series data to TRP data. Priority is not a structural change or deep rooted or attitudinal but is it more about the change in the moods. For capturing populist concerns, this approach is considered good enough.

This is because such a change is easier to track or quantify, given the kind of public communication scenario that the country is trapped into today. This is determined by the type of mass media and social media that is being peddled, the way content is presented, repeated, and scheduled. Moreover, it concerns the conflict of interest that these media, both mass and social, are drowned in. There is also a link between news media and political leadership and the trend for populistic programmes. Such linkages have impacted the social research paradigm that we are stuck in today. Mere data and statistics have become the indicators of impact, which can be put together as required with much ease. The impact of research in the context of public policies must be viewed against this background, the trends in research environment, and its impact.

Denigrating Research and Missing It

Political leaders show their priority in availing and using research in the context of public policies, but almost always only for political considerations or compulsions—that is, to win the next election. The kind of research used on the eve of 2014 and 2019 Lok Sabha and Assembly elections by political parties, leaders, and even by the government, is surprising. The extent of research, the range of research methodologies, and the money spent on these by political parties during the 2014 and 2019 Lok Sabha elections, for example, reminded us of how much political leaders rely on research to devise their electoral strategies. The leaders' realisation about the impact of research in motivating and persuading voters was more evident during these two elections than any that had been held before. The speed at which research was conducted for these elections had never been seen when it came to formulating public policies or assessing and evaluating large-scale national schemes. For every election, new research tools are experimented on. All that should have meant more use of research by the governments that followed in different and larger contexts. But there is no evidence of that happening in the context of governance and public policies. On the contrary, increasingly, we find examples of renewed research focus on political priorities.

What takes only a couple of weeks to cover the entire nation or state in a poll eve study takes months to conduct in the context of a development or welfare scheme. That is indicative of the interest of political decision-makers in better using research tools. Political leaders use survey findings for influencing voters with news media and becoming their collaborator. This has clearly been seen during every assembly and parliament election over the last decade. And yet, news media hardly features research studies in the context of any of the massive public policies or schemes with similar sensitivity as during election. There were, of course, exceptions. This was perhaps because the government was not as anxious to take news media into confidence in the context of formulating public policies or in the implementation of public schemes.

A prominent news item in *The Hindu*,[2] based on a research claim by a Delhi-based 'think-tank', explains the state of research and understanding of research. While writing that 'there has been no independent verification', the news claimed that 'Naxal incidents had gone down since note ban in the country'. The report did not provide even vague evidence for such a conclusion. A closer look at the news item showed that the claim was based on general observations and aimed at the forthcoming electoral requirement.

But the real catch for this 'research' getting such prominent coverage was that it was by a 'Public Policy Research Centre', identified as a ruling party-linked agency, that claimed to have conducted this 'research'. The claim was that the demonetisation had 'led to the shrinking of Naxal activities which in turn made it easier for the government to engage the local population in development venture'. There was no effort made to explain how the two phenomena (demonetisation and Naxal incidents) are connected. The deceptiveness of the claim was that it was more of a PR initiative or a news plant on the behalf of the government. Should we then blame the government or the newspapers that carries the story, or both? This is only one example of how 'research' is misused. Another example of politicalising research was a 'research report', released at BJP office in New Delhi, by a BJP MP and leader critiquing AAP government's education policy in Delhi State. The research report, of course, had not hidden the fact that the research agency (Public Policy Research Centre) was an outfit of BJP activists.[3] But, the point here is politicization of research and in the process denigrating 'research' itself, along with the blatant misuse of news media in the name of research with the belief that people believe something to be 'research'. These examples are given not to indicate that only the party in power misuses research. All parties engage in such games.

On 4 December 2018, *The Economic Times* ran a headline of '89% Indian household now use LPG cylinder', with the government claiming that it was 'as against 56% four years ago'. If true, this was a major story worth global attention. But it was never followed up with details as it was not based on any 'research' or analysis. It was a PR claim to justify public policies, not realising that it meant injustice of public policies.[4]

MNREGS and Swachh Bharat are two massive national flagship programmes. MNREGS, now over a decade old, is limited to those who are seeking work specifically in rural areas. As a demand-driven programme, it was expected to be an 'employment guarantee scheme'. Nearly 13 crore people had registered (2017) under this scheme expecting to be provided with work for 100 days a year (this was initially, but later some states announced that they would increase this timeframe to 150 days). However, hardly half of that percent ever availed the scheme. That is, a lot more people sought work than the government could offer, and even those who were provided worked hardly for a couple of days. This scheme, as envisaged originally based on research, was expected to improve infrastructure in the rural areas and offer supplementary opportunities for the poor. That is, there was something missing in this scheme's target and implementation. An evaluative research, conducted independently, would have suggested correctives to implement of the scheme. Instead, the programme was being propped up based on PR-oriented coverage in news media at the behest of political interests.

In 2005, the scheme was mostly based on prior experiments conducted in one or two states (Maharashtra being one) and as a relief for the agriculture labour who otherwise were unable to find work in the non-agriculture season. But in a matter of couple of years, such an ambitious scheme had gone through a 'crises proportion', which if continues to decline in its importance, could even precipitate an unrest in rural India. How was MNREGS allowed to lose out as a pride project? Why were lessons from short-lived 'food-for-work' scheme two decades earlier not considered? Why was independent research support not considered to rejuvenate the scheme even when such research inputs were available from credible independent and credible professionals?

The conclusion one could draw from the deteriorating

MNREGS status is that either the government was not enthusiastic about it remaining a 'flagship' programme of the previous government or it did not realise the relevance of the programme in the context of the decaying rural economy. Seriously supporting research on this scheme would have saved the country from a 'one step forward, two stop backword' view.

That is, when the political regime changed (2014), the new government should have conducted a review and research for the revival of the farming sector as the programme was seen as belonging to a particular party regime instead of as a national programme. Also, no research has been conducted, for example, on the kind of community assets (until 2019 when water sources were given priority) that were created or whether labour migration trends have changed. But the government promptly presented 'research' that claimed savings by using Aadhar, perhaps because Aadhar was then a contentious and a politicised policy.

This is a classic example of a nation being let-down, particularly in the absence of the government coming up with any other alternative to replace MNREGS. Despite the dilemma, the government had neither conducted evaluative research concerning the larger interest nor was there any evidence of previous research by independent academics being used. How can one interpret such a situation? Although budget allocations were anywhere between Rs 45,000 crore and Rs 60,000 crore, what was the outcome of easing rural unemployment situation in the country? Many of the demands of recent agitating farmers and of the rural poor are known, and yet could not be met. (Dr M.S. Swaminathan's report had hinted at such possibility a few years earlier.) To what can such a situation be attributed? Misunderstanding of 'research'?

The kind of problems that MNREGS has been suffering over the years could have been tackled using research from within as well as outside the government. Research could have helped realise the programmes' objectives. The amounts allocated for MNREGS over the years being high, research would have been a logical initiative to optimise the programme. And yet none of that was considered (as the government went overboard using data and research for some other schemes). Mere monitoring numbers is not enough and may even be misleading. This MNREGS case shows that the union government has not recognised the role and relevance of primary research. Government-monitored figures are believed to be good enough. Or, is it fear that an independent research may 'expose' limitations? Isolated examples of 'social audit' were reduced to 'endorsing tools'.

Swachh Bharat, a favourite national programme, was welcomed by all sections of the country as a much-needed initiative. As a part of this campaign, all public places are supposed to be kept clean, and for this, the prime minister himself had set a good example by participating in the campaign. Chief ministers, ministers, and officers too had taken to showcasing their participation, however symbolically. A flagship scheme of Swachh Bharat is to provide a toilet in every household and to ensure that there is no outside or public defecation.

This toilet or sanitation programme, as part of Swachh Bharat, too was launched on a grand scale with all-out news media coverage on a much bigger scale compared to the family planning campaign decades ago. States, municipalities, and districts have claimed that they have been constructing toilets in large numbers, and many have even claimed to be free from open defecation (by the end of 2018). This requires sustainable change in mind-set and behaviour, for which field research is necessary to ensure key interventions and independent source-based application.

The 2019 Economic Survey (tabled on 5 July 2019) claimed that '99.2% of rural India is now open defecation free',[5] but the finance minister in her speech in the Parliament mentioned 95%.[6] The report also claimed that the first phase of the Swachh Bharat Abhiyan, focussing on toilet construction and use, 'has a positive impact on the health, economy and environment of rural India'. It went on to cite some studies in support of these statements and further stated that 'mind set change is the other major ingredient required for sustained progress in sanitation'. These are much needed good intentions and objectives. Only an evaluative research can establish the ground reality and provide credibility to the claims. (Chaitanya Kalbag, 'Toilet-Training in India', called Swachh Bharat as 'unqualified Success'.)[7]

But the National Statistical Office (NSO) on sanitation debunked these claims, and on 23 November 2019, stated that 71% of rural households were free of outside defecation, with some states having much less than 50 percent households free of outside defecation.[8]

This is not an isolated example of conflicts in data claims on the union's performance indicators. The following table presents another glimpse.

Examples of Variations in Government and NSSO data

Performance Indicators	Government Data	Latest NSSO Survey
Households having access to toilet	98%	79.8%
Households having electricity for domestic use	98.4%	95.7%
LPG connections released under Ujjwala Yojana	100%*	87.6%
Households with LPG	94%	61.40%
Households that received benefit from the government schemes	53%	50.40%
Covered by health insurance	34%	28.70%

Quality and Credibility Problems of Government data

As in the case of the family planning campaign, Swachh Bharat too was taken up with no benchmark or baseline research. There was more focus on numbers generated by monitoring from within the government. But the government took good initiative for independent research. At the end of the first (2016) year, the concerned ministry called for bids to undertake a field research independently in 29 states and 6 union territories.

This process of deciding the research agency, on an open tender basis, took five months and stipulated that the agency complete the research study in all states and union territories within three months. The well-designed study involved a sample survey, a qualitative study with stake holders, and an analysis of the implementation claims of states. The selected research agency conducted the methodology involving the ministry at every stage. The ministry was presented with 36 state specific research reports on ground realities on schedule.

Two months after these research reports were submitted, there was no indication that the Ministry had gone over the reports. The news media had by then already covered state-wise percentage of toilets based on the figures released by the Ministry itself. On repeated reminders by the research agency, the Ministry asked the agency for a presentation of the reports but it took another two months for them to give an actual date for the presentation. When the presentation was actually made, the Secretary of the Ministry was absent. (The presentation was already postponed once as he was not there.) At that point, the officials 'cleared' the study for payment (until then, payment was stalled). But the actual order for payment was issued three months later, and the money was actually paid almost one year after the study reports were submitted to the Ministry. More importantly, the Ministry did not go through the reports that was sponsored by it so that the states could be advised about the types of changes that could be made based on independent field research to assess performance and behavioural change. Their intentions were good. But then, why did they ignore the independent research? Did they presume that the report did not support the declared claims of the Ministry?

This is not an isolated case. It reflects the kind of outlook that officials tend to take when the research is independent and when it may not endorse the claims that political bosses had already articulated. In some cases, such a research is sponsored and conducted more as a formality.

In the case of MNREGS, however, neither did the Ministry directly conduct any independent impact or behavioural study nor did they take into account such evaluation studies by independent or/and academic professionals. Even when they did, it was not acknowledged. Although the ministry took initiative for Swachh Bharat, they were not serious about it.

The year 2018 had seen news media and political parties discussing Cambridge Analytics intensely and excessively. How this UK-based research outfit was supposed to have 'manipulated' elections, including of some state assemblies, was reported extensively and almost endlessly. Has the country's news media ever covered any important national public policy in a similar manner? Research becomes 'big news' only in the context of elections. And it becomes valuable for leaders only for immediate consequences and control purposes. Populism and TRPs are all that seem to matter in politics and news. Rating alone has become the yardstick for assessing the success of a scheme or policy, not the change it brings about in practices and priorities.

Influence of TRP Hoax

On the other hand, the country was taken for a ride by a research hoax some 25 years ago that continues to be the basis for the kind of television India has ended up with. This is what is popularly known as TRP. It has become the benchmark. This has become the criteria for the type of television content, advertising, serials, news, and entertainment formats. No one, not even the academics, the government, or any news media, had questioned the velocity of such 'research' or its relevance or the effects of the TRP system. What questions were asked were about sample size and not about the very research model. And yet, TRP continued to significantly impact our development paradigm, perceptions, and lifestyles, and the kind of upbringing children and leaders alike experienced, with no one correcting the TRP-oriented research outlook. In this process, research has become 'TRP research' where methodologies are used to capture top-of-the-mind or surface impressions and reactions, instead of behavioural and attitudinal changes. This dilemma sweeping across the country was explored in the 2010 film *Rann*, with Amitabh Bachchan in the lead.

There is no evidence of social policies in India ever being sourced to field research. Some policies were based on rigorous analysis of secondary data. Even for a mid-course review, field research is being availed. The idea of introducing social audit in MNREGS as an obligation in some states is an isolated example.

In the earlier decades, there were a number of examples of independent academics basing policies on analysis of secondary data and research, although more in the case of economic policies. Experts like VKRV Rao of School of Economics, Prof B.S. Minhas, Dr Manmohan Singh, Dr Amartya Sen, Dr Bhagwati or Prof. Kaushik Basu, just to mention a few, had a different view and approach to the methodologies of some of the public policies (2005-2020).

Research Utilisation

During 1970-1972, Professor Everett Rogers of Diffusion of Innovation global fame and I visited nearly a dozen premier institutes of the country engaged in research, mostly on public policy issues. It was a Ford Foundation-sponsored project. At each institute, we discussed research concerns, priorities, and pursuit with the functionaries and enquired about the utilisation of their studies. On the way back from Madhurai, after spending three days in Gandhigram Institute of Rural Development, we were excited about the impressive engagement of Gandhigram Institutes. By the time we got down to New Delhi, Rogers worked on a note on 'Utilisation of research' of national institutes. Neither research outcome was put out for larger public for their awareness nor was any effort evident to ensure that research findings benefit someone or affects a perspective. But enthusiasm was very evident in these institutions to publish the research in one or other magazine.

Based on such discussions, Rogers concluded that hardly 15-20% of research on public policies in national institutes was being availed or considered at that time. We never pursued this enquiry any more systematically. Fifteen years later, when the Rajiv Gandhi regime gave a push to the pursuit of knowledge by encouraging research and the use of computers, I made a quick overview of social research utilisation, including by a few national institutes, that I was familiar with in one capacity or other, including the National Institute of Health & Family Welfare, Indian Institute of Mass Communication, and National Institute of Rural Development. I estimated that, even in 1986–87, it was sporadic and hardly 30% of research was considered for further discussion or follow-up. On further analysis, I found that that was because the issues pursued by the institutes were not urgent enough to be pursued and the research was never even put across in context to the Ministry concerned or to any stakeholders. Moreover, there was no credibility and expertise of the research methodology, and more importantly, senior policy makers were not even aware of or sensitive to the research and its objectives.

> Peter King was a marketing specialist with Ford Foundation (1970–74). He coordinated a research by IIM-Calcutta in Hoogly on how condoms were being sold or purchased in the retail network. This study was corroborated by a qualitative validation that Everett Rogers and I conducted in Lucknow's main bazar. We interviewed and observed retail shops (pan and cigarette outlets) on both sides of the street. It was afte the presentation of this research at the insistence of Ford Foundation (1970–71) that the Ministry of Health and Family Planning (as it was known then) went for the idea of 'social marketing' and established a division in the Ministry with one Mr Gupta from the private sector to promote condom marketing in India by involving the top ten marketing companies to take to condom sales (ITC, Hindustan Unilever, etc.). It was an open presentation where research findings were shared with stakeholders (with no political interest), which improved the chance of research utilisation.

About 35 years ago, Eduardo Faleiro, the Union Minister of Electronics, assigned me the task to review the outcome of more than 24 central research labs under that ministry. Many of them had been set up much before 1980. I found that none of their research had resulted in any new product entering the market, nor in any change in ongoing practices or priorities. None of them had ever undertaken behavioural studies either.

But this experience was rare for me. Up until then, I had interacted closely with advertising agencies, advertisers, marketing corporates, and media houses of the country. This was mostly in Mumbai, New Delhi, and Hyderabad (1972–74, 1978–85) when I did landmark studies, mostly sponsored and some on my own, when I was with ORG, Baroda and later with CMS. In association with those in media and Ministries (for example, Roger Pereira of Shilpi advertising, K Kurian of Radius Advertising, A.G. Krishnamurthy of Mudra Advertising), the first National Readership Survey (NRS) and MEMOS (media monitoring) was conducted during the period. During the same years, the first National Family Planning Survey and first ever national surveys on housing and child labour were conducted. Because of the involvement of senior decision-makers in the first two studies, they were taken into account and availed, whereas the latter two studies faced resistance as they were viewed as critical by those in power.

> Once in 1973, on a Sunday morning, I saw in the engagement column of *Times of India* that Union Minister for Information and Broadcasting, I.K. Gujral, was addressing some advertising organisations. Since that place was close to where I was staying, I walked into that meeting. Mr Gujral was telling the audience how, in the absence of any data, his Ministry takes decisions on some policies concerning advertising. At the end, I got up and told what percent of people read English newspaper in some states. On asking, I told him that for the first time a National Readership Survey was just conducted and the report was getting ready. He asked me whether I could share the report. After a fortnight, one Dr K.L. Gandhi, Spl Assist to Gujral, telephoned me in Baroda and asked whether I could give a presentation in New Delhi on the readership survey, which I did 10 days later but only gave the results for Maharashtra to the senior officers, including to the prime minister's office. It was this presentation which lead to more than a couple of public policies in the next one year.

As I have said, my assessment of research of those years was sponsored mostly by advertising and marketing corporates. The advertising agencies and advertisers were using 70% of research sponsored or subscribed by them. They were using it for strategy, planning, targeting or focussing, identifying appeals or themes, and to obtain better returns on their campaign effects and investments made on brands. They were sensitive to the input and output aspects of research and analysis. They were also anxious to use research because, first, the research was task based, was in consultations, and took into account specific needs; second, because they take research seriously when they pay or share the costs involved; third, they were accountable for what they did to their managements; and fourth, the outcome of research often was what they wanted and the studies were mostly instant in nature, not in-depth or longitudinal, as they were intended to meet their immediate requirements.

Advertising agencies benefitted greatly from research because they understood it well. They were in close interaction with the research agency and attended presentations along with their clients. The research findings helped them to convince the client about strategies, campaign schedules, and proposals for the ad budget. In such situations, there is a high percentage of research being utilised formally and informally.

A combination of research methodologies was used to make the findings more reliable in the immediate context, including qualitative and quantitative methods. Client meetings and validating research findings helped the process of research utilisation. Syndicated research practice among competing corporates was another unique feature that increased the potential use of research. In the case of research concerning public policy, such interactivity is unlikely. Public policy makers seek supportive data and research to justify their proposals and initiatives.

How little is budgeted and then spent on data collection, analyses, and social sector research for public policy is not in public knowledge. The crucial contribution of research to public policy is also not made known to the public. What is used from research is never directly acknowledged by governments and most leaders. There would be questions they would have to answer if they did acknowledge this, and if they were honest, about how paltry the funds are that they allocate for such research. For example, decennial census operations cost the country more than Rs 2000 crores. The recent National Register of Citizens (NRC) in Assam alone cost the country over Rs 1000 crores. And now, several chief ministers are planning to carry out a similar NRC exercise in their states; in fact, a union minister has declared that there will be a national-level NRC exercise. These are the same leaders who allot such meagre amounts for social and evaluative research that is needed for welfare schemes and inclusive good governance. Such meagre amounts that they can't be forthcoming about the spending.

Research Revelations, Not Acknowledged

While the Parliament was in session in July 2019, some important research findings came out in news media. For example, a CMS report on poll expenditure showed that 'poll expenditure' was doubling for every election. Another report concerned the number of children who were dying because of malnutrition. NITI Aayog also came up with its report on drinking water and how cities are going to be at a water loss (this was indicated at least thrice earlier by other researchers in two years).

In the 'poll reforms' discussion in Rajya Sabha, members referred to a CMS report as a reminder of the kind of fundamental problem that high poll expenditure meant. But the response was that 'the report [is] not of the government', that it was 'private', thus brushing aside the basic point of its connection to corruption in the country.

No one in this Parliament session has raised the issue of 'malnutrition' or 'water crisis' for a serious discussion to develop action proposals so that people know what initiatives were being taken. Also not raised in the Parliament was the claim in the 2019 Economic Review and in the Budget proposal that

95–98% of the country was 'defecation free'. The fact was far from and tellingly otherwise. Consider any state or city—even the nation's capital, New Delhi. The same week, *Times of India* reportedly prominently how even schools and government offices were lacking toilets for women, and some television channels showed how school toilets were occupied including for cooking or storage. An eminent journalist, Chaitanya Kalbag, even wrote in *Business World* that the government's claims were 'unqualified'.

That is, research revelations and reminders were not taken seriously by law makers unless it had to do politics and elections. Research, from outside or inside the government, is not acknowledged as politicians in power want to take 'credit'. Politicians prefer taking up such basic issues when it suits them for boosting their political interests. Research findings are availed by leaders, not where and when it should be but according to their own preference, and more often in a 'fire-fighting' way rather than to find ways to address the issue. Some leaders even rather prefer for the problem to be recurring so that they can take it on again at another time when it suits them.

The Rise and Decline of Research Signals Larger Malice

There is ample evidence suggesting the decline in social research in vital sectors of development in recent years. These examples are present in many sectors like agriculture, health, demography, and social development. The decline is both direct and indirect. Research environment and architecture depends on how sources of data, statistics, and research such as census, open society provisions, and citizen rights policies are allowed.

Broadcasting services anywhere in the world are closely interwoven with research, particularly with content priorities and programme and time use schedule strategies. Impact assessment of broadcast channels is based on research. Only with primary data can claims of listenership or viewership gain sanctity for their policies on ad tariff, etc. In India, too, the All India Radio (AIR), the only broadcaster until early 1970s, had a research division in support of the service. Initially, research was limited to analysing letters from listeners and monitoring the signal reach, and then the research was extended to actual listening and recall of programmes, followed by proactive field surveys within and outside (outsourced) for programme production. This research had distinct focus over the years. Gradually, the audience research division, which had taken initiatives first, with gaining with commercial broadcasting, and then the competition from private broadcasters took off. Doordarshan (DD) even took to research initiatives like DART. But that initiative was reduced in support of syndicated TRP reports of TAM (and later of BARC). Audience research of a public broadcaster has been reduced to that of a service provider to advertisers and advertising agencies. The research outfit within AIR and DD was reduced to being a public relations outfit, to prepare annual reports, and supply data to the ministry. Research lost it's potential of proactively guiding and offering much-needed evaluative research that is expected from a public service broadcaster.

At the outset, between 1950 and 1970, audience research units were established in major radio stations, and the same were consolidated between 1970 and 1995. With the advent of television, a separate division for television audience research was also set up during the period and consolidated. But after 1995, with the spread of 'ratings' by a foreign commercial outfit, the research concern and pursuit was diluted, and subsequently reduced to being a book-keeper. Proliferation of private broadcast channels had already undermined audience research, both by AIR and Doordarshan. Impact and implications of programme content, which is the essence of broadcasting, was compromised, resulting in the governments remaining mute as if they were not concerned or aware of the implications. By abandoning primary research, the country had allowed an inane or irrelevant Western content model to take root in India. In fact, this model prompted and promoted programmes that went against the Indian ethos and even certain Constitutional provisions.

Without a research environment, no country can expect to stand out as a free, independent, and transparent government. No wonder India stands at 52 out of 129 of the world economies ranked in the 2019 Global Innovation Index.[9] Switzerland and Sweden ranked first and second, respectively, as the world's most innovative countries. China stood at 14 in this ranking. Even on other global indexes, including democracy, India does not have any better standing. In most of those indexes, India lost the score mostly on social development performance indicators, including research support and initiatives.

The decline in primary research was also because foreign management and financial management corporates entered India and took over the research without much the necessary background, and yet, imposed foreign models of appraisal and needs assessment. This rise and decline of research concern and pursuit in broadcasting signalled a larger trend of denigrating evaluative research across different sectors in the country.

The rise and recent decline of freedom of information movement in the country culminated with the dilution of the RTI Act of 2005. This is also a slur on the country's research culture. This Act had unleashed the rights of citizens and became a source for wide range of research, particularly on the functioning of the government and delivery of public services. As such, the way this Act was treated over 15 years (2005–20) also signals the subduing of impact and evaluative research in the country.

The RTI Act and citizen rights in the last decade have given a push to evaluative research, thus opening a new window for varied primary data that has become available, particularly concerning corruption, grievance redressal, delivery of public services, and good governance. Even news media has taken to analysis and research based on RTI activism. In fact, in 2018, 3–4% of news space in the mainstream news media was based on such RTI-revealed information and data. Also, in the last decade, several large-scale surveys were conducted by CMS, Department Personnel itself, NCPRI, and Common Wealth Initiative, among others. These studies on RTI also identified new ways of tracking as well researching how a government functions, ways of improving governance, and how understanding between service providers and the recipients can be improved. Thus, any diluting or clipping of RTI provisions amounted to denting the larger research culture in the country.

During 2005–2010, RTI gained ground in terms of awareness and usage of its provisions. Once its potential become evident, power centre's came up with spokes. By 2015, it was clear that the power centres, including the government, were determined to dilute its potential and reduce the Information Commission to being yet another government department, which showed a retrospective view of transparency in the government.

The two different examples given here reflect how research was sought after initially and how it has denigrated in later years. There are five trends that stand out regarding this rise and fall of research, more glaringly in the social sector. First is the politicisation of governance, particularly electoral politics compelling populism. Second is the craze for populism, compelling the governments with short-sighted decisions and schemes with no concern for long-term implications. Third is the image becoming a priority which led to leaders taking to news media manipulation. Fourth is the increased attraction to control, command, and centralise. Fifth is the shift in the balance of power in favour of political parties and the decline in the representative character of parties. As a result, what is sought and preferred is supportive research and value loaded data, not objective and independent research. An influx of 'foreign consultants' and their entrenchment into ministries with their own modules has further complicated the primary and evaluative research with long term concerns for the country.

Flagships…Good, but More By Modi's Image?

Most of the schemes initiated by Prime Minister Modi and the ideas he advocates are of relevance beyond party politics and have the potential to take India to newer heights. In fact, the best part of Modi's ideas and schemes is that they are meant to change the mind-set of people. Impact-concerned research reflects more reliably the implications of such schemes or ideas and their implementation.

Not all government schemes are expected to be successful or can yield the intended result or make the difference that they are expected to in the same way and to the same extent. Success in quantitative terms need not be the only criteria for judging an initiative or scheme, and it is counter-productive to be overly sensitive about the extent of success or failure. There cannot be failure of good ideas and initiatives, but there may be shortcomings and progress may be slow. In such situations, impact-concerned research points to interventions and correctives better. The leadership is thus required to communicate or convince the people of such a possibility, given the kind of complexities existing in the country and the glaring inequalities present between people and regions.

There are multiple ways to explain the shortcomings and correct the perceptions regarding performance and success and failure. For example, a 30% rate in KAP need not be considered a failure or even as a lapse in implementation. Once people become aware, involved, and participative in the process of implementation, or governance and development, it will lead to a better understanding of the outcomes and even the shortcomings. A comparison of Modi's schemes and ideas on this criterion will be far more revealing. An important factor is the reliability of the interactivity between the people and the present government in the given context, beyond the ambit of political party network. A critical trend is the tendency of the government or the leader to own every scheme and take every credit. The other factor in determining the success or failure of schemes is monitoring, feedback, appraisal, and evaluative practices. The more credible and transparent this process, the less should be the concern or worry of a failure or shortcoming. Swatch Bharat programme, a pet programme of Prime Minister Modi, offers interesting insights. As long as Swachh Bharat remained a government programme, it hardly made headway for future sustainability. Even claims on GDP or unemployment should have gone through such a process. It would have helped avoid controversies and politicisation. A public discussion need not be seen as a criticism of the leader or the government or even of the scheme, as in the case of Skill India and a Digital India schemes. But pre-election sensitivity and temptation to politicise issues has complicated the confidence-building process. With such (political) sensitivities, many initiatives may as well be considered Modi Mantras. This is what I wrote about two years ago in my book.[10]

The present political culture is full of over-claiming and making promises, as that appeals to people who are often unconcerned about the limitations and future implications. Political votary or sycophancy is yet another phenomenon with doubtful concern for the credibility of the leader. This adds to the crisis in confidence and perceptions about performance or success–failure notions of schemes. Research and objective feedback often gets diluted because of such tendencies of political followers. The victim in this process often is research findings when they are in consonance.

Reliance on any one research method to assess performance has its own perils and is likely to disappoint. No source of feedback and methodology of research is without limitations. Its reliability depends on the frequency of validating such a source. Sources like IVR, for example, can be deceptive and have serious consequences. A recent good example is how the Chief Minister of Andhra Pradesh (2014–18), Chandrababu Naidu, publicly claimed IVR medium as his (relied) source for 'high ratings'. He was almost fooled by IVR source. Instead of using it in a supplementary way, he relied on it.

'Dashboard' is a new tool which the then chief minister of AP (2014–19) relied on and popularised to keep track of implementation and the situation on field at any given time (the same way TRP is based on). Dashboard is an impoverished or a hurried way of capturing a dynamic scene. Trying to capture it as and when can be misleading as it can never give a full picture. It can only be an add-on input to integrate into or validate. Dashboard does not indicate **why or how** and even

when. Even numbers which Dashboard provides may not have credibility because transparency is often missing.

Flagship Programmes

Of the approximately 200 'schemes' considered as initiatives of the Modi Government since 2014, some are viewed as flagship programmes. These programmes target or involve a large section of the population, particularly the vulnerable ones. These are unique schemes because of the extensive coverage and complexity of the schemes in terms of the phases involved and the dynamics and multiple changes expected. Such programmes require data and research support to be executed optimally. My 50 years of association with many government programmes indicate that influence and success rate depends on the extent to which various research was availed at different phases such as policy, strategy, or implementation, and in availing of the schemes by targeted people.

Many public policies of the government in recent years are far more populist in terms of their appeal, targets, objectives, and concern 'vote bank politics'. But some of the ideas inherent in these schemes deserve to be assessed on an altogether different criteria and with different research methodologies. Some of these ideas, which I described earlier as 'Modi Mantras', have long-lasting relevance for the trajectory of development, democracy, and governance. These cannot be assessed with conventional research tools and yardsticks of success–failure or popular–unpopular, and in terms of moods of the day.

These schemes can be classified as: 1) aimed at community-level implications in terms of ease of living and quality of life; 2) enriching opportunities for individuals in terms of skills and access to resource; 3) outlook in thinking beyond 'today' and 'me' terms.

The concern in this book, however, is limited to the relevance and role of research in formulating policies, designing programmes, optimising schemes, and their utilisation and ascertaining their impact. Some of the recent (2014–20) schemes viewed as flagship were put through this assessment.

The ones on infrastructure that are routinely administrated extension of an old scheme are not included here. This, I feel, involves complex processes to recognise their potential, and research can significantly help detect the best of the objectives of the schemes.

1. Jan Dhan Yojana (2014)
2. Mudra Yojana (2015)
3. Jeevan Jyoti Bima Yojana (2015)
4. Swachh Bharat Abhiyan (2014)
5. Swachh Survakshana Pros (2016)
6. Ujjwala Yojana (2016)
7. MNREGS (2005)
8. Beti Bachao Beti Padhao Scheme (2015)
9. Awas Yojana (2015)
10. Udaan Scheme (2017)

Not all decisions of the government can be showcased as initiatives of the Prime Minister. An official 'list of schemes' by Narendra Modi till 2019 lists nearly 200 decisions—many of which are routine administrative decisions. Many of these neither involves financial allocations or indicates specifically what is now proposed or who is expected to benefit from them. An objective analysis of these listed 'schemes' can indicate 10 schemes at the most. Not all decisions are necessarily new or can be considered national policies. They may be continuation of an old decision with a new label slapped on them. Nearly 200 decisions were shown as Prime Minister Modi's initiatives or schemes (2014–2019). In fact, not all of them should be described as schemes. Most involve an extension or administrative expression of an initiatives. Some of Modi's ideas, which he had articulated, have significant impact on the mind-set of people. His speeches in Kerala and Tirupati in June 2019 soon after the poll results and in August 2019 addressing party MPs are good examples, and if pursued, suggest a bigger difference to the future of the country and democracy.

Capturing Change, Methodologies Limitations

Results of recent elections in the country and in AP state signals certain trends that suggest that the premises behind research methodologies need to be re-evaluated. The mood of the people tracked before the poll was totally misleading. How is that possible?

First and foremost is the concept of public opinion, as it is viewed hitherto. Today, while public life is dynamic, opinions are static. It is moods that are now relied upon more. They are momentary. Not even 24/7. Capturing them too has to be dynamic.

Opinions remain confined to individuals and are no longer public as they were previously considered. It is external analysis that makes them public. The tools of doing that are too sophisticated today. It is somewhat like a nuclear fission.

Another aspect concerns deciphering responses of sample respondents in a field survey. That it need not be on the face value is known. But the question is about the validity of the responses in terms of time variables. The crux is future validity. The future could be in terms of days, weeks, months, or years. Regardless of how well-structured the format or the questionnaire is, how does one provide validity? This is where Artificial Intelligence (AI) could offer an option.

Similarly, the weightage on experience, as a contributor for formation of opinions, is not as decisive as before. As if we are in a world where not only every moment matters but moods determine the world. Today, opinions and perceptions also are based on mood!

Swinging or changing peoples' moods is much easier than making people change their opinions and attitudes. An emotional appeal is good enough as it does not require logical explanations. For example, factors like prices and jobs, which impacts the opinions of people, are no longer the basis for shifts in moods. In that sense, moods are like clouds. That is how perhaps man is known as an 'weather-clock'? This phenomenon requires new tools to be better understood, analysed, and predicted, particularly concerning the immediate course or direction of moods.

Exposure, not experience, matters in this process. It is accumulated exposures and interactivity that is related to the phenomena of opinion. Not moods. Moods need no logic. The intermediary are aspirations and expectations, which contribute to the formation of a mood. It is similar to a benchmark. Together, the bundle comprises or constitutes opinions, but in a dynamic way. Change implies flux in moods, ideas, and opinions and it involves a *process*. Without capturing or understanding the process, outcomes cannot only be indicative.

A new phenomenon in the process is how exposure to media is accompanied by interpersonal and local group dynamics. TV debates and discussions by themselves are misleading. Social media networks and such other motivated messages may *together* offer insights to interpret field sample surveys. But the fact that perceptions are often managed or manipulated cannot be ignored.

Ethnographic inputs relating to symbols, face-reading tools, etc., can also help in anticipating and interpreting the tidal waves of public preferences or choices.

Artificial Intelligence (AI) is a new discipline that is also being tried in some circles to test or evaluate results and insights, particularly when the sample is large.

So, depending on any one research method of capturing the minds or assessing is misleading, both for researchers as well as for political leaders. The perils of dependence and relying on technology tools, like IVR or wire polls or even TV polls, is often deceptive. It is a trap that political leaders in power tend to fall into. Researchers last longer or beyond tenures of political leaders in power. They cannot afford to be complacent or incomplete in the process.

Such a syndrome was what Professor Mahalanobis, father of applied statistics, had envisioned and cautioned the then Prime Minister Jawaharlal Nehru, more than 50 years ago. He even suggested independent surveys as a better option than relying on the same system that is responsible for implementation. He recommended that a research system should not be under bureaucracy or become routine or taken granted without checks and balances principle. Checks and balances are essential to ensure the reliability of any research, regardless of which methodologies are used.

Poll forecasting today is an altogether different game. It is more about tracking tactics of parties and manipulation and last minute lures for voters. It is not so much about choice, preference, or loyalty. Daily tracking for change in the moods or perceptions of people or melting process of options is more reliable.

Surrogate indicators are often the undercurrents in poll campaigns. In the context of elections, such undercurrents can be identified more reliably in a series of several rounds of field surveys, not in one or even two rounds conducted in a month- or two-month-long campaign. Today, Artificial Intelligence (AI) as a research methodology gives us new ways of envisioning emerging trends in public behaviours.

An individual may be introvert in terms of ideas or opinions but behaviour is not necessarily in isolation. Mass behaviour or crowd behaviour pattern become more apparent. This is what mass psychology is all about. It goes beyond economic and education categories of sample respondents. This is why or how large samples are considered today, contrary to my earlier notion that more is not merrier. To predict moods quicker (before a cloud burst), instant analytical tools are needed to improve sample reliability.

Signals from 2019 polls indicate that researchers need to revisit old methodologies as to sampling, field work, and questionnaire framing and analysis. This obviously is an expensive proposition. As such, this exercise can no longer be independent as it requires research to collude with a sponsor. We need to search for newer tools to save the society from induced influences. The best method is for the key stakeholders (political parties, candidates, the governments, etc.) themselves to change their strategies (for example, it is no longer simple majority, campaigns need not be in solo, and no inducement based pulls).

National Register of Citizens (NRC) became a Pandora's box in Assam that involved continued claims and counter-claims about citizenship and verification and reverification procedures in finalizing the Register. Now that many other states are planning to take up NRC, it is better that we understand the fundamentals involved in the exercise. The first is to create a credible organisation responsible for compiling the NRC. Second is to establish the criteria and the cut-off for determining the eligibility in a transparent manner. Third is formulating a procedure for verification and redressal of appeals and complaints at different levels in a state. Fourth is that the people who are involved with these responsibilities should not have anything to do political parties or leaders.

Considering the sensitivities involved in the exercise, it may be better to have a social audit of the exercise involving independent, responsive, and credible people. The entire exercise is aimed at providing evidence of the numbers and statistics. Which otherwise are likely to become politicalised and lose their credibility.

Since this is an expensive exercise, no effort can go to waste and should be questionable. For Assam alone, more than Rs 12,000 crores were supposed to have been spent for generating the NRC. And 55,000 state employees were supposed to have been involved in the verification and updating exercise, which is nearly as much as what the National Census exercise that takes place once in ten years costs. A member of the legislature of ruling coalition in Assam, who doubted the fairness of NRC, Debananda Hazarika said, 'A fair NRC will be like the magna carta but a flawed one would threaten the integrity and sovereignty of the country'.[11]

Sex Ratio Trends, Missing Girls?

Male progeny trend in the country was supposed to be responsible for variation in the data claims of different agencies on sex ratio at birth. Even the Ministry of Women and Child Development proposed in August 2019 to collate data from several ministries and departments across the country to reconcile fluctuations in various data and arrive at a 'clearer understanding of the numbers' that are criticised for being skewed in favour of male child. Multiplicity of sources and inconsistencies in their numbers is what leads to political leaders taking advantage of the confusion and making whatever claims suit them. On the sex ratio, for instance, there are different data from different surveys and reports, among them:

- Health Management Information System (HMIS) data
- Sample Registration System survey data
- Registrar General of India from civil registration system
- NITI Aayog Reports
- National Family Health Survey

Parliament was told by a Union minister in June 2019 that the sex ratio had increased from 923 to 931 between 2015–16 and 2018–19. But without reliable data sets on the child sex ratio, birth rate, and infant mortality, it is difficult to calculate the sex ratio between the censuses. So the credibility of the minister's claim was questioned by some who pointed to statistical reports which showed that 5% of girls are 'eliminated' before they are born, despite the Modi government's 'Beti Bachao, Beti Padhao' scheme. Both sides were using varying data about the same issue. The data fluctuation results from variation in the sex ratio of births depending on whether the births happen at home, in government hospitals, or in private hospitals. The HMIS data that the Union minister used to make the claim about the increase in sex ratio relied heavily on home and government hospital births and under-reported private hospital births, and it is in private hospitals that sex ratio at birth is majorly skewed, with a disproportionate number of male babies being delivered.[12]

This is an example of reliability and authenticity of data suffering on account of multiplicity of sources and methodologies and inconsistencies in the reference period. One could pick up whichever source suits one claims. The impact and utilisation of research, data, and statistics depends on these various aspects. What difference research has made in public policy depends on how effectively these shortcomings and biases have been recognized and corrected.

CHAPTER SEVEN

Data Is a Life-Line

Claims of good governance and development relies on measurements and quantification of inputs, outcomes, changes, effects, influences, etc. of policies innovations, initiatives, and interventions. A good governance involves credible and independent institutions whose data and analyses would be in public preview and would be shared for their potential use by any of the pillars of the state and the public institutions. Credibility of and timely access to such data is another significant aspect. The traditional indicators of development, growth, and behavioural change are not good enough in a fast-changing scenario, particularly with the availability of newer technologies. In such situations, reliable data, objective analysis, transparency in the process are critical and detrimental for public policies. Data, statistics, and research are even more critical to ensure achievements, fulfil promises, and justify the government's 'performance'.

A prerequisite for development, democracy, and good governance to take root is reliable, updated, and comprehensive data regarding households, citizens, voters, consumers, employees, entrepreneurs, industry, users and non-users, and beneficiaries and non-beneficiaries in an integrated as well as a desegregated manner. Analytics facilitates such a view and helps service providers to remain focused while prompting them about the delivery of public services.

Earlier, census data that is available once in 10 years was the sole basis for many policies. Then agencies such as Central

Statistics Office (CSO), National Sample Surveys (NSS), Directorate General of Commercial Intelligence, Director General of Statistics (DGCIS), and National Crime Bureau (NCB) were introduced. Some of these agencies use different rounds of field surveys, while focusing on specific themes and samples of different sizes in each round. NSS has continuous rounds and its data is used more for appraisal or for a mid-course review of public schemes. There are many other rounds of NSS surveys. In 2017, the 75th round regarded family expenditure as the basis for agencies like NCEAR, and recently ICRIER too came up with a large sample survey that was conducted independent of the potential users. And yet, there is frequent debate on conflicting data regarding the percentage of people below poverty, people who are entitled to subsidies, and targeted schemes, gender ratio, child labour, etc.

From the very outset, policy planners feel the need to conduct post-implementation analysis and research more than they did for the actual planning and design of welfare programmes. The PEO remained an important organ of Planning Commission until it ceased to be active nearly two decades ago, and then the Planning Commission itself was rechristened in 2015 as NITI Aayog.

Good governance requires taking into account the unknown aspects and dimensions of the yet 'unreached', far more than the immediate need-based requirements. Generally, the pursuit has been to seek more of the same again and again. A number of studies have been conducted on the delivery of basic public services but no study has ever examined, for example, the percentage of the country's below-poverty-line population that is unable to avail basic public services as they cannot afford to pay the 'unofficial money' or had no 'contact' to go to until the CMS India Corruption Survey yielded such data, state-wise, first in 2005 and then in 2007. Such new data, analysis, and research enabled public policies to gain relevance and weightage.

On the other hand, with rampant data inconsistencies and contradictions, policies are likely to be bungled up and become misleading with unreliable numbers, claims, and outcomes. This is also when the key statistical indicators get reworked and data is adjusted or manipulated; that is when base lines, benchmarks, and definitions are changed either to adjust to changing lifestyles or to suit political interests while also vitiating national debates as is sometimes seen.

A Data Regime?

The 2019 Economic Survey report detailed a new data regime essential to boost all kinds of research at different levels and contexts. This needs to be seen together with the role the National Research Foundation announced in the 2019 Union budget.

Under this regime, information on different aspects at different levels is expected to be integrated and compiled as databases. The government expects such an initiative to facilitate 'ease of living', improve targeting for welfare schemes, help reach unmet needs, and ensure greater accountability in public services. These intentions and ideas are good. But it is important to note that citizen's expectations are never static. If the intricacies are not decentralised, made transparent, and privacy issue is not resolved, it may boost centralisation and grant more control to the government. Also, as this policy expects to make data selectively available by charging fees to private corporates, this regime may ultimately be in favour of the government and corporates at the cost of the citizen, particularly of the disadvantaged sections.

This proposal must be viewed in the context of other proposals such as the idea of a National Health Register to maintain citizens' health records and databases on education and Aadhar, including of children. Commercialisation of such databases should be a concern in the absence of known safeguards. British Airways was fined 230 million for data breech. No other country has such a system of government selling data on its citizens including data on health and education.[1]

There is an urgent need to promote skills among citizens of

different backgrounds and to inform citizens about locations to access and use databases, how they can benefit from it, as well as informing them that all these initiatives are meant for ease the living of all sections of citizens. In the immediate course of action, all these initiatives will help corporates and tighten the control and command policies of the union government.

Considering the past five years' track record concerning the respect shown for data and research in the country, the implementation of the 2019-20 budget proposals and the 2019 economic survey will have to be seen.

Source of Databases: Databases are likely to be from six or seven distinct sources:

Administrative data: Birth and death records, land records, tax records, etc.

Institutional data: Private or public data on medical, health, education, etc.

Field sample surveys based data: Nutrition intake, employment, etc.

Transactions Data: Agriculture, health, education, basic public services, etc.

There may be 8-10 ministries involved in compiling and availing these various databases at any given time.

Power of Data: The power of data and research depends on the context, timing, independence, and objectivity of their origin, transparency, and credibility. When such data is availed, public policies become in tune with peoples' wishes and aspirations. Such research generates data and facilitates successful implementation of public policies, even when the issues involved are complex and contentious. The more objective and independent the research in any context, the more is its potential.

No responsible democratic government can be expected to perform accountably without reliable data and research backup. It is in the government's own interest to ensure the credibility and transparency of data and data sources. But when a government begins looking at analysis, research, and data as an end in itself and more for justification, that is when the objectivity of analysis becomes questionable, contentious, and may even boomerang.

When results of a research are disappointing, governments tend to suppress, junk or ridicule the findings. Data tends to become political in democracies when governments try to control it. Or when independent institutions, including statistical agencies, come under pressure from or want to please governments and decide to manipulate survey methodologies or doctor the data themselves.

It is important in a parliamentary democracy that research, analysis, and data is not under the sole direction of political bosses or is limited to short-term interests. In today's competitive politics, driven by electoral compulsions, political leaders tend to look at data and research as an *instrument* to justify policies and implementation and claim achievements. Political leaders may become tempted to use data and research for their own ends by misinforming, suppressing, or manipulating data.

With governments presenting massive schemes and achievement claims of political party leaders, it is important to verify the objectivity of research, analysis, and data. The credibility of the outcome of such government efforts depends on the transparency of methodologies and the participatory nature and origin of research. But with politicisation of research and analysis, data becomes dubious and even signals to troubled times, further causing a setback to the developmental endeavours and democratic processes.

When political leaders in the government fail to consider future consequences or implications of data, they tend to mix up the interests of the government and political party, and in that process, ignore the sanctity of statistics. That is when they may even twist the results to suit their own immediate political interests. Data and research has the potential and political power for its findings to be used for image-building and instant gratification and to misrepresent policies and mislead people.

Transparency and democratisation of research can ensure that the processes of generating reports and data analysis are not concentrated at one place or at one level, and when there is no responsibility to explain the basis and share the outcome, the report become vulnerable. That was how employment data of National Statistical Commission (NSC) became a controversy as the report was deferred or withheld to shelve the findings that were considered as not palatable by the party in power. Two examples in 2018–19 were employment data of CSO of NSC and GDP data. While employment data was from a primary survey, the GDP data was based on compilation of secondary sources from the National Accounts Division. Important expert committees like that of Dr Rangarajan had recommended that National Statistics Commission be made autonomous so that such embarrassing situations could be avoided.

The 2019 Nobel winner Abhijit Banerjee cautioned in October 2019 that 'political motivations' in India are vitiating research trends and credibility. He was specific in lamenting the view that 'any data inconvenient to government is wrong'. He reminded recently of that 'fight over data in India' and that it is 'glaring warning' about the economy. Dr Banerjee further noted that 'taking away the rights of institutions and crippling them' is a danger looming with 'extra bureaucratic check' and 'recentralisation' of discussions further prompting the trend.

If the agencies responsible for such vital research and data are not independent or autonomous or are not answerable, political parties may succumb and look for more supportive data.

Independent research, data, and analysis ensure better implementation of policies and schemes and offer a win–win situation to all. The government, naturally, benefits from the positive results, as do the people. But the party in power can also consolidate its base—but only if only it takes a long-term view of schemes and people's aspirations.

If every time a different party or leader comes to power and tries to change the criteria or alter methodology of measuring outcomes with different tools, it can only lead to deceptiveness and even complacency. Even changing the benchmarks for justifying claims of achievement with supportive or sponsored data may be equally disastrous for the credibility of the government.

The tendency of the government and the party is to use internally generated data to endorse their policies and claims. They often view data and research as yet another instrument to manage their political prospects rather than to maximise the outcome of public policies and schemes.

Yamini Aiyar, President of the Centre for Policy Research (CPR), has been independently and objectively analysing the difference made by public policies. She cautioned about country's statistical machinery being on the brink of crisis in recent years and observed that an 'on-going controversy over the credibility and objectivity of India's Statistical system is one of the most damaging legacy'.[2] Aiyar also presented the significant consequences of fiddling with statistical systems to justify the efficient implementation of the schemes at the grassroots and to justify government's claims of achievements. She reiterated the sanctity of data and the role of public confidence in data originating from different sources.

Aiyar suggested that investments are necessary for ensuring reliability of data and quality of research. Her study at CPR found that there was greater tendency of 'over reporting' of administrative data on implementation. A trend today with serious consequences is the government's dependence on 'administrative data'. Of late, ranking and rating government's performance is based more on such internally generated data. Administrative data is collected by the same functionaries who are responsible for implementation. In such an exercise, the trend is supportive of claims or they justify the project objectives. Government accountability and claims of achievement often becomes deceptive when there are no consistencies, independent checks, or verification and validation procedures of such data.

A good example was how the Chief Minister of Andhra

Pradesh (2014–19) relied on administrative inputs and on IVR data claiming 85–95% satisfaction levels with government's public services (against 40–55% levels by independent outside sources). This was also the case with Management Information System (MIS) regarding MNIRGS. While the idea of MIS is good, it helps with proactive initiatives only when it is reliably and transparently derived and validated. With the availability of new technology and digitisation, like GPS, Apps data, dash board, mobile apps, and other alternatives, it can be misleading to rely on any of these and it may even boomerang as was the case with Chief Minister Chandrababu Naidu in AP (2019).

This recent trend is a reminder of the caution that Professor Mahalanobis had observed 60 years ago—'administrative data' and a justification route that the base data is put in. He even suggested to the then prime minister that it is necessary to guard against such survey research. And survey research being a discipline and science, it is important for scientists, economists, and technologists engaged in such services to have an identity and stature where their objectivity is not doubted.

GDP, Growth, and Fundamentals

Role, relevance, and rigidities of research in the context of public policies of a country depends and reflects the soundness of fundamentals, which determine its economy and the social system. These fundamental indicators include GDP, poverty, jobs, savings, and inflation. If these yardsticks are not based on transparent and time-tested methodologies, the very future of the country will be in turbulence and uncertainties will continue to dampen the spirits of its people as well as the global standing of a country's statistics. The rigour of research determines the sustainability of a country's growth path, the success of public policies, and the living standards of its people. A country without a reliable, transparent, and inclusive research legacy to support its public policies deprives itself of opportunities for genuine growth and development.

The standing and status of quantitative indicators cannot be expected to be consistent unless institutes are allowed to be independent and also held accountable. Independent institutes are expected to remain unaffected by political considerations and even by the expectations of the government or the leader in power. Even without constitutional or legislative backup, such efforts should acquire legitimacy. However, in a parliamentary democracy, political factors are likely to be concerned more with the immediate interests of their existence and with control and command objectives. This is a dilemma that every government and leader faces. It is an opportunity to standout and a challenge to cope with and come out of with credibility.

An important question to examine is what is poverty level and how is an individual or a family considered to be above or below poverty level? What variables can be considered to determine poverty? Poverty may be in terms of income or by virtue of consumption pattern in terms of nutritious food or may be a set of composite factors like '*Roti, Kapda aur Makaan*', that is food, clothes, and shelter as well as accessibility to certain services. One could add to these other basics living necessities like health, education, and livelihood opportunities. How can these be determined? Experts on these aspects have conducted research for years and continue to do so on their own in a professional pursuit or as an institutional responsibility. The amount of data that they have come up with have become the indicators of poverty.

Doubling Farm Income By 2022–23

In August 2019, Prime Minister Modi had reiterated his 2016 declaration of doubling farm income by 2022–23; that is, in three years. The growth in agriculture sector during the last five years was 2.9% per year. According to experts, to double agriculture income, this growth rate should be 10.4% per year, while it should be 15% from 2019–20 to 2022–23.[3] Economists like Abhijit Sen and Ashok Gulati have been sceptical of such growth. Even WTO had asked India to explain how it expects to double agriculture income. Of course, its concern was more to do with global market policies. The Minister for Agriculture had already stated in the Rajya Sabha in July 2019 that raising of farm income was not possible with growth in only one sector.

Against this context, the dilemma is how the government expects to double farm income? Considering a number-crunching viewpoint may show that nothing is impossible as it then boils down to the methodology of measuring and the base year or bench mark, particularly when the concern is top-down or has a macro-view, along with the inclusiveness of methodology. That is, what is shown under farm income. By adding non-farm sources of income and allied sectors, the figures will be different. Thus, the method used to measure income in a different manner compared to how it has thus far been captured.

It is a good idea to consider the notion that the past should not limit the future prospects and growth. Modi Government should be appreciated for engaging the country in this 'mindset' exercise. How can a nation of immense potential as India is blessed with otherwise rise to new heights and accomplish unprecedent growth? The idea of doubling should not be brushed aside. I maintained this argument in the book I edited *India 2021* in 1985 and in Andhra Pradesh Vision 2020 in 1993–94.[4]

If the government is determined to present a number or a percent as its achievement or to show fulfilment of a promise, it should not be a problem. All that it needs to do is to come up with a new methodology or new definitions or a new benchmark or a new package as to what constitutes farmer's income. That is, develop new definitions with new methodology of measurement. But, what gives weightage to this concept is the credibility of the source.

An important point is that government should take farmers and the nation into confidence and share how exactly they expect to achieve doubling of income. The government claimed that it proposes to double farmers' income by bringing together four different sources apart from farm productivity and revenue. It can thus be stated that the government plans to include, what could only be, notional transfers to farmers and dole-outs to rural communities.[5]

Then there are socio-cultural and regional differences which cannot be ignored when arriving at these criteria at the national level. Eating habits, for example, in cities are altogether different from those in rural and even tribal pockets of the country. Anthropological and sociological specialisations play a key role in understanding and arriving at these estimates.

Economic data is not the domain of only economists but also of social scientists. Statistics and data are availed by both equally. Both depend on data, primary as well as secondary. Data can be an instrument to combat competitive compulsions, develop strategies, and to have a features perspective.

GDP, jobs, inflation, and poverty levels are always expressed based on benchmarks and in a comparative context. Once they become the medium for government's achievements, the problem gets vocalised as all political regimes try to claim (exaggerated) these achievements. The more such interest, the more the tendency and trend to show off using numbers.

Database

Both primary and secondary data are susceptible to manipulation or 'normalisation'. Database is the basis for formulation of public policies as well as for the implementation of the schemes resulting form that policy. Only based on a research evaluation can the policy objectives be considered as achieved.

Data derived from secondary or primary source gets manipulated and even manufactured when the aim is to chase political opportunities. It can also lead to data wars between different agencies or opposing parties. This trend is what is becoming evident with competition between political parties and leaders becoming too outright and blatant. Data may be free to use, but it may prove to be very costly if misused, which sometimes is not reversible.

The process of creating awareness, sensitivity, and persuasion has become more data-based. This data so availed is not always reliable or has credible origins. Public policies earlier were based mostly on party priorities and promises, but over the years, with politics becoming competitive, it is more promises, public opinion, and popularity than the implementation of promises that have become the concern of parties in power. As a result, data is being sought and searched for persuasive pursuit and for gaining control and command in the government. In this process, research is being looked upon more as a weapon. This trend is one of the reasons for the decline in objectivity of research and data.

Monetisation and politicisation of data and monopoly trends limits the scope of research initiatives. A research can be supportive or endorsive, including of the administrative source. Validation, checks, and balances are no longer availed even when the research and data is being used for key public policy decisions. Transparency is yet another fallout in research despite a transparency regime having come into being for over a decade (since 2005) in the country.

In the past 50 years, a shift has been evident in the sensitivities and priorities of the role and relevance of research in public policies, governance, and in the electoral politics of the country. Between 1950 and 1975, the leaders and the government were anxious to use research for public policies and nation building. The government thus went all-out to establish research establishments and generate data much beyond the census data and even prompted and encouraged independent sources so that research and data would be reliable, validated, and verified and would offers insights concerning national priorities and for motivational endeavours. How else would Dr Lakdawala have been allowed to start the Centre for Monitoring Indian Economy (CMIE) from outside the government and as an independent outfit?

But with democracy becoming focussed on electoral politics and in a combative political atmosphere, the period of 1980–2000 saw a rise of sponsored and supportive research. Foreign research agencies entered the Indian scene, and advertising and public relations became their collaborators, because of which research acquired commercial orientation and support.

But the period of 2000–2020 has seen public opinion being

manufactured to an extent that clearly suggests that research data can be and has been made subservient to political interests and compulsions of the day. It is an option available to the government or the party in power.

Dr Yoginder K. Alagh is a well-reputed, seasoned economist of the country with no political affiliations. He has held numerous positions including as a member of the Planning Commission, Union Minister and has also been the founder of many institutions, including Gujarat Area Development Agency. His research made him pursue agro-climatic zones approach that justified the National Sample Survey as a globally respected and reliable sample survey agency for the size of sample, methodology, and design. NSS is the world's 'most reputed statistician'.[6] At the height of controversy in 2018-19, he called for certain subject areas to be kept away from politics, particularly data, statistics, and research.

Data Doctoring and Manipulation

Data manipulation of all kinds happens all the time, particularly by those who are engaged in persuading or influencing and controlling one or the other section of people. The motivations may differ from situation to situation. It happens in the government, marketing corporations, in foreign affairs, in public services, and even in the academics. The general impression that political leaders and the governments manipulate or misuse research, data, or statistics is true. In fact, an analysis will show that corporates engaged in consumer services, in particular, use research findings favourably, unconcerned of the manoeuvring involved. This happens in different ways and at different points or stages of research. This could be at the time of research design itself or in the very conceptualising or defining of the cause, interpretation of data, or in leveraging the data bases. The manipulation could involve not meeting methodological standards such as sample size or primary source of response or by not adhering to required practices and standards. Data or research misuse may be wilful, dishonest, accidental, partisan or political, biased, or the result of ignorance, or any combination of all these. Political leaders and the governments tend to engage in this as part of a strategy. Deployment of contradictory research or surveys to divert attention or diffuse the situation is another way that governments are tempted to indulge in. Using different time-points as the baseline or reference points (for GDP, unemployment, crime rate, etc.) can change how figures are seen or interpreted.

> Sensitivity to these various possibilities make all the difference in minimising distortion. Depending on the motivation, the data, research, or its findings may be taken out of context. But stakeholders developing an understanding or becoming sensitive to these possibilities can help. Laws and policies against such manipulations or misuse of data are not always good enough to minimise the effects. Nevertheless, preventive measures must be put in place to minimise misuse at different levels. The more emotional the political scene and the more populistic public policies become, the more there is an urge to manipulate data and research.
>
> News media has its own way of managing research and statistics. Their innocence or ignorance or bias gets reflected in the way research findings are covered. Research studies and statistics from foreign agencies are provided better coverage in the media. News media is also involved in data plants, consciously or otherwise. They take to numbers and research to bolster fake news and plant certain content.
>
> The focus in this book is on social research in the context of public policies and the manipulation of data and research in the fields of market research or by corporates or in other contexts.

Manipulation or misuse of research is as old as research itself. Despite concerns and provisions for transparency in recent decades, misuse of data and research continues as if it is eternal. All governments, irrespective of their political structure and stature, have manipulated data at one time or other. The difference being in the degree and in the compulsion. The compulsion for manipulation may be personal for the leader, or it may be political in terms of the command and control, or there may be electoral compulsions or concerns regarding sustaining an image of good governance. Manipulation is not always political; in fact, manipulation of research is as old as persuasion or power politics. The advertising profession thrives on manipulating or exaggerating data and research and on using facts and figures as it suits the occasion.

Over my fifty years of research career, I have first-hand witnessed the advertising profession manipulating data. I have witnessed the governments doing it as well as international corporations, multinational agencies, and think-tanks. The difference between them is the extent or the compulsions, and the objective which may be personal, profit-based, political, or about control. I refer here to a few examples of manipulation of data and research.

Despite the circulation and reach of English news dailies being a fraction of that of Indian language dailies, advertisers and agencies were spending several times more of their advertising budgets on English media for years, and English dailies were being paid several times higher for their space. That was when the first National Readership Survey (NRS) sponsored by advertisers, advertising agencies, and publishers wanted to hide this fact from being included in the report by not providing that finding in the first-ever research. As a researcher, I realised that this was an important finding that demolished a myth. I made the concerned ministry ask for the findings based on a presentation I gave at Sastri Bhavan Press Conference Hall, New Delhi, when that finding was a major talk of the town and could no longer can be hidden as the AAA and ISA wanted. That was how 'exclusive English readers' column was retained in the final report. This meant considerable loss for ad agencies, but it was a turning point in print media in India.

In the wake of the first NRS, a leading daily in Kerala did not like the idea of another local daily being shown close to its readership. It approached me in ORG to correct it by presenting certified circulation. When I refused to change the figures, they wanted a new research. When the field research was taken up after one year, I found from talks with my filed researchers on the phone that the results were somewhat one-sided. Closer scrutiny of the feedback showed that the sponsor had got hold of sample frames of households and started distributing their newspaper to these households without them subscribing so that the survey would show them to be on top. It was a challenge to the research agency to either go along with the sponsor, as it often happens, or take the challenge and call off the survey and lose a couple of lakhs of rupees that they had already spend. It would have been a scandal involving an influential leader of the industry.

In a parliament debate in 1973, the prime minister described certain newspapers as 'Jute Press' (with double meaning) and denied their argument that newspapers were suffering from increasing losses but agreed to reconsider if she found them truly to be in need of government support. As a follow-up, the government appointed a one-person committee with Professor Bhabatosh Datta, a senior economist of Calcutta's Presidency College. Prof. Datta had sent a pro forma to leading newspaper establishments requesting them to fill it. After receiving only three responses despite sending three reminders, he expressed his inability to complete this report and resigned. At that point, the concerned Minister, Mr I.K. Gujral, requested me to help. That was when I studied newspaper economics of over a hundred newspapers. Based on this, the prime minster told the Parliament that newspapers were showing losses by diverting revenue to their other businesses. This agency also reminded that conflict of 'interest' could be an undercurrent for some problems. Only a research could trace and reveal such phenomena.

The World Bank used to conduct 'cost of living index' surveys in sampled countries to determine their lending policies. They would prepare a questionnaire and administer it through a local agency. In the later 1970s, the Indian Statistical Institute was entrusted with this job, who in turn sought ORG's help for field work. After having a discussion with the professor concerned at ISI, I realised that many questions in that format were either irrelevant for India or misleading in the name of uniformity. I took a stand that such surveys must justify subjective policies as they cannot truly reflect the living standards or the cost of living. As a researcher, I expressed my reservation and also suggested changes in the questions, such as the size of rice consumed, whether shoes had laces or not, and whether they received daily newspapers.

Recently, the government was unhappy with the findings of a specialist agency responsible for determining the unemployment rate and even tried to side-line those findings. But when a newspaper leaked this report, they wanted to diffuse the public controversy by floating another research by an industry body that presented contrary data by using new categories for employment and unemployment. This was not the first time that a government had sought such a measure to diffuse uncomfortable data. Earlier, I had seen this happen with independent data on child labour and shortage of shelter or housing in the country.

In the wake of the 1998 Asiad Games, the government realised the role of stadia in encouraging games and sports and took to district-level Initiatives. The HRD Ministry wanted to evaluate this and called for bids from researchers. CMS' study presented certain drawbacks in the scheme and showed how the stadia were being misused and how local enthusiastic youth were going through hardships in the local stadia as well as well included suggestions to correct the problem. The Ministry was sour with the report and shelved it, ensuring that nothing of its findings were talked about.

A decade later, another Ministry acted in similar fashion. This time the research was for another excellent initiative of the government of the time, the Swacch Bharat scheme. The research involved was country-wide and comprehensive, involving households and organisations. This unprecedented research, which was completed in record time and yet with remarkable transparency and the involvement of the entire network of states was also shelved after huge money and effort had gone into it.

I have seen and personally experienced the vitiating effects of attempts by governments as well as multinational outfits to sideline research when it is does not produce the results that will support their pre-decided agendas.

I have also seen around the same time how the Bihar state government adopted a CMS research (2010–12, sponsored by UNICEF) findings for important initiatives concerning poverty alleviation and how a public policy benefited from an independent research.

Leaders in every regime over the last couple of decades have cleverly used—or misused—research and data to suit their political goals. Two classic examples for how research was used by two political leaders in power were seen in 2019. One leader—Prime Minister Modi seeking re-election at the Centre—used data and findings, both from within his government and outside, strategically and did not depend on any single research or one *type* of research. The other leader, an incumbent chief minister—Chandrababu Naidu of Andhra Pradesh—used research in a blinkered way, relying exclusively on machine mode (IVR). The result was as could be expected. The political leader who relied on checks and balances and used data from different sources and methodologies—thus taking no chances—won handsomely, while the other leader, who was complacent and relied only on his own machine-mode set up, failed miserably. Knowing the limits of research and limitations of methodologies is as important as knowing the potential of research.

Concerns of Economists and Social Scientists

Prominent economists and social scientists alleged on 14 March 2019that there was political interference by government in statistical data. In an unprecedented way, a group of 108 Indian and foreign economists and social scientists from premier institutions of considerable standings raised concerns over 'political interference' using statistics and statistical system. They alleged that, 'any numbers that cast doubt on the government's achievements seem to get revised or suppressed'.

Those who raised such concerns include senior professors from IIMs, scientific bodies, and premier academic institutes of the country. They maintained that access to public statistics, their integrity, and institutional independence is critical if users are to have confidence that data has 'not been manipulated for political purposes' and that 'political systems should be seen hands off of the data'.[7]

In their public statement, these economists and social scientists described three specific cases in the previous one year. These include revisions in the uncomfortable or politically unfavourable figures. As the government wanted to show significantly faster economic growth compared to the previous political regime, they intervened in the system. The second was in January 2019, when the estimate of GDP growth rate for 2015–17 was revised. The third instance concerned the first country-wide employment periodic labour force survey conducted by the National Sample Survey Office (NSSO). This report was delayed and deferred from being released, which prompted the resignation of the acting chairman of SNC and its member. That report, published in the Business India daily, showed that unemployment had risen to a 45-year high of over 6% in 2017–18. The academicians stated that, by casting aspirations, the national and global reputation of India's statistical bodies is at stake. They further stated that statistical integrity is crucial for generating data fed into economic policy-making and makes public discourse irrational.

Closer to the 2019 national elections, even Micro Units Development and Refinance Agency (MUDRA) job survey data was put in deep-freeze according to an Indian Express headline of 15 March 2019. The release of this report was deferred under the pretext that some anomalies were found in the methodology used by the Labour Bureau of the Labour Ministry in arriving at the findings. MUDRA was a much-hyped scheme by the ruling party as a job creator. A month earlier, the government had junked the NSSO report on unemployment, and it was obvious that the government was looking for 'supportive data' and anything otherwise was being deferred in view of the impending national election.[8]

These four examples and the way the findings of these were either fudged or deferred and faulted for their methodology shows the intensity of the political fight. This shows that parties and the government succumb to political and electoral compulsions of influencing voters, unconcerned of the impact on the credibility of statistical institutes and systems of the country. The allegation was that research and surveys were viewed as 'handy' for influencing poll campaign. Such political interference hurts official data's credibility, autonomy of statistical bodies, and spreads doubt about field surveys. Primary research too gets ignored and research discipline itself loses its credibility. Any such manipulation of data, surveys, and research signals a larger malice in the fundamentals of the democratic state.

Around this time, two professionals with high credentials too had called for 'credible data' and suggested 'impartial study of data', cautioning about doubts on the accuracy of the country's economic data. The former finance secretary and well-regarded public servant, Dr Vijay Kelkar, and the former Governor of Reserve Bank of India Dr Raghuram Rajan had said that it is imperative that 'the world should not think that in India numbers are being manipulated'. Dr Kelkar even suggested autonomous constitutional status for the NSC in the lines of the Election Commission of India. They also called for establishing 'an impartial and independent body to look into key indicators that determine the health of the economy'. Another group of 46 economists and public policy experts too had echoed the concerns along similar lines.[9]

Earlier, in January 2019, the government had revised its forecast for GDP growth for 2017–18 to 7.2% from the earlier estimate of 6.7%. It also revised the actual growth rate for 2016–17 to 8.2% from the 7.1% estimated earlier. These changes in forecast were not questioned immediately then. But considering what happened in the following months, the forecasts on GDP lost credibility.[10]

The revisions made by the Ministry of Statistics and Programme Implementation in its First Revised Estimates of National Income, Consumption Expenditure, Saving and Capital Formation for 2017–18 were criticised by economists, who said that the numbers did not match with the ground realities. This is especially the case in the demonetisation year of 2016–17, which shows a strong growth in sectors that were widely agreed to have been badly hit by the exercise.

Data Doctoring, Playing with Fire

At the height of controversy (April–August 2019) on CSSO's (then unreleased) report on employment and unemployment rate, some trends became obvious. These trends were indicative of the significance governments tend to give to data and research. This controversy became political at the cost of basic issues and ground realities. It was not only in the parliament but all over the public media. The rivalry between the ruling party and the opposition parties on this controversy remained on-going and became a concern among professionals even during the 2019 national elections.

What does this all indicate?

First, although the government formally commits to the independence of research, it seeks for and prefers supportive research. Second, independence of data and research is not viewed as a virtue but as a problem—depending on whether it is supportive of the government of the day or not. Third, credibility of research agencies and premier institutions of decades is being destabilised and exposed, so that their capabilities are undermined and even questioned. Fourth, the government officials too tend to prefer supportive data for their pet policies. Fifth, a criterion that determines the stature of a research or its report is whether it can be 'used' in an electoral context. Sixth, political interests matter more than performance criteria and efficiencies in the implementation of the schemes or the credibility of an institution or even of the economy.

On 20 July 2018, responding to a no-confidence motion in the Lok Sabha, the Prime Minister told the House that as people are being misled regarding the 'unemployment rate' in the country, the government would now shift to monthly data on 'employment'. Not only was there no arrangement for such monthly reporting on employment, but the 50-year-old credible system was discredited by deferring the release of the report even after the NSC had already endorsed it for release. Regarding that report coming to public attention in the Business Standard, the NITI Aayog chief functionary who otherwise was not in the picture for bringing out these reports of NSSO, came out claiming that the report was not 'approved' to be released to the public. But, with the controversy getting intensified, another professional functionary of NITI Aayog tried to question the credibility of NSSO. Going beyond its mandate, the NITI Aayog official stated that they themselves will conduct the survey so that, 'it will bring out what is expected'. As NITI Aayog intervention and its justification for deferring the CSO report did not end the controversy, two ministers who had no expertise also tried to justify, albeit unsuccessfully. The power of data is such that it can shake a government's credibility, even temporarily. This episode of 2018–19 remind us of the necessity of independence of data or of the research agency and that government should not intervene in the functioning of agencies responsible. Two ministers, the Minister for Employment & Labour and the Minister for Statistics, both failed to explain and justify the reasons for deferring the NSSO's report or of its implications. The government using new surveys and creating new agencies for coming up with supportive data may be a temporary solution but such a view dents the credibility of the country's statistical system and harms the standing of the government. But all of this did not halt the officials and the ministers from such modelling.

As if in a climax, on 31 May 2019, after the poll results were out, the government accepted that unemployment in the country was at a 45-year high, as indicated in the NSO report a few months earlier.[11]

The government was in a denial mode prior to the polls toward the end of May 2019 regarding the decline in the employment rate. But soon after the election, the Economic Advisory Council, NITI Aayog, and RBI admitted a slowdown. The Finance Ministry had made major changes soon after the Budget in July 2019. What more is required to show that electoral compulsions make the government over-claim achievements based on data by the organised sector, when the criticality of unorganised sector and its reliability is far more critical. The estimation methodology involved is what must be looked into (but is ignored). Instead of validating the growth estimates, the government indulged in repeated fallacious claims. This was a good example to indicate what happens when there is no transparency in the data collection and when electoral compulsions dominate research methodologies.[12] This 2019 episode also points to how multiple agencies (Economic Survey, RBI, IMF, Budget, and agencies like ADB) too fall into trap of government data in haste.

Dodgy Data: Fudging data is like a contagious disease. Once one gets into it, it is difficult to get out of the temptation. Even more so when it is a political compulsion. But when the government does this at the insistence of political leadership, it has dangerous implications. Fudging, dodging, and any manipulation of basic facts concerning vitals of the economy or social system has long-term consequences that last beyond political tenures and electoral compulsions. And yet, such instances are increasing, regardless of the public outcry. Recent proliferation and corporatisation of news media, spread of social media, and communication networks have made tinkering of data easier and more tempting. With competing electoral players, it is becoming a compulsion of political parties, particularly those in power, to lure voters with illusionary benefits. This has become a menace to democratic fundamentals. Enlightened and active citizenry and independent bodies are the best bet for saving or safeguarding the economies from such threats and temptations. Even news media can play the role of a watchdog. The recent happenings in India are good examples for a case study of the phenomena to prevent data dodging or to cope with it more honestly.

But this is not a recent phenomenon as is made out sometimes by news media. It is not to do with any one individual leader. One could also say that the tendency for manipulating or twisting facts and data is perhaps not limited to India. It is a global phenomenon. Successive governments in India have been doing this and have even avoided empowering research institutions engaged in putting together vital statistics of the economy, democracy, and development as a professional exercise in the larger and long-term interests of the country.

Data disowning or 'moderation' is also not new. When governments tend to claim achievements and take up schemes in the name of allusive welfare or poverty eradication, data and research tend to become manipulative. The 'Garibi Hatao' slogan (1971) on the eve of elections could be traced to show the origins of exaggerated outlook of data. In 1973, on the eve of the fifth Five-year Plan finalisation, eminent economist member of the Planning Commission, Dr R.S. Minhas, resigned over differences on the misuse of data to present a rosy picture of the economy and poverty numbers. The Planning Commission itself had argued then that results of the surveys were not the best judge of the impact of government policies. That was why the Rangarajan Committee recommended way back in 2001 to create a permanent and statutory National Statistical Commission. In 2004, National Health Survey findings were withheld as they showed high infant mortality. In 2011, the Economic and Political Weekly editorially pointed out that the government was dismissing its own data. Even some tables of 2011 National Census were deferred or delayed. These are only a few examples.

Prime Minister Modi has been reiterating poverty eradication by 2022–23 and doubling of farmers' income. This is good. But is the percent of population below poverty increasing or declining? How do we know? What is the basis and source? Since after 2011–12, no authentic national survey has been conducted, so claiming any number is easy.

In an affidavit to the Supreme Court, the Planning Commission stated that there were 40.74 crore 'poor' people in the country based on Rs 32 per day expenditure for urban areas and Rs 26 in rural areas as the cut-off criteria for poverty. In 2014, Dr C Rangarajan Committee report to the government suggested Rs 47 in urban and Rs 32 in rural as cut-offs and thus claimed that there were 36.3 crore poor people living below the poverty line in the country.[13] But according UNDP report on poverty released in July 2019, 36.9 crore were still below the poverty line (although it claimed that 27.1 crore people were lifted out of poverty between 2006 and 2016). Thus there were three different estimates in media.[14]

NITI Aayog's task force on assessing poverty, with its Vice President Arvind Panagariya as the chair, submitted the report in July 2016 with suggestions on measuring poverty. Three years later, as of September 2019, this report was not considered. In the meanwhile, the concerned union minister announced in the Parliament in July 2019 that the government was going to conduct a 'fresh survey' to determine the numbers below poverty level in the country. Was that to facilitate the claim that the Mudra Scheme (2016) had improved income levels and had lifted many more above poverty level as loans were given under this scheme to 19.24 crore people? But the claim that Rs 25,000, the average loan given under this scheme, offers sustainable productive occupation was not substantiated by any independent research. This was mainly to show that a good number of people below poverty level were provided employment. In the meanwhile, the CSO report had indicated that unemployment was decreasing. A third party field research would have helped avoid such a controversy. Around the time, All India Manufacture Survey for 2014–15 showed that 43% jobs were down in trade, 32% down in small-scale industries, and 35% down in medium industries.

On being questioned about the job loss indicated by CSO (on 29 August 2019), Finance Minister Sitharaman said on 29 August 2019 that the 'country's official jobs data always concentrated on the formal sector only' and that 'Indian informal sector employment has not been appropriately or exhaustively documented'. She even said that NSSO talks about formal sector despite the informal sector being where the majority of employment is. No one can deny her.[15]

Earlier, the government had closed the Labour Bureau in Shimla under the Ministry of Labour which provides updates on organised sector jobs. In 2005, an autonomous National Statistical Commission was given overall responsibility to validate data (and approve reports before releasing to public). The next government diluted this responsibility and its autonomous stature by bringing an ex-officio from NITI Aayog on board and ensured that no data that conflicted with the interests of the party in power was put out.

Political leaders prefer flexibility of data and even in the eligibility criteria. Unfavourable data and research can be found in any period, irrespective of the ruling party. That is when leaders in powerful positions in the government display their wisdom and foresight. Some face the situation squarely and take corrective measures, while others ignore or suppress the signals from the data and devote all their energies in defending their image.

Economist Pronab Sen, the first Chief Statistician of India, acted as the functional and technical head of the NSS in India, as well as Secretary of the Ministry of Statistics & Programme Implementation, Government of India (2007–2010). In an interview, Pronab Sen observed, 'by and large, the political system at the Centre has not interfered very much. There are pressures. Not to change the data, but sometimes…just to suppress or delay release. That pressure does exist. So the data we get is the best statisticians can get out of the system. Nevertheless, it was felt that there needs to be some distance between the government and the statistical system. For ensuring that the National Statistical Commission (NSC) was created. The NSC is the buffer. In States, things are not as good. There is fair amount of evidence of data manipulation, and it is quite understandable. There the issue goes beyond political imagery. Remember, a lot of the transfer of funds from the Centre to the States is dependent on the data, like school enrolment, and so on; all allocations are driven by the data. Now when that happens, there is a very strong incentive with state governments to fiddle with the data—there is good, genuine economic logic. One doesn't blame them. In Agriculture data, it happens all the time, but the final data will usually be okay, but states would say, we are having a drought.'

Sen also said, 'As things are changing fast, keeping data robust is a task. But the problem is we don't measure a lot of things, and for what we do, the frequency is not good enough.' Sen said this in an interview in the context of 108 economists and social scientists having cited in March 2019 three specific instances of the government's interference and manipulation of data which had put the very credibility of Indian statistical bodies at stake. These three instances concerned the country's economic growth rate, GDP growth rate, and differing labour force survey results.[16]

Pronab Sen, who was also Chairman of the National Statistical Commission, is in the best position to sum up the situation at the end of 2019. In an interview to *Mint*, in December 2019, Sen summed up that 'When statistical system is throwing up bad news, the government either suppresses it or tries to discredit it. It impacts not only the credibility but also the morale of the statistical system.' Despite such repeated observations by independent authoritative voices like Pronab Sen's over the last couple of years, there has been no effort to gear up the machinery for a desegregated and credible statistical system at the national level. The situation in the states has not been any better.

The proposed National Register of Citizens (NRC), for example, is likely not only to create new insecurity in a large section of the Indian people, but also result in a fundamental credibility crisis regarding statistics and data. Performance shortfalls, pressures, and biases in the massive nation-wide exercise will bring into doubt and the country's statistical system.

Data Crisis 2018–19 or Crisis in Data?

The fact that data has become politicised has been glaringly evident in recent years with deferring, delaying, or discrediting of data sources and research methodology. But it isn't as if such manipulation is a recent phenomenon. A trend in that direction has been brewing for years with uncertainties in political scene, increased centralisation, and personality-centred politics. In this process, the agencies that were created to ensure reliable or authentic data and research are being diluted, discredited, or side-lined. But this episode also showcases the maturity of the Indian system. Once the electoral compulsions were over, our institutions with committed professionals are usually quick to restore honours.

As general elections approach, governments become more sensitive to data. Political leaders look for figures, findings, and research that support their claims, promises, and prepositions, and anything else has to be suppressed or side-lined, informally or even formally. This political culture is what we need to address with lasting correctives.

Data controversies do not speak well of the political leadership and regimes and may even signal crisis in credibility. On some issues, any numbers that the government comes up with are not taken seriously by the larger public. For example, it may be that the sources for compiling such data are neither independent nor is the methodology transparent. Such a situation suits the immediate political compulsions to get over the poll-time promises or claims. It further indicates a deeper disregard for research. Governments keep announcing targeted schemes for which no desegregated data on implementation can be provided. Unverified administrative data is used to support populist programmes and to publicise welfare schemes as needed.

'Hard facts' are often used by those in power and outside to justify their promises and performance claims. Verifiable evidence that can be validated transparently and independently is absolutely essential for any finding to be credibly accepted as 'hard fact'. Most governments of a controlling nature, however, do not bother with, or have no time or regard for, rigour and transparency. They expect whatever they come out with to be viewed and accepted as hard fact even when there is no expert or independent assessment and validation of the data.

Mahesh Vyas, CEO of Centre for Monitoring Indian Economy (CMIE), an independent professional body founded by Dr Lakdawala, an eminent economist with national concerns, has proved over the past six decades how important it is for a complex country like India to look for independent source regarding fundamental issues and trends concerning factors such as jobs, inflation, growth, and savings. But when things do not go in their favour, the governments, or the leaders in power, find ways to denigrate and raise doubts. This was stated by Mahesh Vyas a week after the controversy on CSO's report on unemployment in 2018–19.

Inconsistent and Unreliable Data—What Are the Compulsions?

During 2015–18, there were series of instances of data being deferred or when data had become contentious. Cumulative effect of a series of doubts on GDP figure, on employment numbers, and on data on suicides in the country is bound to erode the credibility of 'official data'. Some such examples are given below.

1. National Crime Research Bureau (NCRB): The NCRB compiles and publishes information on crimes in India. Its annual report 'Crime in India', in fact, is the only source on different types of crimes that are committed in India. The quantitative data given in its annual report is a treasure for social researchers and academics to pursue follow-up research. The news media has been reporting the highlights of these annual reports promptly.

To a question in the Parliament on 2 July 2019, the minister concerned replied to a question that although NCRB reports are available till the year 2016, such published data was not available for 2017, 2018, and 2019. The 2015 report was a telling story of how suicide count varied among different states. Because Maharashtra was heading for Assembly elections in 2020, the 2015 report received attention as the suicide rate in Maharashtra was the highest in 2015 with 16,970 reported suicides against the country's 13,36,623.[17]

The NCRB released its 2017 report in October 2019, but left out the data on mob lynching, killings ordered by khap panchayats and killings on religious grounds. The government claimed that data on such crimes was not included as it was 'unreliable'.[18] And yet, at the same time, two entirely new and rather vague categories of offences were added—'offences against the state' and 'crime committed by anti-national elements'—and it was claimed that these had increased by 30% since 2016.

Interestingly, the Union Ministry of Home Affairs, whose responsibility it is to bring out these reports, had written to West Bengal Government with crime figures for 2016, 2017, and 2018, showing that crime rate in West Bengal had been increasing. This shows how the government uses its own research reports as it suits their political interests, going to the extent of not bringing out the report. The political rivalry (2018–20) between the ruling party at the Union and in the State of West Bengal had been a priority for the government which dictated the Ministry to not publish the annual report. The 2015 report clubbed 'accidental deaths' and 'suicide', which are two distinct phenomena. This bluff and trickery was to deflect attention from the increasing rate of suicides in the country, particularly in some states like Maharashtra. This is what research faculties in academics should have taken up for a follow-up research so that the phenomena of suicides would have received due attention in public policies. Particularly because 66% of suicides were of individuals between 18 and 45 years of age. If one-third of the suicides are committed by those between 18 and 30 years of age, how can this issue not be included in a larger debate? Further research could have made this issue a national agenda.

2. Monthly FDI (Foreign Direct Investment) reports were deferred for months (until April–May 2019). Normally, this report is released to ensure that it is prominently covered in the news. In May 2019, the FDI figures were put out as having gone up, but marginally. Instead of sharing with stakeholders as to why FDI flow was not kept up, the government deferred the report itself as elections were approaching and poll campaign was on. Only after the poll was over in April 2019 were the FDI figures available formally.

3. Were inflation figures fiddled with? It is possible that these figures were altered by removing one or other item in the food basket. Instead of focusing on measures like market trends, implementing price control provisions, and announcing such initiatives, the government tried to moderate the ground figures, without indicating that the composition was changed even for that round.

4. Unemployment rate: Since there was traditionally no data available from employment exchanges across the country, the main source unemployment figures in the country was what the government itself put out from its direct sources, like the National Sample Survey Office (NSSO), which was a reasonably reliable source, but only as long as the governments and departments using its research believed in the integrity of research data. The unemployment rates articulated by leaders of the ruling party between 2011-12 and 2017-18, for instance, were routinely adjusted and manipulated as an occasion or campaign demanded. With such disregard for the integrity of the important research done by entities like the NSSO, it is not surprising that in 2019 the NSSO was effectively done away with—it was merged with the Central Statistics Office (CSO) to form the National Statistical Office (NSO).

5. Farmer Suicides: The number of farmer suicides across the country are no longer being indicated formally since 2016. The onus for compiling the farmers' suicide rate is on the state agriculture departments. The Union Government is expected to develop initiatives to ensure reliable numbers. Farmers' suicide is not a recent phenomenon. It signals the rising unrest in the farming sector. But political parties have been busy accusing each other. Farmers' suicide figures are no longer talked about because official data has been mixed with other suicides. NCRB reported 'suicides' in general and then mixed the number with 'accidental deaths'. Even the latest (2019) report by NCRB have not been given. In the meanwhile, political parties and news media have used different numbers depending on their political leanings. On 27 November 2019, a question was asked in the Rajya Sabha as to why the government had withheld separate figures for farmer suicides and the reasons for their suicide. Despite the fact that farmer distress has been widespread, despite agitations and demands for relief and action, the government has made no effort to obtain diversified data on farmer suicides. In the absence of this data, the government's promises and assurances to farmers can have no meaning. How will it address a problem that it is not even willing to acknowledge and assess?

This is the latest example of what it means to not have a reliable database, even on the number of farmers in every state. As a result, for example, in 2019–20, the government could not spend one-third of the funds allocated for the much publicised 'PM Kisan Samman Nidhi Yojana' of Rs 75,000 crores. And yet, the government announced that they had quelled farmers' anger before the 2019 poll.[19]

6. Gross Domestic Productivity (GDP) is widely considered as the yardstick for economic status and the growth of a country. GDP figures are **revised** as often as within a week. During 2015–18, the GDP figure lost its sanctity and seriousness except in pink papers and for some TV channels because the growth figures were so often changed by international government agencies, often without credibly explaining the logic behind it.

7. Job Survey: Just before the campaign picked up for the 2019 polls, the Mudra job survey data was put on deep freeze, as noted by *The Indian Express* on 14 March 2019. This was because one of the claims often repeated in the campaign was how Mudra initiative had changed the employment scenario in the country for good.[20]

8. In 2015, the Central Statistical Organisation made two changes—for compulsions we can only guess at. It would appear that the government of the time felt that GDP in the normal course was not reflecting what they wanted to claim, which was a much higher growth rate of economy. Thus, they first changed the baseline from 2004–05 to 2011–12 and then revised the methodology of arriving at the GDP. With that, the GDP for the year 2015–16 became 7.4% instead of 5.5%, thus allowing the government to claim that it had achieved growth surpassing that of China. The government then showed 8.2% growth for 2016–17, in order to claim that during the year of demonetisation the GDP had, in fact, increased. This they did by avoiding the earlier estimates of three years.

On 30 May 2019, just after the 2019 elections were over, the government admitted that in the January–March quarter of 2018–19, the economy had expanded at its lowest pace in 18 quarters, but said that it had still clocked around 6% growth. But then the government's own first term Chief Economic Adviser, Arvind Subramanian, declared on 10 June 2019 that the economy had in fact grown by only 4.5% between 2011–12 and 2016–17—thus contradicting the NDA government's claim of 7.4% growth in 2015–16 and 8.2% growth the following year! Writing in the journal of Harvard University, Subramaniam claimed that there had been miscalculations because 'India changed its data sources and methodology for estimating real GDP for the period since 2011–12, and it was an over-estimate'.[21]

9. No official data on poverty in India are available after 2011–12. Anything given for the subsequent year was projection based on initiatives like MUDRA loan. Poverty was reduced from 268 million in 2011–12 to less than 50 million in 2017–18, with claims that it will come down to 40 million by 2019. This figure was put out often during the three months before the election to justify the achievement claims of the government.

10. PDS claims: Prior to the poll campaign, the government claimed that 2.71 crore 'fake ration cards' had been weeded out, but there was no indication of decline in the off-take of PDS. Because the numbers claimed are that of the states, whereas that of PDS is by the Union Government. The link between the number of ration cards and PDS allocation indicates conflicting figures. This suits political leaders who want to claim the occasion for a political advantage.

11. Promise of doubling farmers income by 2022–23 or even by 2023–24. Thus may be a valid target. But, it should not become part of promise-achievement claim campaign. Particularly when farmers have been agitating against the government's alleged insensitivity. Despite there not being much difference on ground even after three years of that promise, the government has not revised its target.

On 9 September 2019, Prime Minister Modi announced at a UN convention in Noida that the government was focussing on Zero Budget Natural Farming (ZBNF) to make farming 'zero-budget' based. This was despite the fact that a 650-member farm scientists' think-tank involving the senior-most farm scientists of the country stated that the idea was not based on verifiable data or authenticated results from any experiment for it to be considered feasible. They also wrote to the prime minister informing him of the same and indicated that this idea meant that high yielding varieties that had been developed earlier in the country which had trebled India's rice production and increased wheat production by eight times were useless.[22] Why then did the prime minister formally announce what the finance minister hinted at in the 2019–20 budget? Was it part of a strategy of doubling farmers' incomes?

12. Slowdown in consumer expenditure. There is yet again a repetition of what happened with the survey on unemployment status early in 2018–19 of withholding 'adverse' data. In the wake of withholding (on 15 November 2019) NSS report for 75th round that average monthly per capita consumer expenditure has declined, attributing data discrepancies, 200 economists and scholars across the world addressed a letter to the government. The letter advised the government 'to identify sources of and reduce these discrepancies' by making the data public instead of withholding it. This letter by 200 economists further noted that 'it is of fundamental importance for the nation that statistical institutions are kept independent of political interference and are allowed to release all data independently'. The signatories included Pronab Sen, former Chief Statistician of India.[23] The consumption index could be moderated by featuring some indicators in the basket. To get such trends, NITI Aayog plays an active role by prompting others to come up with convenient figures. The idea of ensuring that data is not tied to any specific expert or independent institution dents confidence in it. This was ignored. But agencies, with political appointees at their head, have a tendency to change these figures as it suits them. There will be data at different points with different numbers without explanation and transparency. This index is not a monopoly of any one leader or one party or limited to recent years.

13. Number of Tax payers: After denotification of notes of higher denomination, the government wanted to claim that the number of tax payers in the country had increased significantly. It was claimed on a formal occasion of Independence Day that the number of tax payers was 56 lakhs. But in a written answer in the Parliament, this number was stated to be 33 lakhs. At the same time, the Economic Survey for 2016–17 showed that the number of tax payers increased by 5.4 lakhs.[24] The Board of Direct Taxes had indicated that for 2013–14, tax payers increased by 11.6%. But the growth rate in tax payer numbers for the next two years was only 5%. How can there be such a significant variation?

It is obvious that in such times of frequent data changes, confusion with contradictory or conflicting numbers sways the markets. By taking to such tactics in an era of transparency, it is not only the political leaders who lose credibility but even the institutions responsible for compiling such data on an ongoing basis. This then has a cascading effect on other linked or related data. That is, when governments or leaders tend to make more errors to cover up one error to claim achievements or debunk rumours.

Political leaders prefer flexibility of figures in percentages, even more when they are in power. It gives them an opportunity to justify claims and promise as it suits them, and they can change this data as and when they want. What other rational explanation justifies playing with data? When instances of different versions are there at different times with different numbers and claims, it becomes a 'bubble' of the economy and can even lend to a crisis in data and a setback (even temporary) in the development course of the country.

With frequent changes in political parties in power and even of coalition of parties coming together, better sense prevailed in 2000 when the statistical system became a commission with autonomy. But even after the constitution of the National Statistical Commission in 2004–05, it never functioned autonomously. This showed that such status should have legislative backup. But the 2008 Bill to empower NSSO with autonomy did not go through or was allowed to lapse silently. As anticipated by Mahanalobis 70 years ago, 'overt government interference in the functioning of official statistical agencies' has been off and on. But it has been more on the rise and has been more overt.

The recent developments after 2015 remind once again of the urgency for depoliticising statistical apparatus and safeguarding its autonomy and independence without ambiguities. Also, clarity and transparency in the responsibilities of statistical and research outfits need to be more evident. With an increased grip of political parties on governance, popularity mania dominating public policies, and electoral compulsions becoming an all-out priority of political leaders, such independence of concerned agencies is even more desirable. Data gaps, limitations in estimates, and error margins should always be presented along with or before putting out the data, not after. There needs to be adequate debate about any changes in the methodology of estimation and analysis. The importance of data and its credibility should first be understood by the stakeholder. Institutions should be empowered, arrangements should be transparent, and changes as and when should be shared before and not after. These aspects should not depend on which party is in the government or who the prime minister is or electoral promises or achievement claims.

Voter lists—Data Manipulation: Politicians remind themselves of the significance of data and research as elections approach closer. The interest is not only in demographic aspects but also in the behavioural and aspirational aspect of voters.

In 2018–2019, there were unprecedented controversies concerning voter registration (and deregistration) for the 2019 polls. This was not an isolated incident. It was a glaring phenomenon in two states. The widespread controversy was that either a large number of (non-existing) names were added as voters or a large number of names already on the voter list were removed, closer to polling data. With voter lists available online, it has become easy to track and trace the names of people polling at every booth. The opposing parties had lined up at the Election Commission of India (ECI), New Delhi, and in the State capitals, with complaints that those who were in their favour were being added by a party or names of those who were likely to vote against them were being removed. Such allegations and counter-allegations were submitted to the ECI.

With increased competitiveness between parties and victories or losses of parties becoming narrow or marginal, there is a newfound realisation that every vote matters. This has led to two developments: parties and candidates conducting field surveys anonymously among voters to ascertain their voting intentions or preferences and adding or deleting voters' names based on that information.

Telangana Model: Form-6 is for registering new voters, and Form-7 is for applying to remove a name of a voter on certain grounds. This Form-7 can be submitted by a third-party. And both forms can be submitted online. Political parties had explored both, whichever suits them. The Telangana Assembly Poll of 2018 had left a tempting model to score better where 18 lakhs names were removed from the voters' list. Despite the High Court's intervention to examine these names, the state election officer took no action and apologised, only after the election results, and not for examining the way the names were removed. This is the extent to which political parties have decided to manage elections.

The second method is taking to big data analytics by parties with sophisticated tools and tool-kits to track voting intentions and accordingly determine voters' profiles until the last minute of polling. And all that without any transparency, and even clandestinely. There were also complaints that this data on voter profile was being linked to Aadhar IDs, which are central to welfare schemes.

The political war went to the extent that certain IT companies were raided and software experts arrested by the police. One of the allegations was that the software company of a particular party was in possession of government data. But such data could already easily be found online or accessed from various apps like DashBoard. Besides, several governments anyway use private company consultants for their data management.

Both, the party in power and the opposing party, accused each other of conspiring to influence or manipulate electoral outcome. The case of Andhra Pradesh is another example. As the state is full of IT wizards, in Hyderabad and outside the country, use of new technologies and application has been far more than ever before.

Shifting of loyalties from one party to another after elections has also lead to such poll manipulation allegation, thereby vitiating poll atmosphere by giving an impression that polls are not fair or free. Migration of people from one state to another or from one constituency to another has also caused provocations and accusations. All these recent (2019) developments pose new challenges for the objective use of data and research for public policy-making.

Misuse of online data: Instead of improving efficiencies and representative character of elections, online provisions have facilitated manipulation by middlemen. In no time, 5–10% of voters' names can be deprived of their right to vote, giving them no chance to protect and correct such fudging.

In Andhra Pradesh, according to the state election officer, of the 7.75 lac applications for voter registration, 1.48 lacs were found to be 'bogus'. And, on finding that these were online applications on Forms-7, criminal cases were filed against 45 of more than 250 complaints.

Databases for various public services are put online by most departments and are updated online for anyone to verify and ask for any changes including for address or number of children. Beneficiary databases are now public information.

What happened in March 2019 in Hyderabad data analytics company based on databases of Andhra Pradesh did not occur for the first time. It showed that there is an emerging electors scenario in the country with convergence of data services and sophisticated apps. These data sources include voter registers, Aadhar, voter identity, phone number, lifestyle, and bank account number. Most of these data are available commercially or in one or the other app of the government. Such open source data is linked to Aadhar, voting intentions, and 'beneficiary profile' for focussed persuasive campaigns.

Desegregated analyses of booth-wise voters lists by political parties is not a crime. It is part of political campaigns. But doing it glaringly, remotely, and on such a large scale is what caused ripples. In one Guntur district alone, for example, one lac voters were supposed to have applied to get their name removed from the voter list. Verification of these online requests cannot happen as fast without validating such requests.

These recent developments further indicate that parties are more concerned and preoccupied with manipulation of public opinion using technology to exploit much-needed numbers in the electoral constituencies. In that process, polls are becoming increasingly impersonal and have been reduced to numbers and persuasion, not concerns.

CHAPTER EIGHT

Need Is a Research Echo System?

The 2019 Union Budget apparently had the potential to become a landmark move towards boosting research initiatives in the country. The budget had provided for National Research Foundation (NRF) to integrate research efforts from various ministries to create an overall systemic research echo in the country. This foundation was expected to assimilate, promote, fund, and coordinate research efforts. This is expected to identify 'national priorities' and research programmes for funding in selected areas. The funds available with these Union Ministries were expected to be pooled into NRF. The idea of such a foundation was originally proposed by the prime minister's Science Technology and Innovation Committee and was also endorsed by the New Education Policy of 2019 drafted by Dr Kasturirangan's committee. This was expected to work as a course-correction with centralised funding that would promote quality and multi-disciplinary research across academics. This appears to have been developed in response to the fact that none of our universities stand in the global hierarchy on innovation or knowledge or research. This foundation was to be chaired by the prime minister. The thrust areas identified for the foundation were energy security, environment and climate change, health care technology, water resources, habitat, nanotechnology, and artificial intelligence.

While it is good that the government realised that such scientific climate must be inculcated and research in academics needs to be revived, the way NRF was outlined implies centralisation of research and giving control to the government. This means that the government would decide the very scope of research endeavours in the country in the guise of a roadmap for the country as well as the 'relevance' of topics. It is necessary to promote an independent research echo system that is not controlled by the government or is a directed research echo system. Can we expect a centralised research foundation under the chairmanships of the prime minister to promote innovations? Maybe it will take a couple of years to know whether such initiatives become a turning point for unleashing research potential or whether it further snubs academic initiatives. ICSSR is already part of the Ministry, and by converting a 70-year-old UGC under an Act into a Higher Education Commission of India (HECI), the funding function rests with the Ministry. The government can thus set the agenda and tenor of research in the country.

For research to be transformational, it cannot be centralised and be under the nose of the politically elected leader of the government. This initiative should not hinder DST, CSIR, HECI, (UGC), ICSSR, ICMR, and similar government bodies currently promoting research. It is crucial for these agencies to be revamped and liberated from bureaucratic clutches. As envisaged by the National Education Policy, the research foundation should help build research capabilities and a research culture across academics as well as the way the government departments avail research services. Scholars should not be deprived of intellectual property rights, for example. The idea of having 100 universities focusing on research by 2023 is not possible. How can they make a difference unless opportunities for research become uninhibited? There is already large infrastructure created in the country for research, development, and training by high-end institutes, research labs, centres, councils, etc. These need to be consolidated and revamped first, and their independence assured.

The country's research architecture includes institutes of the ministries; nodal agencies like ICSSR, UGC, HECI, and National Research Foundation; special interest research institutes such as the 26 tribal research institutes; or R&D bodies like the CSIR, Electronics, and telecom. There are, of course, premier bodies of the country like the Indian Institute of Science, Indian Statistical Institute, and Tata School of Social Sciences, as well as universities, the IIMs, IITs, think-tanks, civil society bodies, etc. that influence the research environment of the country. This research architecture should also include census operations, NSS data, PEO, and DMEO studies.

Research Institutes of Ministries

On the initiative of the Planning Commission, the earlier governments went about very systematically, first with think-tanks, next with sector-wise national bodies, and then with social science faculties in the universities. The next logical step towards promoting a research culture and logistics was for the ministries to promote research institutes as per their unique needs. This foresight ensured that such institutes become the early research and training hubs of many ministries. The seriousness in this pursuit was evident from the fact that these various institutes were set up as societies (instead of as government departments) but with continued support of the concerned ministry. However, outside experts or professionals were associated in the management committees of those institutes. Today, many of them have been established for 50 years. Instead of totally depending on government funding, they were expected to earn revenue from their services at least in 20 years. Most of those institutes, however, continue to depend on the government. A pertinent question then concerns their role, contribution, and the difference they make to justify their continuation.

In the initial years, these institutes did serve the ministries, in either putting together the relevant primary numbers or in appraising the concerns of the ministry. They also helped monitor the implementation of the ministry's schemes. Many of these institutes were active in the initial years in training the personnel engaged in the operations of the ministry and their units, either by offering full-time or short-term courses. But an analysis of these institutions in recent years show that they no longer relied on or engaged in any such role.

Almost two decades ago, I was requested to review at least six of these different institutes. I also served on the executive committees of as many institutes at one time or other a few years ago. Based on my reviews, I forewarned the respective ministries of how they were ignoring the institution or were treating them as an extension of the ministry's bureaucracy, and how some institutes had become redundant in the changed market scenario or were suffering from the lack of direction regarding their priorities. I found that the situation had become glaring with the change in the political regimes. In fact, every time there was a change in the minister or even a secretary of the ministry, some institutes ended up having different priorities. In some cases, the institute was even viewed as a dumping ground of unwanted officers or a place to sideline some officers of the ministry. There is also confusion at the policy level regarding the role of these institutes. Are these institutes expected to be earn major part of revenue from the market or are they expected to be dedicated to the ministry? Are they offering any service which is unique in the changed market scenario?

Today, there are more than 50 such institutes set up by various union ministries some fifty or more years ago with an enthusiasm to avail independent research support or as sounding boards on contentious public issues so that they could help the government take proactive initiatives. These institutes were expected to offer reliable feedback to the ministry as and when required. Some of these institutes were reviewed once or a few times over the decades but their accounts are audited annually, as required by the Accountant General of India. There is no evidence of any of the institutes undergoing any change in mandate. I suggested to more than two prime ministers to close down or restructure many of these institutes which have become redundant after the 'market' has become preferred, and the governments themselves have started preferring outside agencies, even foreign origin ones, for feedback, research, and even for assessing their public policies. These institutes, with only a couple of exceptions, no longer are part of a research environment that was initially envisioned.

It is high time that, as a part of less government and more governance, these research and training institutes are reviewed and repositioned or redeployed where necessary, particularly the social sector ones and the ones concerning socio-economic development tasks. It would be better if independent and public representatives, not from political parties, are involved in their managements so that the institutes are not bureaucratic.

Most Union Ministries have one or more institutions under them with a mandate to provide research and training support, to offer think-tank support, and be their database. Most of them continue to be funded fully or are 90% funded by the Ministry. However, only a couple of these institutes are earning more than 25% of their annual budgets. Most of them have well-established infrastructure, annual budgets, and even experienced cadre of staff at their head. All of them were appointed by the Ministry, directly or indirectly.

An analysis of operations of some of these national research and training institutes shows that there has been no instance of these institutes coming up with any policy propositions or interventions for the ministry. Some of these institutes conduct field research and even provide feedback on an ongoing basis to their respective ministry. And yet, there are not many examples of the Ministry taking initiatives based on these institutes' inputs. There may be a couple of these that have acquired their own standing for their services, and only exceptional cases have become reference points in the field of their specialisation.

Some Institutes Founded and Funded by the Union Ministries
1. V. V. Giri National Labour Institute, Noida
2. National Institute of Urban Affairs, New Delhi
3. National Institute of Science Education and Research, Bhubaneswar
4. National Institute of Science Communication and Information Resources, New Delhi

5. National Institute of Rural Development, Hyderabad
6. Indian Institute of Public Administration, New Delhi
7. National Institute of Public Finance and Policy, New Delhi
8. Indian Institute of Personnel and Training
9. National Institute of Nutrition, Hyderabad
10. National Institute of Design, Ahmedabad
11. National Council for Educational Research and Training, New Delhi
12. International Institute of Population Studies, Mumbai
13. Administrative Staff College of India, Hyderabad
14. Indira Gandhi Institute of Development Research, Mumbai
15. Indian Institute of Social Welfare and Business Management, Kolkata
16. Indian Council for Social Science Research, New Delhi
17. Indian Institute of Mass Communication, New Delhi
18. Indian Institute of Forest Management, Bhopal
19. Indian Institute of Foreign Trade, New Delhi
20. Centre for Development Studies, Thiruvananthapuram
21. Indian Council for Industrial Research, New Delhi
22. National Institute of Health and Family Welfare, New Delhi
23. National Institute of Public Cooperation and Child Development, New Delhi

Apart from these, there are nearly 30 tribal research institutes in the country, many of them over 50 years old. Upwards of a hundred crores is budgeted annually for these institutes (according to 2019-20 data). They claim to undertake about 3000 research and evaluation studies, despite half or more of the sanctioned staff for most of these institutes remaining vacant. There is no evidence of them developing any unique research or evaluation methodology or making a difference with their proactive research initiatives or even implementing public policies specially designed for development and empowerment of tribal population or pockets.

A quick review of R&D establishments of Ministries such as the industry, electronic, and telecom indicate that they hardly ever availed social science research to enhance the scope of their services or products or R&D initiatives. For example, there are about 35 labs under the Ministry of Electronics that have been around for over 40 years. I reviewed their operations more than two decades ago and sampled a few recently for this review. I observed that they have never even considered the relevance of social science research to enhance user-orientation in their designs or discoveries or marketization.

Research environment is made up of not only the government or government-sponsored agencies but independent, industry-sponsored, and academic bodies. Their practices and standards do make a difference to the overall research environment and architecture.

Civil Society, Academics Research

Public policies acquire their durability and accomplish objectives when they are backed by civil society and independent research. The role of civil society depends on how active the citizens and their voluntary organisations are. Many public policies are initiated from such sources and become legislations. It is not always a show of strength in the Parliament but the power of an idea or a cause and concerns that drives it to become a public policy.

These active citizens and civil society organisations are motivated because of their own concerns, experiences, and insights gained from data, analyses, and research in the public domain. There are instances of civil society itself taking to research to substantiate their concern and its larger relevance. In fact, initiatives of civil society are boosted by analysis and research. A recent good example includes the RTI Act and Mahatma Gandhi National Rural Employment Guarantee Scheme (MNREGS). Much earlier, 'Midday meal' and 'Family Planning' policies also received such support.

Think-Tanks and Lobbies: Both think-tanks and lobbies have been traditionally engaged in influencing public policies. They often try to influence formal decision-makers, legislatures, and the bureaucracy to sometimes go against existing legislations or a government's decision. Sometimes, they help the government's decisions to be implemented. Some think-tanks are also lobbies.

Independent research organisations often become think-tanks when they take to public issues and research concerns in a transparent way for larger sensitivities and the larger good. Lobbies tend to cater to businesses or political interests more than the public's interests. Think-tanks think beyond temporal concerns or sectional interests, which is what the lobbies are for. Lobbyists are likely to rely on data and analysis in public domain, while think-tanks depend on their own research and analysis in a proactive way.

Think-tanks have always existed in every country. They try to influence public policies and decision-makers and enjoy enormous influence on the course of pursuing power, although not always overtly. Most often, this is not acknowledged. A think-tank's role depends on the transparency and integrity of the professionals involved in these think-tanks and their research initiatives. A number of self-proclaimed think-tanks are set up by or include retired bureaucrats or former public persons who have vested interests and come with political and ideological affiliations. The more their conflict of interest is known, the better they become at channelling their 'potential'. The source of funding of a think-tank or its dependence on a political outfit—usually the ruling powers—is a determining factor in its work and effectiveness in the kind of public causes or public policies that it takes up in a proactive manner. Most think-tanks rely on existing data, analyses, or research studies, while a few take up new research studies. Elected representatives tend to seek and benefit from think-tank reports and analyses.

Think-tanks end up as lobbying outlets at one time or another or in one or the other context. The future of think-tanks has been on the decline, with many of them having a conflict of interest or a political orientation. Most of them are funded or supported by foreign sources, and most do not have their own source of data to avail secondary data.

Lobbyists influence public policies irrespective of any

regulation. In fact, lobbyists influence in a roundabout way, if not directly. Their reliance on primary research is also declining.

In India, lobbying is carried out more through public relations, advertising, and corporate consultants. Of late, think-tank groups are registered as foundations and trusts even though they are fronts of an industry or other interested groups. Many of these lobbyists directly or indirectly are in favour of one or the other industry or business house and in favour of or against certain public policies, as in the case of insurance, export–import policies, entry of foreign interests into the country, foreign policies, tobacco interests, taxation policies, etc.

Israel, USA, Japan, Germany, for example, have formal and informal lobbies in India. These include think-tanks, public relations corporates, research outfits, news media, and even academics.

The modus operandi of lobbyists is to form 'personal contacts' through persuasive discussions and push-and-pulls that work with news media and decision-makers. They also use research when it suits them and in a supportive way. Sometimes, they also sponsor research by well-known research agencies. For example, as online lottery business is prohibited in many states, a lobbyist would get a research study to show the advantages of online lottery. Lobbyists look for 'supportive data' and research, the same way political leaders do.

The tendency recently is to go to a lobbyist rather than sponsor a research project as the requirement is of 'supportive or endorsing data', which they are not sure of getting in a primary or freshly sponsored research. 'Foreign hand' is often heard about, both in the case of lobbies and think-tanks in India.

Government Initiatives to Revamp Research in Academics

The government's new 'PM Research Fellowship' scheme of 2018 was a timely initiative. This scheme did not, however, specify the need to focus on research. It was to attract more PhD programmes as the number of students going for PhD in social sciences in the country was declining and quality of research has come under criticism. Lack of qualified faculty, even in premier institutes, is yet another issue, with too many vacancies than ever before. To encourage research, the government came up with special initiatives. In 2018, under this national fellowship programme, the government announced 1000 fellowships (but could get only 135 qualified aspirants). According to Dr Kasturiranjan's report on new education policy, there were only 30,000–40,000 patents registered in India, of which 70% were by NRIs. (This was against 6–7 lac patents in the US.)

The initiatives of the Department of Science & Technology to set up five Centres of Policy Research with research thrust on economic, energy, climates, education, and health have somewhat revived hopes. These are at IIT Delhi, IIS Bangalore, IIT Hyderabad, and at Ahmedabad and Lucknow. For the Centre at IIT, Delhi, Tata Trust had given a grant of Rs 50 crores (2018–19).

Dheeraj Sanghi, Professor at IIT Kanpur (2018), wrote that the prime minister's scheme for encouraging research attracts students from poor quality colleges and the selection was based on discriminatory procedures, which was likely to further add to the problem of quality.[1] On 16 January 2019, about 2000 students and researchers converged and protested in Delhi, where 700 of them were even detained. They were arrested by police for protesting in front of the Ministry of HRD for demanding a hike in their research stipend.[2]

Union HRD Minister confessed in June 2018, speaking in Shirdi, that academics and research in the country is suffering from plagiarism. He said that it is an increasing phenomenon in PhD theses. Instead of looking into the root causes, the Minister said that a new software was being used to detect such trend![3]

Dr Deshpande cautioned against 'Western research models' based on tool-driven research methodologies, which are predominantly statistics and survey preoccupied. And yet, no one has cautioned against the increasing trend of 'copy catting' in academic research. Such trends have further contributed to the decline of research discipline in academics.

An acute shortage of academics is, of course, a recurring problem at IIT, IIMs, NIT, and Central Universities. Realising this, in November 2018, the government launched a leadership (LEAP) programme involving three weeks at premier institutes and one week at two selected US universities. This is a good initiative. The HRD Ministry intends (August 2019) to post these select few participants at important educational institutes as deans and department heads. Under this scheme, the HRD proposes 'to induct the specially selected' to lead the premier academic institutes. This obviously meant the new crop of academic heads in the country are directly handpicked by the ministry. Can we expect independently oriented researchers coming out of our education stream in the coming years?

Market Research Base for Policy Research

The story of market research in India is the story of policy research. Applied social research, in fact, grew out of market research. That perhaps explains why social science and public policy research, in particular, has 'market bias' in conceptualising and field research methodologies. In the initial years, market research was a function of advertising whose objective was and is to influence consumers. Although social research is more concerned with change and motivations, it is also interested in the process of influence. When advertisers were mostly interested in those with 'deep pockets' (that is, consumers who can afford to buy), they were interested in knowing their size and obtaining data on their demographic, lifestyles, and socioeconomic features. In that pursuit, the advertisers collected secondary data and generated primary data required to experiment their products or services and expand distribution and size of their market. Around the mid-1960s, major marketing corporates engaged in a range of consumer products believed that, with the competition growing, they needed reliable, specific, and latest data as well as a primary analysis of households, consumers, and markets.

In the next decade during 1975–85, there was proliferation of market research agencies. The big ones being the Indian Market Research Bureau (IMRB) and the MARG as affiliates of London-based global corporates. They thrived while initially catering to multinational corporates and then became entrenched into the Indian market and the government. Continuation of a 'preference for foreign' helped this process. Overall, the contribution of these market research agencies is important, particularly for consumer behaviour research and generating a wealth of primary data. The key differentiators of two research models include speed, depth, and the shelf-life of research.

Since I'm familiar and also directly involved in several pioneering studies at ORG, I can present an example of ORG's contributions during 1970–85 years and its support of public policy research, with India-specific research methodologies and a wealth of primary data bases on various aspects, including on public services. Many of its initiatives were sponsored by one or the other government agency.

Research Institutes that made a difference: Big changes and turning points in a country or a field of study or in governance comes from ingenious and visionary initiatives of individuals, as well as the institutes in the course of a nation's endeavours. This is true for roping in research support for public policies. During 1960–75, India witnessed the birth of many research organisations including some outside the government that played a pioneering role. I have outlined only four of many such examples here.

Way back in 1944, JRD Tata had advocated prioritising investments into education including, more specifically, in 'scientific education and research'. His proposition in 'A plan of Economic Development for India' along with G.D. Birla and other pioneers was very timely. Even after 75 years, that advise holds. Jawaharlal Nehru and other national leaders of the time took note of JRD Tata's and Mokshagundam Visvesvaraya's insights. That was how Tata's initiative and support laid the foundation for research culture across disciplines.

The idea of the first research house in the mid-1960s was that of Dr Vikram Sarabhai. The organisation, Operations Research Group (ORG), was initially a support service at Sarabhai Group's enterprises. Within five years, India's first market research organisation had become the fountainhead of socio-economic market research. It emerged because Sarabhai entrusted the responsibility to a team of graduates from the Indian Institute of Statistics, Calcutta. This team made a difference with D.V.N. Sarma as its director. R. C. Bhavsar, S. Rajgopal, S. Tyagarajan, Sahasrabuddhe, N Bhaskara Rao, DN Bose, and B. Samantha were some of the pioneers who built ORG into an independent pioneering research house, despite retaining its identity with Sarabhai. A series of national sample surveys of ORG, with a large sample size, had become the benchmark during 1970–85. It was the first National Readership Survey with 45,000 households, (today some such surveys are based on over a couple of lacs of sample size) the first National Survey on Family Planning with 75,000 households (until 1970, a sample size of 5000 was considered big), and many more on a range of social economic development issues, apart from introducing market research in India with store audit and pharma audit. It was ORG that introduced the idea of 'syndicated' studies, thus presenting a level playing field. Research until then was confidential or exclusively sponsored. It was ORG that engaged full-time trained field researchers across the country to collect primary data. I had the privilege of carrying out my best research with the organisation. A no-confidence motion by George Fernandes against the Congress government in the Parliament was based on primary data on several social sector issues that was collected and presented in a book edited by me—*India 2021*[4]—based on studies conducted at ORG.

However, after 25 years of playing a pioneering role, ORG was destabilised and dissolved by a profit-driven multinational research and consultancy corporate which grabbed ORG and MARG of Titoo Ahluwalia. By 1974, the other leading market research agency, IMRB, was also a profit-driven multinational (now known as KANTAR IMRB).

Two foreign research corporates tried to backdoor entry but did not succeed because of my resistance as I was sure that Indian researchers had a better idea of the impact, evaluation, and behavioural research. Foreign agencies had better presentation and storytelling skills and certainly better marketing strategies. Ministries of Indian Government went all-out preferring foreign corporates, not realising what it meant.

Centre for Policy Research (CPR): The Centre for Policy Research (CPR) is now 50 years old. It was an idea of a person who had seen how public policies were being developed in the previous decade. In 1970, Dr V Pai Panandiker, an academician who was associated with economic reforms, launched this CPR for an independent appraisal and evaluation impact of social development. It was created out of concern and commitment for independent research with a conviction and belief that research support impacts the relevance and sustainability of public policies. Trusting him in his pursuit was T.A. Pai, then Minister for Industry, and Finance Minister Morarji Desai. With campus in New Delhi's prime diplomatic area, CPR had initiated several analytical studies and inducted senior bureaucrats and experts. CPR went on to become a think-tank as its services were availed by successive prime ministers and governments and international agencies for the next 40 years, even after Dr Pai retired to Goa and Pratap Bhanu Mehta and Yamini Aiyar became its CEOs.[5] Each of the CPR Chiefs further strengthened the agency. All three were equally active, concerned, and communicative. Yamini Aiyar even added a new strength to CPR by taking to social development and governance issue with renewed focus on citizens, the system, and implementation of programmes. Pratap Bhanu Mehta was most vocal with his regular columns and media activism. With CPR (1970) becoming a model, many similar sounding initiatives sprang up in New Delhi. Most remained centred on one or two individuals and functioned on project-to-project basis.

Rajni Kothari, political scientist, founded the Centre for Society and Developing Societies (CSDS 1963), another non-profit research agency. It took to public policy issue in an independent manner and as a research pursuit. With Rajni Kothari, C.D. Singh, Bashiruddin Ahmad, KGK Murthy, Bhutt, etc., CSDS emerged in no time as a think-tank. It is now 60 years old and has made its mark with a focus on political parties and elections, starting with their first study on Kerala elections in the early 1960s. After Rajni Kothari, it was Yogendra Yadav, in particular, who has added to its credibility and has taken CSDS to newer heights in research initiatives for public policies. A major contribution of CSDS was its network of concerned academic-researchers. It nurtured certain research discipline in academics around the country. Sanjay Singh continued its legacy of sensitizing the larger public.

Durgabai Deshmukh, doyen of India's social welfare movement with a focus on women's and children's development, was another pioneer who realised the role of research and founded the Centre for Social Development (CSD) in 1970 with Dr Pradipto Roy, a sociologist who was part of Everett Rogers's global project on diffusion of innovations. It was initially supported by the Ford Foundation and Tata Foundation. I had the privilege of being personally engaged in discussions with the founders or chiefs of these pioneering research agencies of India (1970–90).

ORG was the first organisation outside the census to use their 'sample frames' and 'cluster maps' in the early 1970s, and after considerable deliberations, the census agreed to sell these sample frames. After analysing the census data for 1941, 1951, and 1961, it was obvious that there was error in capturing the number of 'females in the work force'. This number varied between less than 10% to over 20%. Credit should be given to the census officials then as they promptly asked ORG to look into the problem. A resurvey was used to observe how the questions were framed, how they were asked by the investigators, recorded, and analysed, and how it all varied from one region to another. That was when the census corrected and revived the probes for the 1981 Census. This saved the census from a major embarrassment.

It was ORG studies that corrected numerous anomalies and assumptions in public policies. For example, the NRS corrected the myths about the reach and potential of regional language newspapers compared to the English newspapers. Based on this study, advertising strategies made significant changes, new media planning models were developed for advertisers, and media development plans of the government went through corrections. It was ORG's first reports on rural markets, consumption trends, and retail network that changed the face of marketing strategies and priorities. It was an ORG study that corrected Rural Electricity Corporation's contention on villages being electrified by bringing sensitivity in data analysis and providing household-level reach as the criteria, instead of considering the village as a unit.

The government was in a dilemma in mid-1970s about shortages of drugs and the spiralling drug prices in the country. ORG came to the rescue by offering its services to monitor the retail network drug-wise and market-wise and suggest policy interventions including the Drug Price Control Order (DPCO) in 1982. Moreover, it was ORG's proactive initiative that put child labour on the national agenda by indicating, for the first time (in 1974), that 42 million children were engaged in child labour. It took a couple of years for the government to come to grips with the issue, even as the Supreme Court intervened and asked for state- and region-specific surveys on child labour. The dropout rate of girls from school in Madhya Pradesh (in 1982-83) was another study done by ORG. Based on this study, for the first time, UNICEF identified the absence of toilets in schools as one of the main reasons for the high dropout rate. The government itself had ignored or refused to acknowledge this finding even some after the study, until UNICEF took it up seriously.

At the national level, the focus of India's family planning campaigns shifted, as we have seen before, to 'hard, core couple'—the rural, agriculture-dependent and often unlettered couple—based on an ORG research (1974-75). Again, it was ORG that introduced a unique methodology of crop surveys in the country to help estimate yields based on pre-post sowing harvest surveys and estimation methodology. This approach today could have helped minimize farmer suicides or at least sound an early warning for the government to step in promptly with relief and corrective measures. The Planning Commission and the National Council of Applied Economic Research (NCAER) considered some of the research pioneered by ORG. A pioneering initiative of the Planning Commission on climate zones was the work of a ORG researcher (D.N. Basu) along with Dr Y.K. Alagh. There are dozens of more such examples regarding how research helped government take initiatives or correct some of the ongoing policies. It was because of such active contribution by ORG that it was taken over by a multinational agency as it was the source of primary data on various aspects of India, its people, and the markets. By 1990, ORG ceased to exist and became part of a multinational corporation.

Corporates in India are known for lobbying for favourable policies. It is to the credit of the Tatas that, from early years of independent India, they have been taking initiatives for public policies based on research—the Indian Institute of Science in Bangalore and the Tata School of Social Sciences in Mumbai are only two such examples. After a couple of decades, Tata's had come forward in 2019 to support public policy research, as if they had realised the vacuum that existed in this regard in the country.

The education scene in the country in 2019-20 has been marked by disruption and uncertainty, particularly concerning higher education. This is in the context of the proposed winding up of the 70-year-old University Grants Commission (UGC), replacing it with a new commission to regulate higher education—the Higher Education Commission of India (HECI). The announcement of 100 universities with a focus on research and the launch of the National Research Foundation also added to the uncertainty and disorder. Signals from the field have also been contradictory. Change should be for the good and should be welcomed. But the apprehensions are that these proposed changes are for centralisation, which may inhibit independent research and innovation in the faculties of social sciences. For research to acquire a professional standing and to flourish, universities play a key role.

The fact that research architecture must be encouraged to play a more active role was recognised by many early pioneers of India, beginning with the first (1953–54) education commission to the more recent report (2019) by Dr Kasturirangan on the new education policy as well as the immediate previous committee of Subramanyam (2017) for the same purpose whose report the government had abandoned. All these reports had observed the need for renewing research discipline in the country as an important part of the educational system. The 2017 and the 2019 reports recommended that a National Research Foundation be constituted with special funds and suggested that there should be 100 universities prioritizing research. Earlier, several reviews had indicated the need to revamp and renew the Indian Council for Social Science Research (ICSSR), which was established more than 50 years ago specially to sustain social science research in the country. There were also indications that the quality of research in the country has declined and that, over the years, public policies are no longer based on data, statistics, and research. The signal of this decline was when the Programme Evaluation Organisation in the Planning Commission was wound up years ago. Private and foreign research outfits that have been swaying research priorities since then made little difference to the paradigm of public policy formulation as they are 'market driven' and based mostly on a 'foreign model' of research in terms of the methodology and conflict of interest.

The NDA government recently (2018–20) took certain initiatives signalling the repositioning of research. Research fellowships have been repositioned with more numbers, and there has been an increase in the number of scholarships. Social research grounded in sound social science should receive attention and support, as in the case of technology and impact of public policies. In a first of initiatives, the NDA government declared 20 universities as 'eminent'. Nearly half of these are private institutes. These are expected to excel in research. (The fact that a couple of private institutions had not even taken off at that point (2018–19) is a different story.)

However, repositioning and shifting the research paradigm comes only with initiatives in the larger sense and across academics, public services, in the government policies, and in governance.

Reorienting Evaluation, Government's Niti!

The Programme Evaluation Office (PEO) was part of the Planning Commission from its very outset, in 1952. It was described as an 'organisation' within the Commission but it established its own field setup of researchers to initially evaluate community development schemes, and its role was later extended to evaluating Central government schemes. It was deactivated after 1995, although no formal notification was issued to that effect. In early 2000, an 'Independent Evaluation Office' (IEO) was created which was supposed to provide the same service as the earlier PEO did. The new IEO was guided by an Evaluation Advisory Committee from 2004, so that it would gain credibility. The Cabinet Secretary even advised all Ministries to get their ongoing schemes evaluated by the IEO and advised the IEO to strengthen itself in order to take up these tasks. But the NDA government in 2015 repositioned IEO as Development Monitoring and Evaluation Office (DMEO) under the newly formed NITI Aayog. This new Office was assigned the task of 'outcome monitoring', and in 2019, the NSSO, as we have seen, was made defunct, being merged with another organisation to form the National Statistical Office (NSO). Each time there is a change in the political party in power, these 'eyes and ears' of the government are also re-calibrated!

Within a few months of the change in government at the centre in 2014, PEO was scrapped. The DG of PEO, who still had two more years of service left, was removed and most of the regional evaluation units were closed. But then, in September

2015, DMEO was announced that merged the earlier PEO and IEO to 'coordinate' sponsored research. What its role would be once the National Research Foundation takes off after 2020 needs to be seen.

Earlier, in 2014, the new government wound up an open forum review of the functioning of the ministries. This 'Task Force of Cabinet Secretariat for Performance Appraisal' was a high-level group of experts set up before 2009. It reviewed Ministry-wise mandates, mission, schemes, strategies, priorities, and outcomes in an open format. It was experimented (2009–14) as 'Result Framework of Ministries'. This format brought in transparency and independent appraisal of the functioning of the ministries, besides field research. The group consisted of senior retired functionaries and independent experts. Headed by a senior secretory in the Cabinet Secretariat (*Dr Prajapati Trivedi*), this group validated the idea of 'outcome orientation' of Ministries. Soon after a new party came to power in 2014, this idea of open review was disbanded even though this was not a politically appointed group. Instead, this function was then shifted to the prime minister's office. Even the Indian Economic Service (IES) was disconnected from such performance evaluation activity.

The new government indicated its concern for the effectiveness of centrally sponsored and central sector schemes and made monitoring and evaluation mandatory a part of the national development agenda and an obligatory responsibility of NITI Aayog. The objectives of DMEO were formally announced in 2019 as 'long term impact of development' and included making policies data-driven, improving sustainable outcomes, and the impact of different schemes. Although DMEO was announced in 2015, it became functional only in 2017. DMEO outsourced evaluation studies on centrally initiated schemes, for which it even invited technical consultants through an open competitive bidding process. There was still preference for foreign consultants so that no Indian experts could qualify.

Considering 'informal briefings' of NITI Aayog officials to the news media about DMEO in 2015, 2016, 2017, and 2019 shows the sensitivity with which 'monitoring and evaluation' was viewed at the highest level in the NITI Aayog and in the government. The ideas indicated to the media and in the note of 2019 on DMEO were well-articulated. One thing is obvious during the four years (2015–19) of dismantling and regrouping the structure and functions of PEO and IEO that there was better control of research and evaluation functions in the government and that such efforts should be supportive of the government.

The trend was that the government was trying to avail or gear up research, monitoring, and evaluation to control, command, and centralise. This is evident from the fact that DMEO is more an office in NITI Aayog than an organisation with its nose to ground. It is more a nodal office to outsource and provide grants for selected projects with priority and focuses more on the infrastructure schemes. It was an 'umbrella' approach such that the reports are made in NITI Aayog, not in the field or by individual commissioned consultants.

The 'international standards' and 'global norms' were claimed to be a virtue of DMEO's concerns. As a result of this, its approach and modus operandi may become 'out of context'. What else can explain DMEO's preference for 'foreign consultants' and 'corporate consultants' who chase bigger profits? Its conditions of eligibility to outsource and assign monitoring and evaluation projects is discriminative. It ensures that no Indian researcher or experts get qualified. It has not only fixed Rs 50 crores minimum income per year from professional fees for the three preceding years (which no Indian researcher could have), but the more the revenues goes beyond Rs 50 crores, the more weightage is given. This 'bigger the better' consultant idea is a misnomer and poses a questionable criterion. Such criteria may apply in tendering by civil and engineering projects, not in the social sector. It ignores the fact that India has well-established institutions with expertise, experience, and specializations in research and monitoring and far more appropriate evaluation capabilities. I am reminded of the fate AP CM Naidu met more than a decade ago by taking similar approach of engaging foreign consultants indiscriminately.

Another contentious element is reliance on 'measurable indicators' which more often are surrogates. Such symptoms never make us wiser or come up with correctives for proactive initiatives. There is also no initiative to rope in a network of academic institutions to build skills and capabilities within the country for monitoring and evaluation. Research thus becomes more relevant regionally. In the anxiety of global norms, copy catting becomes prompted. It can only add to the animated competitive spirit, not aid the much-needed sustainable development.

Fund for cutting edge research: On return to power in 2019, Prime Minister Modi stated his concern for quality in research. The government thus announced Scientific and Useful Profound Research Advancement (SUPRA) to attract quality research proposals with new 'out-of-the-box' proposals. Funds under this scheme aim to promote long-term impact on science and technologies. However, this scheme was not even formally announced as of November 2019. Earlier in 2017, Science and Engineering Research Board (SERB) was announced as a scheme for funding 'High Risk–High Reward Research' (HRHR), but this scheme was withdrawn even before it took off without any explanation. This was the second such scheme that was meant to promote research which was withdrawn or never took off. The earlier one was DMEO under NITI Aayog (2015) which took four years (2015–19) to take off.

No wonder then that a senior ruling party leader alleged on 20 August 2019 that 'NITI Aayog is being run by foreign experts who have no idea of the on-ground reality' and that 'foreign funded agencies are sitting there'.[6]

Going by this track record of the government regarding research-supporting schemes, there is no guarantee that the National Research Foundation, as announced and provided for in the 2019–20 budget, would take off anytime soon. Despite the prime minister's indication, the government has no policy outlook for encouraging evaluative research in the country, particularly in social sectors.

Census of India: The government was quick to reposition the planning commission as NITI Aayog and change the scope of PEO as DMEO, come up with National Research Foundation, and announce a proposal to set up 100 universities with research focus. But then why were the census operations in India never revived and repositioned to match the changed socio-economic and political compulsions?

The British were using census as an instrument to control and administer India. Many of their strategies can be traced to census as in the case of language, religion, and regions or states, migration, new born, etc. Censuses continues to be administered by the Home Ministry of the Union Government similar to how they were before independence. Even after 1947, independent India continued the legacy of decennial Census from 1950, using the same framework but with certain variables of development added. Census reports earlier took three-four years to come out. The 2011 census was out within a year, but certain aspects of 2011 census data were released in 2019.

Why should the periodicity of census be limited to once in 10 years? State governments and Ministries have recently been conducting their census-like operations and doing so competently. Why then should census operations be under the Union Ministry of Home? With the government concerned about migration from across borders, terrorist activities, and the eligibility issues for targeted schemes, it is perhaps time to review the census operations independently, to have an empowered commission that could suggest changes in the scope and structure of the census.

AI, Without Research!

New technologies like Artificial Intelligence (AI) and 5G are expected to influence the research methodologies and the type of research that the government, corporates, and media indulge in in the coming years. As of 2020, many countries have indicated strategies to adopt AI to their advantage. According to PricewaterhouseCoopers (PWC) consultancy, India is also among the list of countries with a national strategy for AI. PWC is supposed to know what they noted because they are the consultants to NITI Aayog or/and the concerned Ministry. As early as in 2018, NITI Aayog had constituted panels and came up with a national strategy. For the next year, there was no indication of this national strategy. But the government announced a National Centre of Excellence in AI and stated that there would be centres around the country. But there was no attempt to communicate what the strategy was or what the themes of concern were. The only public discourse (until mid-2019) on AI was a CMS-organised 'national Colloquium' on 18-19 February 2019 at New Delhi's India International Centre. This was the first open discussion between experts from academics, industry, civil society, and senior policy people. It is known from the very outset that AI has implications on larger public, lifestyles, and public policies. Yet there was no research on the type of disruption that AI implies or the impact of these technologies on research methodologies, feedback, and evaluation strategies. Even the CMS meet did not recommend research support which would be essential for identifying and applying the best features of AI to social impact initiatives and governance.

This despite the fact that Prime Minister Modi had referred to AI twice in one month in January 2019, including at the Indian Science Congress meet, claiming how life is going to be 'easier' with AI. But no one explained what 'easy life' meant. Since no research was undertaken on how AI would make life and living easy and productive, it is not possible for people to be prepared to avail newer opportunities.

As of mid-2019, there has been no research on the appropriateness of India opting for 5G technology. With mounting pressure from the US and China, India appears to be rushing to expedite its decision. When the use of 4G in India continuous to be limited, why is India considering 5G, particularly as it involves heavy investments and health hazards as indicated by WHO, and it is unknown whether social justice and socio-economic divides in the country will be narrowed.

CHAPTER NINE

Could Research Be a Third Eye?

If numbers lose their credibility, what is the basis for their standing and relevance? If statistics have no reliability, what is their sanctity? Yardstick for both time and scale involves numbers. Today, values, basis, and criteria increasingly depends on numbers, figures, and statistics. Both exploitation and cooperative situations arise from numbers. The world crumbles when numbers decline or cease or even when change. The basis for both problems and solutions are numbers, as in the case of 'performance'. This being the reality today, the sanctity of numbers has to be a concern. Data, statistics, and research offers a perspective, opens a window for solutions, and becomes a 'third eye' for stakeholders.

Esteemed applied statistics Professor Mahalanobis had envisioned 70 years ago the kind of dilemma the Indian state was going to be preoccupied with regarding numbers and data. He also foresaw the circumstances for their manipulation. To cope with this, he suggested that data and statistics should go through checks and balances and should not be under subordination of anyone, particularly bureaucrats. He did not, however, foresee that real threat to the country's statistical system would come from political leadership and political compulsions. This reality is what determines research culture, traditions, and standards today.

Analyses of data cannot be the same for all, at all times, and in all contexts. Data is not always used with good intentions. In fact, today, data is used more often to influence or motivate or for individual interest. What could be a worse (disaster and) crisis in credibility?

How do we insulate analysis and research from frequent conflicts of interest and the push and pulls from different sources or lobbies, or political, economic, or bureaucratic interests? On this depends the sanctity of data, analysis, and research. There is no particular corrective that can ensure data credibility, data neutrality, and research objectivity, regardless of who is in power or what the equations are.

First, a common understanding as to what data or measures are is important. Second, precedents and practices in the country towards such quantitative outcomes should be established. Third, the prevailing laws and legal environment must be determined. Fourth, the prevailing academic standards and concerns must be adhered to. Fifth, professional standards that data generators and researchers observe and maintain should be respected.

Laws of the land: Laws of the land provide certain legal standing to data and statistics. But that alone may not give the credibility or reliability that data must have for sustainability. In fact, in some instances, data may have much-needed weightage, irrespective of legal backup, and vice-versa.

Political Parties: Political leaders and parties, particularly those in power, need to show concern and restraint from entrenched political interests. Parties and leaders tend to exaggerate figures, data, and statistics to suit their interests. In the trap of achievement mania, the party in power, particularly, will brazenly misuse data, statistics, or research for immediate electoral gain.

Professional: Professional functionaries and bodies have a responsibility to consider or constrain data, statistics, and research to meet the temporal push and pulls interests and validate their outcomes. They should be aware and sensitive to the way in which research, data, statistics, and outcomes are availed by various stakeholders.

Academics: Academics are supposed to be the backbone of the research system in any country. Colleges and universities are expected to sustain and strengthen research, and sensitise society about the scope of research. They are expected to broaden the scope for independent research and even offer much-needed critical appraisal and minimise the scope for misuse or misinterpretation of research and data. Open debates and robust deliberation enhance transparency and credibility of research.

The mix-ups: Certain mix-up about what the state is all about and how it is different from the government of the day in a parliamentary democracy must be understood at large, specifically by those in electoral politics. It should be understood that the state continues on while the government may be different each time there is a general election. While the government too is ongoing, the party in the government is there for a tenure. The party that wins in the election runs the government for a certain period. The data and statistics should serve or cater to the state and not be limited to the interests of the party in the government. The value and criteria of data and statistics cannot be different each time there is change in the party in government.

Data and statistics should be institutionalised not only for the sole interests of elected office bearers but also for the competency of the government, the state, and the citizens. Data and statistics, however, are being tailored to the advantage of the political party in power. As an institution, they are expected to cater beyond their tenure concerns and last beyond the tenure of a party of the existing government. Data and statistical system should always be an outcome of the checks and balances process. They are expected to stand up to validation, even by an external agency.

Data and statistics should not be solely based on laws or government rules. Precedent and rules of transparency should be the guiding principles. Data and statistics should be immune from partisan priorities of the political party or group that is in power and has control of the government. That the incumbent party will use or misuse data and statistics has long been considered inevitable; but governments are not expected to fiddle with or try to manage the scope, structures, and processes of data and research. When credibility is in doubt, how can data from different sources be relied on? Not surprisingly, often it is data from sources outside the government that is believed more.

Precedents and Perceptions: Every country has its belief systems. For example, traditionally, people tend to believe the government more as a source of information than a private source. But once credibility of leaders in the government is doubted, information from that source also gets doubted. That is when institutions which operate beyond their immediate interests are likely to be believed more. Institutions such as the Indian Statistics Institute or the Indian Institute of Science or even the Tata Institute of Social Science or the Indian Institute of Nutrition, with their own credibility, tend to be believed more than other sources because of their professional standing and reliability of long-standing concerns and research pursuit.

Divides: Every time there is change in the government, there is a tendency to divide people further based on numbers in one or the other category for some political advantage. For example, BC, SC, ST has been further categorised in 2019 in some states into eight categories which are SC, ST, BC A, BC B, BC C, BC D, BC E minorities, presumably to provide them with economic assistance. These groups are further divided by their age into 45–60, 18–35, and so on. For the numbers in each cell, a task or assistance is proposed. Since the Mandal Commission, dependency on numbers is no longer the same. Reservation, subsides, targeted schemes, and populism have changed the weightages and craving for data and surveys.

Three-Pronged Initiatives

To restore and revive research to its pride in India's growth path, a three-pronged effort is needed.

First, the role and relevance of research needs to be reiterated and made evident to decision-makers at the highest level. They should become sensitive to criteria for research and to what or how independent research is different from sponsored or supportive research.

Second, some transparent regulatory mechanism is essential in the research architecture of the country, not through government control and centralisation but by combining voluntary and self-discipline obligations such as professional validation, social audit by independents, etc., and in a balanced manner.

Third, promotional campaign for inculcating research culture or understanding data sensitivity is crucial. Awareness of basic desirability to identify the virtues of research, data, statistics, and analysis is important. This has to be the responsibility of multiple stake holders, not just of the government.

There is an urgency in the country to reverse the trend of the past decade so that independent research, assessment, and evaluation of public policies is not on an extinction course. Most public news media today are either sponsored or supported or at function at the behest of an interested stakeholder. Data and statistics in the context of governance must acquire their sanctity back. All this is possible only when we have a national policy on 'research culture'. The policy should specially indicate a space for social science research, more specifically in our national pursuits and the trajectory of democracy, development, and governance.

Foundations for a data regime: No country can be expected to have a reliable, credible, and state-of-the-art statistical system, databases, and analytical advantage without academic backup and a cadre of professionals. Indian Statistical Institute in Calcutta was the fountainhead of Indian statistics. It had earned India's global leadership in statistics, which made it possible for India to have 400 universities offering an opportunity to study statistics at the post-graduate level and also for many Indian scholars to lead global academics. There is a cadre of functionaries in the Union Government known as Indian Statistical Service (ISS) to man services in the government concerning data, statistics, and research. This service needs to be revived, revamped, and strengthened. The number of ISS cadre officers remained static, despite the needs having increased manifold in the recent years. Their recruitment and training should be reassessed and repositioned based on the changed requirements and new technologies, both software and hardware.

The 2019 Economic Survey presented to the Parliament devoted a considerable number of pages to outline a 'data regime' that the country is in. To appreciate this timely reminder, we need to take an overview of how such a data regime could, in fact, be a potential source for growth, change, and development and offer a new perspective for future research architecture. This becomes the foundational base for accomplishing holistic targets and long-term objectives. A main source for statistical base and fundamental knowledge is social sciences.

For better understanding and appreciating statistical rigor, related subjects such as analytics should be made compulsory for PhD and post-graduate courses. This is already the case for certain courses like psychology and economics. A quick cursory analysis of those in research organisations in the country including those who are engaged in various field surveys that appear in news media shows that these individuals hardly have any academic grounding for their professions. Even those in the government services, being posted for some data acquisition, analysis, and research functions, have no background. For example, one reason why Chandrababu Naidu, chief minister of Andhra from 2014 to 2019, missed the grassroots reality altogether—and paid the price by losing the 2019 elections very badly—was that the functionaries in charge of surveys, feedback, and evaluative research had little or no professional knowledge of statistics and analytics and other means to gauge public opinion.

Today, practically everything in policy-making, governance, and public administration involves data, analytics, and statistics. It requires not only sensitivity but also some fundamental knowledge. Functionaries involved in policy formulation process must have certain knowledge of to the basics of research and methodologies. Those in the Ministry of Programme Implementation should also be aware of the significance data, analytics, and research methods. But there is no indication that this Ministry has any official with special background to assess the implementation of policies and programmes.

Orientation courses to functionaries in governance today requires individuals to have the basic fundamental knowledge of surveys, data, analytics, and research methodology. The way the research services are outsourced by some senior functionaries in important ministries indicate a lack of understanding of the fundamentals of reliable research such as what constitutes credibility. Research without credibility can have boomerang consequences sooner or later.

The Economic Survey should also have examined the basic issue of whether it makes sense for the census operations to remain with the government—under the control of the Ministry of Home Affairs—as has been the case since the British colonial era. Despite being conducted once in 10 years, census operations continue to be treated selectively and exclusively when it is, in fact, a key source for analytics, evaluative research, and long-term concerns.

In a democracy, the role and relevance of research is as significant as any of the pillars of the state, particularly the Fourth Estate. When research culture is ingrained in a society, the 'We, the people' credo of the Republic of India is consolidated in reality.

Transparent and independent research can be a reminder of the vibrancy of the institutions of the state, and government agencies and institutions can reliably and credibly implement policies. The present government of India should, in its own interest, restore the healthy tradition of Independent India's early decades and facilitate, support, and sustain good and impartial research. The leaders at the top should express their belief in research and not only acknowledge—which they rarely do—but also *share* the knowledge gained from impartial research findings. They should welcome independent research inputs for important national schemes and policies, while pointing out any deficiency in research as and when it comes to their knowledge.

The government should indicate a certain percent of budgets for research. This could be both in terms of the percent of the public schemes budget, as in the case of budget outlays of Swachh Bharat, and in terms of the percentage of overall development or welfare budget. What is spent now for social and evaluative research, even for flagship schemes, is too little for conducting reliable research. Depending on the nature of the scheme and its target, 1–3% should be allocated and spent on data, research, and analysis.

The government should not depend on any one source for research, particularly when evaluating major schemes like MNREGS, Mudra Scheme, or Swachh Bharat. The government can identify specialist agencies for research within the government or outside to assign a particular responsibility based on their expertise and experience. The government should also not put all its bets on any one source or research methodology. A recent glaring example for this phenomena was how a state government relied on the CVR method to assess its public services which made them believe that its schemes and programmes had an 85–95% success. Over-reliance on one method of getting feedback backfires. (Methodology should have cross-check programme.) We need to develop alternative ways of measuring the same thing.

The idea of 'L-1' as the basis for assigning a research project in an open tender may be appropriate for physical supplies or civil works but not for assigning research studies for qualitative assessment. The selection should be based on a three-stage process. Priority should be given to the technical pre-qualification of the research agency regarding its capabilities, infrastructure, specific scheme of research in the context, and maybe then the cost factor should be considered.

The political leaders should not meddle with the functioning of the organisations responsible for developing with periodic reports on vital parameters of the economy, demographic, GDP, employment, performance assessment, consumption, saving, inflation, etc. But, of course, they should express their views and suggestions without attributing values to data and statistics. The government should ensure their budgets annually, and the tenure of key functionaries of the data, statistics, and research organisations should be fixed. These positions should not be coterminous with election schedules.

All governments should uphold the transparency principle in the functioning of such vital organisations concerning data, monitoring, feedback, and research. For this, certain promotional initiatives should be taken. A consultation group for each of these vital function or a standing advisory with outside professionals and stakeholder personalities can help avoid lapses, and in some cases public hearings and social audit may be of greater help. Social audit by outside professionals such as academics or retired functionaries could be made obligatory as and when an issue or scheme becomes contentious.

The government should be aware that while 'authenticity' may be present for certain messages if the source is the government, there are cases when an independent or outside source will be better. As such, significant public policies and public programmes are better appraised or evaluated by independent agencies, even by an academic group or by a consortia of experts. Such an assignment to an independent body is likely to be more credible and generate better outcomes.

The newly launched (2019) National Research Foundation by the government should be a catalyst, facilitator, and beneficiary, and not a controller of research faculties and studies in the country. The government should be sensitive that it is in its own interest to ensure that research is not constrained and centralised.

The proposed National Research Foundation should specifically include social science research as an area of specific relevance and provide for its coverage. ICSSR could be the nodal or a coordinating body. This foundation should be a professionally moderated body, and not politically and or bureaucracy-led body, as is proposed. A re-evaluation of this can enhance the relevance of NRF itself.

Research architecture in the country is at a cross-road. Challenges and opportunities for all kinds of research in different contexts, with the potential to take the country to newer heights, are neither recognised nor being focused on. We need to listen to and learn from the Nobel Laureate Abhijit Banerjee who has spoken about and shown the immense importance of social research in making the world and India more equal, just, and humane through informed and enlightened policies.

The Third Eye of Governance

Research means different things to different people. It also has different meanings at different points of time. The idea of research is also used differently depending on their profession or even their location. Context makes all the difference in research. My concern in this book is independent India's growth path, development pursuit, and the future course for accomplishing its cherished goals. This obviously is in the context of public policies in pursuit of social, human, behavioural, and holistic change. While India has made significant strides in technology and infrastructure, commensurate change is not evident in the social and behavioural respect as successes have remained islands.

This vacuum should concern every one. It is in this context that a missing link is research on opportunities and options. Are we a research-based country or an irrational and subjective one? Can we expect, in the coming years, to excel without harnessing research in all its potential? How else can we become a knowledge society, as well as become, once again, a country of innovations, prosperity, and flourish in a holistic way?

Research should not be viewed as a panacea. It is merely a window to understand the world and its concerns better and take better decisions. In that process, research enhances sensitivities and the perspectives of stakeholders. Research should not be viewed as a solution by itself or a way out of a crisis or conflict situation. Instead, it helps provide options and alternatives for more appropriate and objective decisions. This is even more so in the case of social science research.

Research—evaluative research, in particular—is not event-driven but process-driven and data-based. Process cannot be captured in one shot or with one methodology; it has to be a pursuit, a multi-pronged one. The extent to which processes are captured is the extent to which research becomes relevant and reliable. This 'research as process' view requires an understanding of the linkages and relationships between the different facets of a process and their weightage, which are variable and contextual. Such an understanding determines the tools or methodologies on which research should be based. Data, statistics, databases, research, and analytics help this process. Artificial Intelligence and digitalisation can now enhance the scope further.

Research acquires relevance and credibility depending on how well it is based on certain critical features like data sources or origins, transparency, reliability, ethical and social responsibility, and future concerns. When research becomes commercial or a branded service, it has to follow certain self-acquired disciplines more seriously. Research should never be unconcerned in terms of who benefits or who suffers or is deprived by research. There should be mechanisms for self-correction. Research should be viewed as a passion and pursuit and a prerequisite for good governance.

Cause and effect can be an exceptional phenomenon in social and behavioural contexts. It is a process and a dynamic one of linkage and relationships. And certain theoretical insights or understandings are essential for research to organise itself and make a difference. Sound academic concern is an essential element to sustain this culture.

Research can also become a meaningless, repetitive, and futile process when it is based on static or asymmetrical methodology. One reason for this is the mistaken notion of a strict duality—'right' and 'wrong'—when, in fact, social systems are fluid and they are about plurality and multiplicity. And yet policy makers tend to view research in fixed and black-and-white terms. One often finds both leaders and researchers trapped in such fallacies. Public opinion surveys also become entrenched in such fallacies. In this process, it is more likely that there is a gap in how political leaders look at the idea of research compared to its potential as a liberal idea for justice, equity, and offering a level playing field, which leaders may not always be in favour of.

An Agenda—A realisation is a prerequisite: Economic growth cannot stand on research indicators in vogue. It is, of course, essential for a country's development, but not sufficient. In fact, development is incomplete or irrelevant without social development and accomplishing indicators of a holistic growth path. But social research is far more important, much more so in the case of diffusing and adopting infrastructure and technology. There are more research options in the case of social sector schemes.

Recognising that social research is a missing link in India's development pursuit is critical. And this is one reason for India not yet scaling its success stories. The story of Punjab and Haryana is a good example for how they failed to apply social research to determine that social factors pulled down the overall development despite high economic growth. These states remained low on the social development indicators.

This can happen with the prime minister and chief ministers as well as key decision-makers calling for social research on one or the other appropriate public occasion talk of the virtue of independent feedback and evaluation. But governments must also provide increased budgetary provisions for social and evaluative research and predictive or proactive research.

The immediate need is to consolidate the existing infrastructure for social research in the country. This includes ICSSR, UGC, HECI, universities, and other institutes created over 70 years by various ministries along with many outside organisations. All of them need to be repositioned and revived rather urgently. Only then can India expect to stand out in the global assessment.

It is vital to compile and consolidate data bases, digitize them, and entrust the responsibility for updating and allowing open access to these databases. These databases should be available for AI and such other new technologies to be explored further.

The statistical service, as one of the civil service, needs to be upgraded, expanded, regrouped, and reassigned in Ministries. These should be reoriented with research methodologies for monitoring, feedback, appraisal, and evaluative sensitivities.

The entire statistical system in the country at various levels and in different sectors needs to be reviewed. The way methodologies were being formulated and the way their reports are finalised needs to be re-examined in terms of the emerging 21 century scenario centred on transparency, citizens' rights, and governance issues. This review should consider alternatives in the wake of populism, competitive politics, and electoral trends.

Simultaneously, data, statistics, and national survey organisations need to be repositioned and empowered with support, independence, and transparency. They need to be liberated from bureaucratic and political involvement. The government should consider the merit of the census operation out of the Home Ministry, maybe under the Ministry of Statistics or Programme Implementation. The National Statistical Commission, NSSO, etc. should be brought together, perhaps under an apex council.

Social research should have a budget separate from overall research and development. More specifically, a certain percentage, approximately 2%, of budgetary allocation for major projects, schemes and programmes can be indicated, similar to how corporates are expected to get involved in CSR annually. Social science research by prominent organisations should be eligible for CSR funding.

NITI Aayog should reformulate DMEO to incorporate distinct responsibilities as was the case decades ago in the

Planning Commission. The Finance Ministry, Programme Implementation Ministry, and other social sector Ministries should restructure research, computer, evaluation, feedback, and related sections in the Ministries. All civil service cadres should be sensitised about the role and relevance of research as well as the opportunities involved. In fact, the programme content at all training institutes, including at the Missouri Academy, should reposition research, data, statistics, feedback, and monitoring (MIS) courses.

The Union Government should review the role of foreign consulting agencies in these ministries—how they conduct research; their accountability; the kind of methodologies they are using; and what impact their presence, and the preference they receive, has on Indian social scientists.

Various research and training institutes that exist under different ministries over the decades must also be reviewed and renewed. Special institutes like the Tribal Research Institutes should be relooked at in terms of their functioning and modus operandi. Their social science research capabilities need to be augmented.

There are several research bodies, including under CSIR, numbering over 40 research centres under various technology ministries. All of them must be reviewed concerning why they are not able to make a difference. These centres and labs should have sociological and social research specialisations to take their work forward. Many of these R&D centres under tech ministries will benefit if only they strengthen their social research capabilities.

News media plays an important role in positioning data, statistics, research in their coverage. But this role often is double-edged. That is, they end up presenting facts in a tinted way and stories are often planted in the garb of a research or a survey. Media should become sensitive to the intricacies in their own interest and credibility. Some initiatives, preferably by professional groups, occasionally may help bring more responsible coverage of research. Impact and implications of data, statistics, and research should never be lost in the news media.

Media is also pivotal in expediting research culture directly and indirectly. It is also an immediate beneficiary of research. Research and revelations from RTI is a good example of this, as is research on MNREG, but media often trivialises research data, statistics, and surveys to their advantage. They often themselves pick up what is sensational in research. The use of the term 'survey' has made it lose its sanctity. Media should not cover a survey or research without identifying the agency responsible, the methodology involved, the timing, and the sponsor, if any.

Conflict of interest in statistics and research is an eternal issue. Quite often, one does not know the roots or source of research or data in the public preview. This must be addressed, perhaps both by the government and the professional bodies and civic groups, so that it becomes obligatory to declare or indicate any conflict of interest in the research and its findings.

Rating and ranking of public services, infrastructure, and various public systems and services has, of late, become a preoccupation without realising the implications of such an (misleading) assessment. It is an instant and half-baked method of promoting competitive spirit (or is it copycatting?). It is not a substitute for evaluative research, and is at best a surrogate exercise. Ratings and ranking preoccupation, however misleading they may be, should have promoted 'linkage analysis' or revived the 'factor analysis' methodology. Even this pursuit would have led to futures research. That also is not evident today. With so much data and databases available in the country, regardless of its compatibility, we should have various applications, for example, to take proactive initiatives in the farm sector. It should also have been possible to curb farmers' suicides. Analytics now brings new perspective in this process. The new India Research Foundation should take up such tasks as missions.

Research becomes more productive when there is a long-term perspective instead of a concern only with temporal interests. Governments should also realise that they cannot apply the same policy and procedures for outsourcing social research as they would for acquiring goods and physical services. The L-1, or lowest-bid, system that is the norm for the latter process is not ideal for assigning evaluation studies to outside agencies. The L-1 approach ignores the relevance, context and reliability aspects of social research, and therefore undermines quality.

In addition to this, research operations, particularly of social research, should never be allowed to become centralised or become a monopoly service of any single agency. Also, the findings of research on public policies and any research conducted with public funding should have protection from manipulation and misrepresentation.

Rejuvenating Research Culture and Environment

Research-based public policies are considered a better reflection of the state of affairs in a functional democracy. Global indexes on factors such as democracy, development, good governance, innovation, and knowledge society have 'research culture' and 'research architecture' as key indicators. India lags significantly and is considered average in such global indexes as its research concerns and initiatives are not considered up to the mark. India's innovation and knowledge standing is viewed as based on its standing on education. In many instances, research is viewed as a part of the educational system. But how well public policies are based on data, feedback, and evaluative research is also integral to these indexes. Apart from research in fundamental disciplines, research in functional sectors such as for behavioural, motivation, governance, education, agriculture, health, social change, development, etc. constitute a research culture and research architecture. The stature of such research in terms of independence or validation or checks and balances should matter.

For governments, 'research' more often means technology or engineering or scientific research. Yes, this research is important, but social and behavioural research is also critical in a pluralistic country with development pursuit based on social justice, equity, and a level playing context. Social science research can make a difference in accomplishing many of the overall national goals and in a holistic way. In fact, we lag behind in many respects of change and development because we did not realise the significance of social research and the insights it can offer for motivational and behavioural changes. This is even more relevant and critical in the context of evaluation and impact of technologies, infrastructure initiatives, and public policies. Impact and implications and the kind of change aspired and claimed requires to be tracked and studied to ensure timely corrective measures can be implemented. All this requires social science research support. Similarly, legislations by themselves cannot bring about the required change. Even social and communication and motivation skills need social research methodologies. And such a support cannot be fixed or constant for all occasions and situations. They need to be evolved locally. The former President of India Pranab Mukherjee lamented recently in 2019 that universities are not mere degree-awarding centres but can bring about significant changes in the outlook of the people of the country. But there is no indication of that in the prevailing paradigm. Why did he come to such a conclusion at the fog end of his long political career? Also, in the last two years (2018–19), a number of eminent scholars at home and abroad have written to the government to not withhold data, even of specialised agencies with an impressive track record.

Would the proposed 100 universities for research address such a vacuum today? For that, first, the significance of social science research must be recognized. Certain academic courses at the graduate level and specialisations should include social science research methodology courses. Field-exercise-based project reports should also be made compulsory for all post-graduate courses. The research methodology adopted and the analytical skills availed of must be specific to the subject of the project and the region where it is to be conducted, and should be informed by social, cultural, and economic context. Whether this can be achieved through strictly syllabus-based courses taught inside walled campuses with little exposure to the outside world and lived realities is debatable.

The research fellowship programme so far has made no difference to the pursuit of quality. As the HRD Minister announced in 2018 and as observed by the UGC committee on the 'copycat' phenomena in PhDs, the country's research project system needs a thorough review. Of over 30,000 PhDs awarded annually, hardly one-third are original initiatives.

ICSSR requires restricting and repositioning with a revamped mandate and much higher budgetary allocations. It needs to be depoliticised and de-bureaucratized. There should be transparency and much wider participation and partnership in its operations. Its institutional support approach can be replaced by subject-centric concerns. This requires a fresh look at its institutional association. ICSSR network should not be limited or confined to the ones currently in its patronage.

Research and evaluative operations should be brought under transparency laws and should be periodically assessed and reviewed by independent academics and civil society activists—in fact, independent experts and activists with ground experience should be involved in the very designing of plans for public schemes and policies. Monitoring, feedback, and evaluative data, past and present, should never be controlled or used in a monopolistic way. Why is the learning of lessons from what the Tata Foundation did in 2018 to promote credible and reliable research in public policies limited only to the Indian Institute of Technology, Delhi, or to Wipro or Infosys? Such funding and parameters for research on public policy formulation should also be emulated by other foundations in the country.

Research culture cannot be expected to flourish without transparency, freedom of information, multiplicity of sources of data, series of publications, frequent debates, discussions, and conferences. This also need not be promoted only by the government. Professional bodies like the Indian Association of Econometrics should be in the forefront. Some of these bodies created earlier by the government should be activated with more support and less interference. They also need to be depoliticised.

The more the number of databases, the more the chances of research. The more there is primary research, the more primary data gets generated. Transparency and access to these databases is critical. Analytics is a key tool to make the most of databases functional. Access to these databases reduces the chances of manipulation and politicisation.

Major sources of primary data, statistics, evaluation, and research in various fields or respects should be preserved and strengthened, and their annual or periodic reports should be maintained, not fiddled, deferred, or their scope changed without the involvement of stakeholder groups. Public libraries, social audit of MNREGS, or national crime report bureau, or annual reports of an information commissions, for example, should not be meddled with as it suits the leaders or the party in power.

Data, statistics, monitoring, feedback, and research often suffers from political interests and concerns becoming the first priority. In fact, political leaders have a weird outlook towards research. They tend to think that research limits or constraints their opportunities to be popular and hinders their freedom. Prime Minister Narendra Modi proved that such perceptions are misplaced. No other political leader has availed research for proactive initiatives as much as Modi, both before and after the elections. He benefited (2014–2019) by using research. Research can also be used for unleashing good governance for larger and long-term advantage. Today, governments tend to have a lukewarm outlook towards evaluative research and data sources. This trend has been responsible for the decline in research in the country.

Governments are also responsible for prompting 'supportive research' or 'endorsee data' or even 'justifying evaluation' without transparency. This is when the concern of the government becomes temporary and short-term and even partisan. Political leaders ignore or bypass the credibility criteria of data, statistics, feedback, and research. They need to realise that a third party feedback is far more credible than its own, particularly by the same source that is responsible for implementation or a beneficiary source or a source with a conflict of interest. This distinction must be understood and respected by leaders and decision-makers of public policies. Governments should not scuttle or meddle with institutions that have been established 40–50 years ago by robbing their autonomy or depriving them of their professional teeth. Instead, the government should extend them support.

Foreign management consultants specialising in consumer markets, financial auditing, and share markets have become the policy 'researchers' in India to assess and appraise development schemes, like rural employment and motivational projects such as the Swachh Bharat. They provide very impressive reports with good graphics and charts and have links to rating agencies. Two implications, however, are ignored. First is what this outright indiscreet preference of these foreign firms means to the Indian ethos and research environment. Social science research is driven more by anthropology, sociology, behavioural sciences, statistics, and political science. Second, such quantitative and ranking-oriented reports, riddled with conflicts of interest, are misleading in the long-run and add to complacency, thereby inducing India into models inconsistent with its ethos, culture, and constitutional compulsions.

Any data, statistics, and evaluative research from any source with conflicts of interest, directly or indirectly, should be known to the stakeholders. In fact, this should be an obligatory. Even if the government of the day is not concerned about it, professional and academic bodies should be. Eventually, it is the credibility of research that is at stake.

Public-funded research should follow certain protocols. First, the topic and the field work should be confined to certain ethical considerations and should indicate conflicts of interest or the context for the study as well as the outcome in whatever form should be accessible to specific publics. Transparency should be evident. For whom or at whose instance or service the study was taken up should be known. Some organisations like CMS have an Ethical Review Board with outside subject experts in responsible positions to vet the concept of the study, methodology, and outcome objectives before the study is conducted. Such ethical review should be an obligation on the part of evaluative research studies being taken up by foreign consulting, specifically by market research firms.

Field surveys and primary response collecting practices from primary sources should be validated to certain specifications and transparency. Public responses should not be collected without respondents knowing the context. The way the public opinion and election studies are conducted by known and unknown and profit-driven organisations calls for a review of their accountability. The respondents should have the obligatory right to seek the outcome or the findings of the survey for which they have cooperated, voluntarily or otherwise.

Different research methods often used in the context of welfare and development policies should be promoted so that citizens are sensitised about what to look for in a field survey and research. When independent research organisations conduct annual or periodic studies on issues of significance referred to in news media, they must hold open house or a public hearing for the public to learn about how the findings were derived.

Social research is futile without considering the larger societal context. Researchers must thus be sensitive, for example, to universal human values, development concerns provided in the constitution, and cultural considerations of the community in context.

The impact of a policy or a programme intervention or their future implications should never be out of sight of policy-makers and the attention of researchers. 'Futures research' is in a nascent stage and has not yet taken off despite isolated studies since 1976–78, 1985,[1] and Abdul Kalam's book as well as my own book, *India 2021* of 1985, along with the first vision 2020 exercise of Andhra Pradesh which I steered (1992–93).[2] TIAFAC, created by the government for forecasting technology trends four decades ago with Dr Y.S. Rajan as its chief, is not heard so much about today. The attention, even of the NITI

Aayog, now is on ratings and ranking which obviously meant concerns of temporal nature. This is one reason for the rise of populism recently in political parties and the governments. Populism, in turn, boosts propaganda. Propaganda tends to rely on manipulated data, feedback, and research evidence. It is necessary for ongoing research to consider this phenomenon. But there are hardly any such studies being conducted. Organisations such as ICSSR should be concerned about this.

Research Should mean Win–Win

Has social research made any contribution to any of the basic problems confronting the country for years? A quick review of some different topics shows a bleak picture. All these basic issues involve beliefs and behavioural, attitudinal, motivational, and lifestyle aspects. Deep-rooted attitudes cannot be changed only through policies, legislations, or even subsidies and incentives or awareness.

Water-crisis, road safety, violence against women, impact of media, and farmers' distress are not new issues; they have been the concern of the country for more than a decade. And yet, how did we approach these concerns over the years? What measures have we taken? We did take several initiatives. But the missing link in all these is a sociological perspective and social research involving citizens and stakeholders, their motivations, concerns, sensitivity, beliefs, behaviours, and attitudes. A serious and holistic view would have made a visible and lasting difference.

Water crisis: Shortage of both irrigation and drinking water has been in public discourse for a long time, and in more recent years, it has resulted in a crisis proportion. It is also known that shortage of water is caused by attitudes and behaviours and concerns lifestyles. And yet, no behavioural study of consequence is known. Neither the Planning Commission nor NITI Aayog or ICSSR or any of the IITs or IIMs had examined ways to cope with this in the coming years from a sociological perspective. A sociological or anthropological research would give insights to develop models that can motivate different sections of society and regions of the country to alleviate this problem.

Farmers distress and rural unrest: The prolonged suicides, distrust, and unrest is not an abrupt phenomenon. It has been brewing for a couple of decades and was forewarned about by experts like Dr M.S. Swaminathan. In fact, he had even submitted an action plan based on his years of research, including social research. And yet, there has been no reversal of the trend despite the government claiming that it took initiatives by allocating huge budgets through dole-outs or compensation and subsides.

That there is a problem which we are not able to address is obvious. Not all the accumulated problems concern the government's compensation or support or crop insurance, but there are also sociological aspects concerning lifestyles, societal value systems (like marriage and health expenditure), consumption priorities, individualisation from community orientation (each one for himself or herself), migration, government policies, and priorities. Research on these aspects is isolated and sporadic. Several surveys have scratched the surface. The zero-budget organic farming being promoted recently should have been backed up with field research.

Media effects: It is widely known that mass media impacts different sections of people differently at different points of time in different contexts—positively, negatively, directly, and indirectly. Only time series studies can unfold such effects. Such studies have to adopt methodologies that are neutral and local. Academic institutions and specially created bodies like ICSSR are expected to be concerned about these media effects. Interested sections like the advertisers, marketing strategists, and even politicians would obviously be interested and would evolve tools or methodologies to suit their interests. NITI Aayog should have taken a proactive interest.

India has around 1000 journalism or communication schools, but at different levels and streams. More than a dozen of them like IIMC and Film & TV Institute are pioneering and at the forefront. And there is a minister in New Delhi and one in every state concerned with the media. Yet, I have not heard anyone using research studies—as if no one is bothered about it. Even more surprising is the fact that none of the academics, societal leaders, or governments have ever bothered about the TRP system, despite it moulding the content model of Indian media. The TRP had denigrated all other research on mass media and dominated the media scene. The TRP was based on push on and push off 'instant response' to media exposure and was designed to impose a content model alien to India and going against the ethos of the country.

A related phenomena sweeping across the country today is fake news, with rumours swaying and sweeping people's sentiments. Is word of mouth relied on more now, despite the proliferation of mass media? Has the agenda setting moved from mass media to social media and to rumours? This situation is because there is greater concern with image, ratings, news management, and consensus building than with motivation, persuasion, and involvement. Instant 'surveys' are sweeping all across the country rather than KAP studies on experiences or beliefs or behaviours. Instant surveys have gained more traction as they fit into the round-the-clock news model. Only an in-depth social research unfolds the psyche and yields lasting options.

Crime and Criminalisation: The National Crime Reports reveal crimes of different nature, suicides of different origin, etc. This annual report offers a wealth of data for sociological, anthropological, psychological, and philosophical research. Neither ICSSR nor any other academic body has bothered to analyse the trends from a sociological or psychological perspective, even when it was revealed that adolescents are taking to crime and cybercrime increasingly. The role of electronic media in spreading deviant behaviour among children and adolescents must be examined.

These reports are being used mostly by news media in an exaggerated manner, sometimes even by political leaders.

The way the crime report is structured limits its desegregated analysis. For example, why has there been an emergence of suicides of different types? Examining suicides of farmers separately yields specific insights. If there were active researchers using this data, it would have improved the potential of these crime reports for preventive or proactive initiatives. Headlines such as 'India number one in sexual violence' and 'India is most dangerous country for women'[3] in 2016–17 have not made us want to conduct follow-up studies. Why has social science not been availed? Why have sociologists and psychologists not examined this issue?

Road Safety: Despite 1,50,000 people dying and a million seriously injured every year, road safety has remained a concern for police or law and order. The Motor Vehicle (amendment) Act 2019 recognised that all stakeholders including the community should be aware of safe road use practices. It is not merely about speed, using seatbelt, drunken driving, or signals but also about attitudes, lifestyles, and exposure to media. Sociological studies are useful for understanding such phenomena and developing serious interventions. India has made impressive progress in road infrastructure but commensurate efforts were not made for making a difference nor building into social research support.[4]

Student Suicides: The phenomenon of youth disaffection and despondency in the country has resulted, among other things, in increased suicides. A lancet report in 2012 indicated that the suicide rate in India is the highest in the 15–29 age group. The 2018 NCRB data indicated that 27 students had killed themselves in the IITs alone. Every year, there are reports of students committing suicides after the board exam results. Should this not prompt serious, structured research?

Futures Research

Pursuit of 'futures research' sets a good base for research culture in the country. The methodologies for projecting and prediction models are important for developing a research architecture. Despite initiatives in this regard by visionaries like Dr Abdul Kalam, Dr Y.S. Rajan, and Dr R.A. Mashelkar a few decades ago, India is nowhere near pursuing this research, even in the academics. Even in the case of demographic model, no new research is heard of. India needs to take special interest in this regard.

Research methodologies based on field surveys in any specific context require consideration of certain important factors in order to ensure reliability of their results. These include, apart from intelligent, scientific sampling, the credentials of the researchers and their familiarity with the respondents. The researchers should not have any links with those in power, so that they are not, or are not perceived to be, biased either willingly or due to any coercion. Other factors need to be factored into the process—for instance, the competitive scenario in the political campaigns which may result in 'bandwagoning'. There is also the possibility in some cultures of respondents being reluctant, for reasons ranging from fear to suspicion, to share with strangers their opinions on sensitive issues, especially political issues. They may not give clear answers to questions, or may even give answers contrary to what they feel or believe. And yet, such responses are routinely taken more seriously than they should be.

The much needed corrections, revamping, and renewing cannot be done by the government alone. But governments must be concerned and take initiatives more seriously, with a holistic outlook. 'Control and command' view is the very antitheses of a healthy research culture. Civil society and active citizens too have stakes to ensure that research in the country plays an objective and proactive role. In fact, they should be more involved in the social audit of research, particularly social research in the country in specific contexts. The role of mass media and social media is unique and is a double-sword. It can save research from its fall from sanctity and credibility. The professional bodies, associations, and councils must ensure that they do not come under moral questioning. They should take proactive initiatives such that there is no government intervention in research practices. They must have certain restrains regarding professional standards, ethical concerns, and in bringing transparency to any conflicts of interest.

Professional study and survey for gathering social data is an essential service towards sustaining democracy, and making fair, enlightened governance and genuine development possible. Autonomous and transparent research is the best safeguard against inadvertent or deliberate bad governance. Scientific, non-partisan research is truly the third eye of governance.

NOTES

CHAPTER ONE

1. Narendra Dabholkar, *Please Think: Practical Lessons in Developing a Scientific Temper* (Madison, MS: Context Publishing, 2019)
2. Economic Times & National Education Policy, March 16, 2018.
3. Jairam Ramesh's Lecture on Mokshagundam Visvesvaraya https://www.theweek.in/news/india/2019/09/15/one-nation-one-language-will-never-be-reality-jairam-ramesh.html
4. Shriman Narayan Agarwal, *The Gandhian Plan of Economic Development for India* (Palala Press, 2015)
5. Prabhash Ranjan, 'Still a Developing Country,' *The Hindu*, October 31, 2019 https://www.thehindu.com/opinion/op-ed/still-a-developing-country/article29834940.ece

CHAPTER TWO

1. Abantika Ghosh, 'Gender gap in AIIMS OPD: Four lakh women missing in 2016, say researchers,' *Indian Express*, August 9, 2019 https://indianexpress.com/article/india/gender-gap-aiims-opd-four-lakh-women-missing-in-2016-researchers-5890479/
2. Shriman Narayan Agarwal, *The Gandhian Plan of Economic Development for India* (Palala Press, 2015)
3. J. C. Kumarappa, *Gandhian Economic Thought* (Varanasi, India: Sarva Seva Sangh Prakashan, 2010)
4. 'Panel to frame code of conduct for MLAs, MPs in 2 months,' *Economic Times*, August 29, 2019 https://economictimes.indiatimes.com/news/politics-and-nation/panel-to-frame-code-of-conduct-for-mlas-mps-in-2-months/articleshow/70884927.cms?from=mdr
5. 'Interim Budget 2019: Rs 61,398 crore allocated for health sector; Ayushman Bharat gets Rs 6,400 crore,' *India Today*, February 1, 2019

https://www.indiatoday.in/business/union-budget-2019/story/interim-budget-2019-rs-61-398-crore-allocated-for-health-sector-ayushman-bharat-gets-rs-6-400-crore-1444725-2019-02-01
6. Satellite Instructional Television Experiment, 1975–76

CHAPTER THREE

1. Esha Roy, 'Six cities picked for Centre's project to link research, industry,' *Indian Express*, August 13, 2019 https://indianexpress.com/article/india/six-cities-picked-for-centres-project-to-link-research-industry-5899865/
2. Minority Report, Status of the Muslim Community in India, Muslims for Secular Democracy (MSD) https://casi.sas.upenn.edu/sites/default/files/iit/Minority%20Report.pdf
3. Prabash Dutta, 'What is Swaminathan report that has kept farmers vs govt battle alive for 12 years?' *India Today*, June 1, 2018 https://www.indiatoday.in/india/story/what-is-swaminathan-report-that-has-kept-farmers-vs-govt-battle-alive-for-12-years-1247810-2018-06-01
4. Uday Bhatia, 'Shyam Benegal: It is not the job of the CBFC to function as a moral custodian of the public,' *Livemint*, July 14, 2018 https://www.livemint.com/Leisure/5pxKY6ItuKwUThuUAyMG5I/Shyam-Benegal-It-is-not-the-job-of-the-CBFC-to-function-as.html
5. The National Family Health Survey (NFHS) is a large-scale, multi-round survey conducted in a representative sample of households throughout India. Three rounds of the survey have been conducted since the first survey in 1992–93.
6. The ASER Centre approach has its roots in Pratham's work across urban and rural India to help children acquire basic skills in reading and arithmetic. ASER Centre was established as an autonomous unit within the Pratham network in 2008.
7. Milind Sohoni, 'Shyam Benegal: It is not the job of the CBFC to function as a moral custodian of the public,' *Indian Express*, October 16, 2019 https://indianexpress.com/article/opinion/columns/a-need-to-democratise-science-6070639/
8. Vasudha Venugopal, 'Global consultants to audit over 125 centrally-sponsored schemes,' *Economic Times*, September 26, 2019 https://economictimes.indiatimes.com/industry/services/consultancy-/-audit/global-consultants-to-audit-over-125-centrally-sponsored-schemes/articleshow/71304344.cms?from=mdr
9. 'Deposits in Jan Dhan accounts cross ₹1-trillion mark,' *Livemint*, July 10, 2019 https://www.livemint.com/industry/banking/deposits-in-jan-dhan-accounts-cross-rs-1-trillion-mark-1562752764534.html
10. Himanshu, 'Demystifying poverty: which estimate and why,'

Livemint, January 19, 2010 https://www.livemint.com/Opinion/UhxQYjZ7tqxw6bMQfISCSK/Demystifying-poverty-which-estimate-and-why.html
11. Nidhi Sharma, 'Ayushman Bharat awareness 80% in TN, barely 20% in Bihar and Haryana,' *Economic Times*, September 3, 2019 https://economictimes.indiatimes.com/industry/healthcare/biotech/healthcare/ayushman-bharat-awareness-80-in-tn-barely-20-in-bihar-and-haryana/articleshow/70953467.cms
12. Bindu Shajan Perappadan, 'Malnutrition claimed 244 lives in 4 years in Delhi hospitals, reveals RTI inquiry,' *The Hindu*, April 2, 2019 https://www.thehindu.com/news/cities/Delhi/malnutrition-claimed-244-lives-in-4-years/article26706599.ece
13. 'India Has Highest Number Of People Without Basic Sanitation: Report,' NDTV, November 17, 2017 https://www.ndtv.com/india-news/india-has-highest-number-of-people-without-basic-sanitation-wateraid-report-1776912

CHAPTER FOUR

1. *Economic Times*, May 19, 2019
2. M. V. Nadkarni and R. S. Deshpande (ed.), *Social science research in India* (New Delhi: Academic Foundation, 2012)
3. 'IIT-Delhi gets Rs 50-crore grant for School of Public Policy,' *CNBC TV18*, January 16, 2019 https://www.cnbctv18.com/economy/iit-delhi-gets-rs-50-crore-grant-for-school-of-public-policy-1983001.htm
4. Anubhuti Vishnoi, 'Govt ádvised' central Universities to ensure 'national priorities' in research, documents show,' *The Economic Times*, March 25, 2019 https://economictimes.indiatimes.com/news/politics-and-nation/govt-dvised-central-universities-to-ensure-national-priorities-in-research-documents-show/articleshow/68566316.cms?from=mdr
5. Amitabha Bhattacharya, 'The government is within its right to question the quality of PhD research,' *Hindustan Times*, April 16, 2019 https://www.hindustantimes.com/analysis/the-government-is-within-its-right-to-question-the-quality-of-phd-research/story-sLITiQTloemXpHGSYYLEuL.html
6. 'Reaching for the Stars', *India Today*, July 1, 2019
7. Shyamlal Yadav, 'Research published in pay-and-publish journals won't count: UGC panel,' *The Indian Express*, June 21, 2019 https://indianexpress.com/article/india/research-published-pay-and-publish-fake-journals-wont-count-ugc-panel-5791656/
8. N Bhaskara Rao, G.N.S. Raghavan, *Social Effects of Mass Media in India* (South Asia Books, 1996)

9. Nidhi Sharma, 'Govt readies report card on 'smart cities, big impact', *Economic Times*, August 19, 2019 https://economictimes.indiatimes.com/news/politics-and-nation/govt-readies-report-card-on-smart-cities-big-impact/articleshow/70728762.cms
10. *Economic Times*, August 16, 2019
11. 'Prime Minister Modi addresses the nation from Red Fort n 73rd Independence Day,' Narendra Modi, August 15, 2019 https://www.narendramodi.in/pm-modi-at-73rd-independence-day-celebrations-at-red-fort-delhi-545967
12. Dr N Bhaskara Rao, *The TRP Trick: How Television in India was Hijacked* (India: Vitasta Publishing Pvt. Ltd, 2019)
13. Bindu Shajan Perappadan, 'Kerala, TN, Himachal top India child well-being index, says report,' *The Hindu*, August 28, 2019 https://www.thehindu.com/news/national/other-states/kerala-tn-himachal-tops-indias-child-well-being-index-says-report/article29272084.ece
14. *New Indian Express*, January 2, 2019 http://www.newindianexpress.com/nation/2019/jan/02/large-number-of-posts-at-tribal-research-institutes-remain-vacant-1919527.html

CHAPTER FIVE

1. List of countries by research and development spending, Wikipedia https://en.wikipedia.org/wiki/List_of_countries_by_research_and_development_spending
2. Sukhadeo Thorat and Samar Verma (eds.), *Social Science Research in India* (India: Oxford, 2017)
3. Sayantan Bera and Elizabeth Roche, 'Budget 2019: FM cultivates farmers with ₹6,000 in hand every year,' Livemint, February 02, 2019 https://www.livemint.com/budget/news/budget-2019-fm-cultivates-farmers-with-6-000-in-hand-every-year-1549003772968.html
4. 'With district-wise data, Assam govt pushes for NRC,' *The Hindu*, August 1, 2019 https://www.thehindu.com/news/national/with-district-wise-data-assam-govt-pushes-for-nrc/article28787767.ece
5. Union Budget (2019–20), Ministry of Science and Technology https://openbudgetsindia.org/dataset/department-of-science-and-technology-2019-20/resource/54671a2d-d886-4221-9919-dd3ce7734dbd
6. Ministry of Human Resource Development https://openbudgetsindia.org/dataset/616beae6-f007-4f17-8828-10fab535cc9f/resource/c8450332-fdcc-40e6-888c-4467c6118631/download/department-of-higher-education.pdf
7. Ministry of Agriculture and Farmer's Welfare https://openbudgetsindia.

org/dataset/4949e3c4-59c1-4280-a47d-3a6af6c914f2/resource/ 4153e6f2-87dc-4ef8-ac03-f7e4c65a5c87/download/department-of-agricultural-research-and-education.pdf
8. Ministry of Health and Family Welfare https://openbudgetsindia.org/ dataset/ebac5fff-5c0a-4696-962d-efb2734907ea/resource/56b3f2dc-de58-4ec5-aed3-0d71967e1e79/download/department-of-health-research.pdf

CHAPTER SIX

1. Centre for Economic and Social Study (CESS), Hyderabad Study on impact of their research on policy making. Edited by Sukhadeo Thorat and Samar Verma, Social Science Research in India, (Oxford, 2017).
2. 'Note ban weakened Naxal movement: BJP think tank,' *The Hindu*, November 1, 2018 https://www.thehindu.com/news/national/note-ban-weakened-naxal-movement-bjp-think-tank/article25384049.ece
3. *The Hindu*, July 4, 2019
4. Sanjeev Choudhary, 'A record leap: LPG cylinder now used by 89% households in India,' *The Economic Times*, December 4, 2018 https:// economictimes.indiatimes.com/industry/energy/oil-gas/lpg-cylinder-now-used-by-89-households/articleshow/66930092.cms?from=mdr access done 28-08-2019
5. 'Economic Survey 2018–19: Private funds needed for Swacch Bharat,' *The Hindu*, July 4, 2019 https://www.thehindu.com/business/Economy/ economic-survey-2018-19-private-funds-needed-for-swachh-bharat/ article28285864.ece (accessed on September 7, 2019)
6. 'Budget 2019 Updates: Sitharaman calls for structural reforms, relaxing FDI norms,' *Livemint*, July 5, 2019 https://www.livemint.com/budget/ news/union-budget-2019-live-updates-1562297269692.html
7. Chaitanya Kalbag, 'Toilet-Training India,' *Business World*, October 1, 2019, http://www.businessworld.in/article/Toilet-training-India/01-10-2019-176943/
8. Priscilla Jeberaj, 'Open defacation-free India: National Statistical Office Survey debunks Swachh Bharat claims,' *The Hindu*, November 25, 2019 https://www.thehindu.com/news/national/open-defecation-free-india-national-statistical-office-survey-debunks-swachh-bharat-claims/article30070689.ece
9. Rhthma Kaul, 'India moves up on innovation index,' *The Hindustan Times*, July 25, 2019 https://www.hindustantimes.com/india-news/ india-moves-up-on-innovation-index/story-jvoYrGRFz9C90Jx6tq4stI. html
10. Dr N Bhaskara Rao, *Sustainable Good Governance, Development and Democracy* (SAGE, 2019)

11. Bikash Singh, 'NRC stirs intense debate in Assam Assembly,' *The Economic Times*, August 02, 2019 https://economictimes.indiatimes.com/news/politics-and-nation/nrc-stirs-intense-debate-in-assam-assembly/articleshow/70493017.cms?from=mdr
12. Sabu M. George, 'Finding the data on missing girls,' *The Hindu*, August 2, 2019 https://www.thehindu.com/opinion/op-ed/finding-the-data-on-missing-girls/article28787720.ece

CHAPTER SEVEN

1. Paul Sawers, 'British Airways faces record $230 million GDPR fine over data breach,' *VentureBeat*, July 8, 2019 https://venturebeat.com/2019/07/08/british-airways-faces-record-230-million-gdpr-fine-over-data-breach/
2. Yamini Aiyar, 'Data is useful but only if credible,' HTDS Content Services, March 28, 2019 https://www.htsyndication.com/ht-mumbai/article/data-is-useful-but-only-if-credible/33753861
3. Zia Haq and Saubhadra Chatterji, 'Centre plans wider method to measure income of farmers,' *Hindustan Times*, August 26, 2019 https://www.hindustantimes.com/india-news/centre-plans-wider-method-to-measure-income-of-farmers/story-xSQOdAEDCbGtsuW8lRefFL.html
4. Dr N Bhaskara Rao, *Andhra Pradesh Vision 2020*, AP State, 1993–94
5. 'Modi govt promoting agri allied sectors to achieve target of doubling farm income,' *Business Today*, July 26, 2019 https://www.businesstoday.in/sectors/agriculture/modi-govt-promoting-agri-allied-sectors-to-achieve-target-of-doubling-farm-income/story/368173.html
6. Yoginder K. Alagh, 'The National Sample Survey needs to be kept above the realm of politics,' *Indian Express*, February 28, 2019 https://indianexpress.com/article/opinion/columns/national-sample-survey-data-fake-news-5603794/
7. 'Economists allege political interference in statistical data,' *Economic Times*, March 15, 2019 https://economictimes.indiatimes.com/news/economy/policy/economists-allege-political-interference-in-statistical-data/articleshow/68418232.cms?from=mdr
8. Amitav Ranjan, 'Even Mudra job survey data put in deep freeze,' *Indian Express*, March 14, 2019 https://indianexpress.com/article/india/even-mudra-job-survey-data-put-in-deep-freeze-pm-modi-5625399/
9. 'Raghuram Rajan raises doubts about India growing at 7%, says cloud over GDP data needs to be cleared,' *Economic Times*, March 28, 2019 https://economictimes.indiatimes.com/news/economy/indicators/raghuram-rajan-raises-doubts-about-india-growing-at-7-says-cloud-over-gdp-data-needs-to-be-cleared/articleshow/68581012.cms

10. 'GDP growth rate 2017–18 revised upwards to 7.2% from 6.8%,' *The Hindu*, January 31, 2019 https://www.thehindu.com/business/Economy/gdp-growth-rate-for-2017-18-revised-upwards-to-72/article26140013.ece Access done 20-5-2019
11. 'Joblessness at 45-year high? NSO puts a caveat,' *Times of India*, June 1, 2019 https://timesofindia.indiatimes.com/business/india-business/joblessness-at-45-year-high-but-nso-adds-a-caveat/articleshow/69604908.cms
12. Arun Kumar, 'Why India's growth figure are off the mark,' *The Hindu*, September 16, 2019 https://www.thehindu.com/opinion/lead/why-indias-growth-figures-are-off-the-mark/article29425194.ece
13. Mahendra Kumar Singh, 'New poverty line: Rs 32 in villages, Rs 47 in cities,' *The Times of India*, July 7, 2014 https://timesofindia.indiatimes.com/india/New-poverty-line-Rs-32-in-villages-Rs-47-in-cities/articleshow/37920441.cms
14. 'India lifted 271 million people out of poverty in 10 years: UN,' *The Hindu Business Line*, July 12, 2019 https://www.thehindubusinessline.com/economy/india-lifted-271-million-people-out-of-poverty-in-10-years-un/article28403303.ece
15. 'Nirmala Sitharaman on job losses: Data talks only about formal sector, not informal,' Indian Express, September 2, 2019 https://indianexpress.com/article/business/economy/fm-nirmala-sitharaman-on-job-losses-data-talks-only-about-formal-sector-not-informal-5957380/
16. Seema Chishti, 'Interview with Pronab Sen: There needs to be some distance between govt and statistical system,' *The Indian Express*, August 12, 2018 https://indianexpress.com/article/business/interview-with-pronab-sen-there-needs-to-be-some-distance-between-govt-and-statistical-system-5302506/
17. 'Telling numbers: How suicide count varies among the states, across age groups,' *Indian Express*, July 3, 2019 https://indianexpress.com/article/explained/telling-numbers-how-suicide-count-varies-among-the-states-across-age-groups-5811771/
18. *Times of India*, October 22, 2019 https://timesofindia.indiatimes.com/timestopten/msid-71703745,card-71709858.cms
19. Kabir Agarwal, 'Exclusive: 30% of PM Kisan Funding to Go Unspent as Centre Doesn't Know How Many Farmers India Has,' *The Wire*, October 2019 https://thewire.in/economy/pm-kisan-30-of-funding-to-go-unspent-as-centre-doesnt-know-how-many-farmers-india-has
20. Amitav Ranjan, 'Even Mudra job survey data put in deep freeze,' *The Indian Express*, March 14, 2019 https://indianexpress.com/article/india/even-mudra-job-survey-data-put-in-deep-freeze-pm-modi-5625399/
21. 'India's GDP growth overestimated by 2.5%, says former CEA Arvind Subramanian,' The Hindu Business Line, June 11, 2019 https://www.

thehindubusinessline.com/economy/indias-gdp-growth-overestimated-by-25-says-former-cea-arvind-subramanian/article27788143.ece
22. Harish Damodaran and Parthasarathi Biswas, 'Top agricultural scientists body rejects zero budget natural farming,' *Indian Express*, September 10, 2019 https://indianexpress.com/article/india/zero-budget-natural-farming-government-scientists-question-5981236/
23. Somesh Jha, 'Over 200 global economists seek junked NSO report details from govt,' *Business Standard*, November 22, 2019 https://www.business-standard.com/article/economy-policy/over-200-global-economists-seek-junked-nso-report-details-from-govt-119112101222_1.html
24. '56 lakh new taxpayers added, no inconsistency in government data: CBDT,' *Times of India*, August 18, 2017 https://timesofindia.indiatimes.com/india/56-lakh-new-taxpayers-added-no-inconsistency-in-numbers-cbdt/articleshow/60123042.cms

CHAPTER EIGHT

1. Dheeraj Sanghi, 'Why the PM's New Research Fellowship Scheme Is an Utter Disaster,' *The Wire*, February 25, 2018 https://thewire.in/education/why-the-pms-new-research-fellowship-scheme-is-an-utter-disaster
2. Shyna Kalra, 'Delhi police arrests researchers protesting outside HRD Ministry,' *The Indian Express*, January 30, 2019 https://indianexpress.com/article/education/delhi-police-arrests-researchers-protesting-outside-hrd-ministry/
3. 'Centre to use 'Turnitin' software to curb PhD plagiarism: Prakash Javadekar,' *The Economic Times*, July 27, 2018 https://economictimes.indiatimes.com/industry/services/education/lack-in-innovation-quality-research-foremost-challenge-for-nation-hrd-minister-prakash-javadekar/articleshow/65166584.cms?from=mdr
4. Dr N Bhaskara Rao, *India 2021*, ORG, 1985
5. Yaminin Aiyar, Centre for Policy Research www.cprindia.org/people/yamini-aiyar
6. Kumar Anshuman, 'Harvard-influenced Niti Aayog killing jobs: RSS' Labour Wing,' *Economic Times*, August 21, 2019 https://economictimes.indiatimes.com/news/politics-and-nation/harvard-influenced-niti-aayog-killing-jobs-rss-labour-wing/articleshow/70760746.cms?from=mdr

CHAPTER NINE

1. Dr N Bhaskara Rao (ed.), India 2021, ORG, 1985
2. Dr N Bhaskara Rao, 'Andhra Pradesh Vision 2020', AP State, 1993–94
3. Angela Dewan, 'India the most dangerous country to be a woman, US ranks 10th in survey,' CNN, June 26, 2018 https://edition.cnn.com/2018/06/25/health/india-dangerous-country-women-survey-intl/index.html
4. Piyush Tewari, 'Awareness among all stakeholders key to safer roads in India,' *Livemint*, August 14, 2019 https://www.livemint.com/news/india/awareness-among-all-stakeholders-key-to-safer-roads-in-india-1565721670515.html

www.ingramcontent.com/pod-product-compliance
Lightning Source LLC
LaVergne TN
LVHW091715070526
838199LV00050B/2416